M000084033

Nobody
Calls
Just to Say
Hello

———

Nobody Calls Just to Say Hello

Reflections on Twenty-Two Years in the Illinois Senate

Philip J. Rock

with Ed Wojcicki

Southern Illinois University Press
Carbondale and Edwardsville

15   14   13   12   4   3   2   1

frontispiece: Rock making a point in the Illinois Senate,
1989. Photo by Michael Fryer, *Chicago Tribune*.

Library of Congress Cataloging-in-Publication Data
Rock, Philip J., 1937–
Nobody calls just to say hello : reflections on twenty-
two years in the Illinois Senate / Philip J. Rock ; with
Ed Wojcicki.
      p. cm.
Includes bibliographical references and index.
ISBN-13: 978-0-8093-3071-3 (cloth : alk. paper)
ISBN-10: 0-8093-3071-7 (cloth : alk. paper)
ISBN-13: 978-0-8093-3072-0 (ebook)
ISBN-10: 0-8093-3072-5 (ebook)
1. Rock, Philip J., 1937– 2. Illinois—Politics and govern-
ment—1951– 3. Illinois. General Assembly. Senate—Bi-
ography. 4. Legislators—Illinois—Biography. I. Wojcicki,
Ed. II. Title.
F546.4.R63A3 2012
328.73'092—dc22
[B]   2011013793

Printed on recycled paper.♻
The paper used in this publication meets the mini-
mum requirements of American National Standard for
Information Sciences—Permanence of Paper for Printed
Library Materials, ANSI Z39.48-1992. ∞

To my four children,
Kathleen, Meghan, Colleen, and John (Jay)

To my grandchildren,
Emily, Erin, Lily, Ellie,
Kyleigh, Connor, Maggie,
Jack, Owen, Kate,
Julia, and Sarah

And of course, to Sheila,
"the wind beneath my wings"

Contents

Photo gallery following page 118

Preface

I FIRST APPROACHED FORMER ILLINOIS STATE SENATOR PHILIP J. ROCK in 2002 about writing a book. His response did not surprise me.

"Who cares what I think?" he asked.

A lot of people do, I told him.

Phil Rock was one of Illinois's most influential politicians in the 1970s and 1980s. He served as Illinois Senate president for fourteen years, longer than anyone in Illinois history. His career overlapped those of such Illinois legends as Chicago mayor Richard J. Daley, Governor James R. Thompson, and House Speaker Michael Madigan as well as Mayors Jane Byrne, Harold Washington, and Richard M. Daley and Cook County powerhouses George Dunne and Edward Vrdolyak. Rock interacted frequently with all of them. Coming from the West Side of Chicago, he has an insider's perspective on Chicago politics and Illinois history of the last quarter of the twentieth century.

Conventional wisdom might not predict that a loyal product of the Cook County Democratic organization could emerge as an ethical voice for the voiceless or as an Illinois leader who gave Republicans the courtesy of having their points of view heard, as Rock did. Rock's story makes it clear that one can be a loyal partisan and a highly principled public official. His contemporaries agree that he was a statesman with great integrity.

Rock's perspective needed to be recorded and remembered. Or so I thought.

But Rock, the man the *Chicago Tribune* once described as "the man for all sessions," briskly shrugged off the idea of a book.[1] His proclivity for privacy made him wonder whether a book about his career would sound like he was bragging, which he is not prone to do. He was reluctant. A year after I first inquired, he asked me, "If I did a book, how would the process work?" I talked about possible approaches: biography, autobiography, memoirs, an oral history. The final product is none of the above, because none fit the way he reflects on his twenty-two years in the Illinois Senate. He breaks the mold, and his story is compelling.

He agreed to start with an oral history, and I began interviewing him in 2004. I also consulted with and interviewed about two dozen people who knew him well, some on the record and some for background. Only a few declined to be interviewed.

Then I began writing. Because of Rock's colorful way of spinning stories, I chose to put this book together in the first person, by him. I captured his language and thoughts as well as I could, though I know that some will disagree. Early drafts confirmed his original concern. "It seems too self-serving," he told me after reading the first couple of chapters. I then suggested, tongue in cheek, that to balance any apprehension about making himself look too good, he write an opening chapter that would include everything he's ever done wrong so that people would know he is not a saint. We laughed about that and just kept going. I interviewed him twenty-eight times between 2004 and 2010 in his Chicago law office, first at 350 North LaSalle Street, just north of the Chicago River, and in his current office at 321 North Clark. Many of the transcribed interviews will be featured, with the audio, as part of the "Illinois Statecraft" series of the Abraham Lincoln Presidential Library's Oral History Program.

Rock has a profound reverence for the institutions of government, especially the Illinois Senate. He never stopped trying to teach that the Illinois Senate is an institution as well as an assembly of elected members. He enjoyed reflecting on how such an institution should operate and on how its members should behave. In his career, he received both praise and criticism from fellow Democrats for having a great working relationship with Governor James R. Thompson, a Republican. It is clear to me, after many conversations with Rock, that a big part of that relationship was his regard for the office of the governor. At the same time, his loyalty to the Democratic organization of Cook County also emanated from his respect for a particular political institution, the Democratic Party.

Two themes emerged consistently from those who spoke about Rock's career.

First, he always tried to do the right thing. I would ask those I interviewed directly to confirm whether that was true, and most enthusiastically said yes. Rock believed that government should help people, especially those in greatest need. He paid special attention throughout his career to children, to people with disabilities, and to people threatened by their social conditions, such as abused women, neglected children, and kids in trouble. His last chief of staff, Linda Kingman, said that the genius of Rock's career was that he not only did the right thing but also knew how to use power wisely.[2] As examples, Kingman mentioned the Illinois Domestic Violence Act, which Rock helped to fashion on behalf

Table 1
Illinois General Assembly breakdown by party, 1959–93

Year convened	GA no.	Senate	House
1959	71	33R | 24D | Vacancy R1	86R | 91D
1961	72	31R | 27D	89R | 88D
1963	73	35R | 23D	90R | 87D
1965	74	33R | 25D	59R | 118D
1967	75	38R | 20D	99R | 78D
1969	76	38R | 20D	95R | 82D
1971	77	29R | 29D	90R | 87D
1973[a]	78	30R | 29D	89R | 88D
1975	79	25R | 34D	76R | 98D | 3i
1977	80	25R | 34D	83R | 93D | 1i
Rock as Senate president, 1979–93			
1979	81	27R | 32D	88R | 88D | 1i
1981	82	29R | 30D	91R | 85D | 1i
1983[b]	83	26R | 33D	48R | 70D
1985	84	28R | 31D	51R | 67D
1987	85	28R | 31D	51R | 67D
1989	86	28R | 31D	51R | 67D
1991	87	28R | 31D	46R | 72D
1993	88	32R | 27D	51R | 67D

Sources: State of Illinois, Illinois Blue Books 1959–93, published by the Illinois secretary of state; see the Illinois Digital Archives at http://www.idaillinois.org/. Table compiled by Kyle Dooley.

Note: GA = General Assembly, D = Democrat, R = Republican, i = Independent.

[a] The number of senators increased from 58 to 59 due to the 1970 Illinois Constitution.

[b] The number of House members decreased from 177 to 118 due to a "cutback amendment" approved by Illinois voters in 1980.

of abused women, and the Illinois Women in Government conferences, a creation of Rock's staff while he was Senate president.

The second reason that so many contemporaries have such a high regard for Rock is that he held together a fragile, divided, and unruly Democratic caucus in a manner that allowed the senators to pass significant legislation. Rock never had a large majority; in fact, he always had just barely more than a majority of the fifty-nine senators needed to pass a bill (see table 1), so he always had to keep close tabs on every vote. Very troublesome for him were the rivalries among his own members and the grief that some, such as Jeremiah Joyce and Frank Savickas, poured on him regularly. After Rock had been Senate president for ten years, the

Chicago Tribune's political reporter, Tom Hardy, described the Illinois Senate of Rock's era as "an assemblage of 59 raging egos."[3] Hardy delineated the Chicago blacks and the white ethnics, the North Shore liberals and the south-suburban conservatives, and the downstate members who did not trust their Chicago brethren. Holding that group together was, by most accounts, a magnificent political achievement. For fourteen years as Senate president, issue by issue, Rock pieced together coalitions of a fragmented caucus—sometimes needing Republican support, too—to pass remarkable and innovative legislation. Rock's career exemplifies what a statesman can accomplish.

Another of Rock's gifts was his oratorical skill. "He was the most articulate public speaker I've ever served with," said Senator John Cullerton of Chicago, who became Illinois Senate president in 2009. "He was persuasive."[4] It's a shame that nobody kept or compiled copies of Rock's many speeches given at conferences and meetings of trade associations, civic organizations, and many interest groups. He tailored his remarks for such diverse groups as bankers, organized labor, and the Illinois Farm Bureau, and he also spoke at the funerals of several of his colleagues and friends. His remarks were masterfully crafted, often with quotations from Alfred Tennyson or John F. Kennedy. Copies of most of his speeches evidently disappeared when Rock left the Senate or when he finally shut down his political office in Oak Park. Fortunately, transcripts of his legendary floor speeches are preserved. I studied them often when putting these chapters together. What Cullerton meant and what others mentioned in reminiscing about Rock was that when Rock would rise to address an issue on the noisy Senate floor, the chamber often would halt in abrupt silence. Rock would have a few words scribbled on the back of an envelope, on a small piece of paper, or on the Senate calendar for the day, and when he began to speak, people really listened. Some of his best floor speeches are quoted throughout this book.

Of inestimable value in putting this volume together were hundreds of newspaper and magazine articles from the 1960s to the 1990s—too many to cite individually—as well as official transcripts of Senate floor debates and other government documents. But ultimately, the reflections in this book are grounded in the recollections of one person: Senator Philip J. Rock.

Historians would remind us that some decisions made in the past "grate on modern ears" because all leaders belong to their own eras.[5] Rock's years in full-time public service spanned three different eras in Chicago and Illinois politics. First were the Mayor Richard J. Daley years, when the mayor's personal blessing opened the doors for many projects and jobs. Rock considered Daley not only one of the most powerful people in Illinois but also one of the most powerful Democrats in the United States. The second era, after Daley's death in 1976, involved changes in the composition of the Illinois Senate, with the rise of independent state senators known as the "Crazy Eight" along with the emergence of the black caucus. That era also saw the election of Chicago's first woman mayor, Jane Byrne, in 1979, then the city's first black mayor, Harold Washington, in 1983, and eventually the state's first Latino senator, Miguel del Valle, in 1986.

That era blended into the one that continues today, an era in which the four legislative leaders—Senate president, Senate minority leader, House Speaker, and House minority leader—dominate the legislature and outweigh the importance of the individual members and the two major political parties at the state level. In Rock's last ten years in the Senate (1983–93), the four legislative leaders stayed the same—Rock and Republican James "Pate" Philip in the Senate and Speaker Michael Madigan and Republican minority leader Lee Daniels in the House. Rock's insights into his relationships with those leaders and Governor Thompson are likely to be among the most-discussed topics in this book.

In twenty-two years in the Senate, Rock handled thousands of bills and was the main sponsor of 450 of them. He worked with hundreds of legislators, dozens of staff members, four governors, five Chicago mayors, and two interim mayors. That's what makes his unique insider's perspective on both Springfield and Chicago Democratic politics so compelling. Many Illinois leaders are most prominent in one or the other, but Rock knows both very well. In this book, he focuses on the issues of greatest significance to him and of his time and on the people who made government work in Illinois.

—Ed Wojcicki
Springfield, Illinois
November 2010

Acknowledgments

THIS BOOK WOULD NOT BE POSSIBLE WITHOUT THE ASSISTANCE, guidance, and support of many people.

Among those who provided early direction or guidance along the way were former members of the Illinois Senate Democratic staff Bill Holland, Judy Erwin, Rick Schoell, Linda Hawker, Cindy Davidsmeyer, and David Joens as well as two journalists of my era, Charles N. Wheeler III and Mike Lawrence. Ed Wojcicki and I thank them for their insights and assistance but assess none of the blame to them for any oversights or inadvertent errors.

We are also grateful to the Illinois Senate staff photographers, whose work was wonderful during my time in the Senate and was made available to us by *Illinois Issues* magazine and the Illinois State Archives.

Providing valuable research assistance were two University of Illinois Springfield students who have since graduated: Kyle Dooley, then a graduate assistant in the Center for State Policy and Leadership, and Greg Bishop.

Many thanks, also, to those interviewed by Ed Wojcicki or Kyle Dooley as part of the oral history project related to these memoirs: Governor James R. Thompson; Governor Jim Edgar; current or former Senate presidents John Cullerton, Emil Jones, and James "Pate" Philip; Speaker of the House Michael J. Madigan; and Senators Ken Buzbee, James Donnewald, Dawn Clark Netsch, and Patrick Welch. Others interviewed included Pat Arman, Peter Creticos, Linda Hawker, Bill Holland, Linda Kingman, John Lattimer, Gerald Shea, Bernard Sieracki, Father John Smyth, Paul Vallas, and Katie Newsham. Other interviews are continuing for the Philip J. Rock Oral History Project as the book goes to press; either time or scheduling conflicts prevented them from happening yet.

Other thanks go to Herman Bodewes, Barbara Ferrara, Mary Ellen McElligott, Tom Wood, Charlene Lambert, Andrea Winland, Joan Sestak, Sara Wojcicki, Jill Rock, Dan Fusco, Bonnie Ettinger, Tim Mapes, Steve Brown, Andy Manar, Pat Coburn, Pat O'Grady, Amanda Bly, and Sherry Hutson and to the staffs at the Illinois Legislative Research Unit, the Municipal Collection on the fifth floor of the Harold Washington Library in Chicago, the Springfield *State Journal-Register* library, Brookens

Library at UIS, the municipal Lincoln Library in Springfield, the Illinois State Historical Library in Springfield, the Illinois State Archives, and the University of Illinois Springfield Archives.

Much gratitude goes to Southern Illinois University Press and its editor in chief, Karl Kageff, who believed in this project, to other editors at SIU Press for their insights and wonderful editing, and to Jim Nowlan and Paul Kleppner for the reviews and critiques of the manuscript.

And for personal support that could never be described adequately, we offer our heartfelt thanks to our wives, Sheila Rock and Sally Wojcicki.

Chronology of Senator Philip J. Rock's Career

1937 Born May 4 in Chicago

1964 Receives law degree (JD) from Loyola University School of Law

Marries Sheila Graber

1965–69 Named assistant attorney general, state of Illinois

1969–71 Named assistant state's attorney, Cook County, Illinois

1970 Elected to the Illinois Senate

Elected to the Democratic State Central Committee

Begins private law practice with Daniel R. Fusco

1971 Named Outstanding Legislator in Illinois General Assembly (shares the recognition with Senator Tom Hynes)

1972–82 Equal Rights Amendment to U.S. Constitution debated in Illinois (Illinois never did ratify it)

1973 Appointed assistant minority leader on Senate Democratic leadership team

Regional Transportation Authority (RTA) created

1975 Appointed assistant majority leader on Senate Democratic leadership team

Sponsors Horse Racing Act of 1975

School for deaf-blind children created

Sponsors Abused and Neglected Child Reporting Act

1977 Moves family from West Side of Chicago to Oak Park, Illinois

1978 Elected Democratic committeeman, Oak Park Township

1979 Elected Illinois Senate president (first of seven consecutive two-year terms)

Sources: Philip J. Rock, Illinois Legislative Research Unit, and official Senate journals, published annually

1980 Backs state bailout loan to help save Chrysler plant in Belvidere, Illinois

Illinois opens legislative office in Washington, D.C.

1981 Takes Governor James R. Thompson to Illinois Supreme Court and wins on the issue of the election of the Senate president

Sponsors Illinois Domestic Violence Act

1982 Elected chairman of the state Democratic Party

1983 Temporary income tax increase passes (higher rate effective for eighteen months)

1984 Runs unsuccessfully for Democratic nomination for U.S. Senate

First Illinois Women in Government conference held

1985 Sponsors major education reforms, a package of forty-seven issues

Sponsors package of bills to support Alzheimer's victims and their families

1986 Illinois Sports Facility Authority created to help White Sox stay in Chicago

1987 Illinois Senate gets first woman secretary of the Senate (Linda Hawker)

1988 State renames deaf-blind center in Glen Ellyn, Illinois, as the Philip J. Rock Center and School

Attends first night game played at Wrigley Field

1989 Temporary income tax surcharge passes, increasing the tax for two years

Undergoes successful double-bypass heart surgery at age fifty-two

1990 Riverboat casinos approved for Illinois

1991 Temporary income tax surcharge of 1989 made permanent

1992 Receives Loyola University School of Law Medal of Excellence

Receives Lawrence O'Brien Democratic Party Achievement Award

Receives Illinois Third House Distinguished Service Award

1993 Retires from Illinois Senate; engages in full-time law practice in Chicago

Named Celtic Legal Society of Chicago Man of the Year

1999 Appointed chair, Illinois Board of Higher Education

2002   Receives President's Medal, Loyola University Chicago

      Receives In Service of One Another Catholic Humanitarian Award, St. Mary of the Lake University, Mundelein

2005   Turns law practice over to a new firm, Rock Fusco, LLC, and he and Fusco become "of counsel" to the new law firm

2010   Sells house in Oak Park and moves to Chicago

*Nobody
Calls
Just to Say
Hello*

———

Introduction: Try to Be Fair and Evenhanded

I'm never voting for you as Senate president unless
you give me the Empire State Building.

IN MY FOURTEEN YEARS AS THE SENATE PRESIDENT, from 1979 to 1993, I never had what I considered to be a solid majority of Democrats. The Senate had fifty-nine members; it took thirty to have a majority. We Democrats had between thirty and thirty-three members in various years, but I never had all their minds on my side. There were factions; there were individual egos; there were people with agendas far smaller than the big picture. I had more difficulty with my own Democratic caucus than I did with members on the other side of the aisle. That was just a phenomenon that I learned to live with. Of the seven times I was elected Senate president at the beginning of a legislative session, every two years from 1979 to 1991, only three went without a hitch. A few disgruntled members who were upset with me would hold out for something, maybe a leadership position in the Senate Democratic caucus. It was as if those members were each saying, "I'm never voting for you as Senate president unless you give me the Empire State Building" or some stupid thing. So I dealt with those people, talked to them, and worked things out.

Others weren't happy with me because they wanted me to beat up on Governor James R. Thompson, a Republican. They thought partisanship was more important than doing the work we were sent there to do. I had to remind my members that on any given day, they might want me to go down to Thompson's office on the second floor of the State Capitol, one floor down from us, and ask him to sign their bill. "Why are you so eager for me to criticize him?" I would say. "After I do that, you want me to ask him to sign your bill, which he probably doesn't care about?" That didn't make sense to me, and I told them that. Some of my members also wanted me to afford no opportunities for legislative success for their Republican colleagues.

1

I did my best to tell them and teach them and show them that it's possible to be partisan and fair at the same time. In my twenty-two years in the Illinois Senate, I respected the fact that every member of the Senate had been elected to office, just as I had been. All of them represented many thousands of Illinois citizens and had a responsibility to make government work for those people. So if any member wanted to raise an issue, Republican or Democrat, he or she had a right to raise it. That's the process I believe in.

Don't get me wrong. I was proud to be a regular Democrat—a member of the Democratic organization of Cook County and the state of Illinois. So while I was fair to the Republicans, I also made it known that we, in turn, could work to defeat any Republican idea, and that's the process. I just never believed that it was fair to toss them aside and not give them a hearing.

If you're always fair, then people know where you stand. There was a time in history, for instance, when parents could not get their newborn babies insured. There was a waiting period of a week or a month or longer, depending upon one's insurance policy. That didn't seem fair to parents who suffered financial hardships because their infants got jaundice or some other medical condition. So I set out to change Illinois law. The insurance companies opposed me. But they knew where I stood, and I told them they were going to look foolish if they opposed this too publicly. I also indicated that it would be fair to adjust insurance premiums to allow for this coverage, as long as the coverage was there. It was common sense. They battled me for a while, but the General Assembly prevailed and got this law passed in 1975.

The insurance issue is a good example of what I mean when I say the number one function of government is to help people. Government exists so that we will have an orderly society. It should improve or enhance the quality of life for all who live under its jurisdiction. It should not impede free enterprise, but government should have a special role in helping people who otherwise can't help themselves. I have to admit that my view of government over the years has tempered a little bit. When I started, I would have been called a flaming liberal. I now would be a little more conservative, I'm sure, on the liberal-conservative spectrum, but I still think fundamentally that government has to help people. Once we forget that or transfer our energy to something else, such as pursuing a personal agenda, seeking additional power, or falling to one of the many sins and temptations that elected officials face, we lose a lot.

So in addition to being fair, the next essential ingredient for a public official, especially someone in leadership, is that you have to care. You have to give a damn. If you do, the rest will come. You have to care passionately about your own values, care about the people you deal with, care about the people you serve, care about your constituents, care about the institutions of government, and, most of all, care about what you view as your responsibility. As a leader, everything else flows from being fair and trying to care.

You also have to be willing to accommodate the views of others. You don't have to adopt others' views, but certainly you can try to understand them. That was part of my role as caucus leader. When I talk about my caucus, I'm referring to the Democratic members of the Illinois Senate. The Senate Republicans have their own caucus, as do the House Democrats and House Republicans. When I was caucus leader, I respected the fact that members felt torn; they had competing interests. They had their individual interests, whether from the district or from a lobbyist friend or from some group that supported them. Collectively, their interests were disparate, and someone had to corral them in order to make an impact on the bigger picture. That role also fell to me.

I was transparent with my caucus. I would tell them what was happening, whether it was good news or bad. I used to make little notes to myself on the back of an envelope so that I knew what news to deliver, and I would walk around with those notes. I would say, "We're going to be here three days this week, from Tuesday to Thursday, and in those three days I expect to pass this, this, this, and this and to kill this, kill this, and pass this, and the House will send us some bills." So everybody knew what to expect for the next three days. They knew what I had planned. "If you've got anything you want to add, let me know," I would advise. "If you've got anything you want to subtract, let me know." I gave them what I called full disclosure. I told them if they wanted to know what the negotiations were with Governor Thompson, just ask and I would be happy to share that information. "There are no great state secrets," I said. "We're just trying to hammer it out." My members respected that. They knew I wasn't deceptive; that was not my style.

Another thing I did was to meet one-on-one with my members quite a bit. Sometimes they would come to my office, and I would go to theirs, too. Most of them had something from their district that was important to them—a special issue, a pet project—and I recognized that and tried to help them with it. I learned that in order to be successful, I had to know where my members stood. I appreciated that they might have a different point of view from mine. I also reminded them that I was in a position to affect their agendas or jettison their bills. I could arrange to have Speaker

Mike Madigan amend a bill and send it back, or have the governor amendatorily veto it and send it back, or have him veto it altogether. In all such cases, their bills could be killed. I also told them never to forget that I could walk to that second floor and ask Thompson to do something with a bill, and he would do it—sign it, not sign it, or send it back—because he knew I was going to be there the next year and the year after, and so he was better off working with me than doing something just for them. From time to time I would quietly visit with my members and remind them that I had helped them with their agendas, and I would say, "Now, I could use a little help here. This issue today has nothing whatever to do with you. It's something for the city of Chicago"—or for the mayor of Chicago or for the Democratic Party. "It means something to me, and if you don't have any serious, strong objections, why be a horse's ass? Just get on board and let's move it out of here." And they did, to a surprising degree. As long as they were getting the information that they felt comfortable with, from time to time they would give me a vote that they otherwise probably would not have. The fact that I would take the time to listen also helped.

I made great use of a little office off the podium in the Senate chamber. The chamber is on the Capitol's third floor, on the north side of the building. Members can enter through the gigantic, ornate double doors from the public area, or they can enter from one of the back doors, behind the podium. There is a hallway behind the chamber, along with some offices, one of which is the office of the Senate president. There also are a couple of small conference rooms back there. It was easy for me to duck into one of those rooms without anyone particularly noticing. If I had to have a chat with one or a few of my members, I'd get their attention and whistle them up to the side of the podium and go into a meeting room for a few minutes, and when we were finished—or *I* was finished—they would filter back out onto the Senate floor. They used to call it the woodshed. From my perspective, though, we got a lot accomplished in that room. That's where I could have candid, private conversations with members and find out exactly what they wanted—and to be sure, they would find out what I wanted them to know.

I liked the one-on-one meetings, but every year a few members would complain that we didn't have enough formal caucuses with all of our members. Frankly, a caucus was one of the last things I ever wanted to have because of our volatile mix. Some of my members seriously didn't like one another. When they would complain about not enough caucus meetings, I explained that one is too many; I wouldn't call for a caucus unless it was absolutely essential. I wasn't going to meet for the sake of meeting. But every two years it came up when I would go around and literally ask each one of them for his or her vote for Senate president. "This is a personal request from me to you," I would say. "If you've got a gripe, I want to hear about it now; otherwise, I expect your vote. I don't know of any other candidates for Senate president, and I need thirty votes and you're one of them, and so you've got to vote for me." Ten or twelve of them would say, "We've got to have more caucuses." I said, "We'll have caucuses when necessary, but I'm not going to promise one a week because you and I both know there are some people in our caucus who don't like one another. There's certainly a group in there who don't like me particularly, so why am I going to stir that pot unnecessarily?" I did not want to do it, and so that's the way we left it.

Sometimes during a session, particularly when the pace of business was picking up, I could tell when they really wanted to fight with each other. So, I would leave the Senate floor and ask my assistant leader, Vince Demuzio of Carlinville, to preside at the podium and handle all the Senate business. I'd say, "Vince, let them go. Let them yell and scream and pee in their pants, whatever they want to do." He would grumble and say, "Ugh, I get to listen to all that stuff!"

"I know," I told him. "When it gets bad enough, I'll walk back out and take the gavel and get them quieted down. But it's cathartic; just let them go."

Then I would leave the floor and turn them loose. I would duck back to my office and turn on the sound system and listen as they chewed one another out. They would really go at it, but after awhile, it calmed them down. The same thing happened in a caucus from time to time. I would let them go at it and really argue with each other. For the most part, it did not get too out of hand, although there were touch-and-go moments.

I had to be a good disciplinarian on the floor when I was presiding. I could literally look out and see who was talking to whom and the little subplots going on. If I saw some unlikely huddling of two or more members, I knew trouble was coming. For instance, when I saw Walter Dudycz, a Republican from Chicago, talking to one of my members, I knew that something was going to happen and that a group commonly called the "white ethnics" from Chicago was rising up, and I would step in to quell whatever they were cooking up.

Part of the advantage I had with an unruly caucus, I think, was that physically I was big enough to literally stop some fisticuffs. We had, for instance, Senator James "Jimmy" Taylor of Chicago, who had been a sparring partner for boxer Joe Louis. Taylor and one of our other members almost got into it one day, and the other member was, well, a bit goofy. He could have gotten himself killed for taking on Taylor. I saw them start to go at it, and I stepped down from the podium, walked down their aisle, and stood between them. I sat them both down, and that was the end of it.

Another time, we were on the floor near the end of a session and one of the white ethnics got mad as hell with me. He was using his position on a conference committee to sabotage a bill. I found out from the conferees that he had a personal agenda, and it included killing that bill. He was causing trouble. So I yanked him off the conference committee, and he got really upset. I could see him burst through the back door of the chamber, and I watched as he flew down the center aisle about fifty miles an hour. To get to the podium, which is raised up a few feet, you have to go around the side, then up the steps. When he hit the bottom steps, I said quietly to him, "You take another step, you're going to get this gavel right in your forehead." He stopped but was swearing at me, and I said: "I took you off the conference committee, yes, that's right. That bill has to pass, and what you don't know is that there is a companion bill in another sequence that we're going to take up, and that other bill is going to solve your problem. So just lighten up. You didn't even give me a chance to tell you what the hell was going on." He backed off but kept grumbling. But I will say this: the way he was racing at me, I sure felt like hitting him right in the head with the gavel.

Being fair and caring about the issues were the two big factors that allowed me to serve as Senate president for fourteen years. Several other principles about public service and leadership emerge in these reflections about making Illinois government work, and I want to mention a few more.

First, it can take years to get what you want—if you ever get it—and even then, it's usually not *all* that you want. Some people complain that changing a policy takes so long and is incremental; they always say we're not doing enough today or this year. They might be right in some philosophical way, but that's the legislative process. I have seen it happen with numerous issues. I accept it. Solving problems with education funding, for example, was a high legislative priority before I got to the Senate in 1971. It was on everybody's mind every year I was in the Senate, and it's still not solved today. But we always worked on it, and we did what we could to increase funding for education.

Another good example is how the state deals with abused and neglected children. I sponsored the first Abused and Neglected Child Reporting

Act in 1975, and we kept tweaking it over the years as we became aware of new ways to protect children in the state of Illinois. We would discover, for instance, that we forgot to include a group of persons who should have to report child abuse, or that the law was misinterpreted, and so we would tighten up the law. Some issues that I strongly supported—like moving the primary election date from March to September—came up several times. I pushed two or three times to move the date, but we never managed to get it done.

Second, it is important not to lock down so hard that you can't accomplish something that needs to happen. I tried to keep the conversation going on many issues over the years. I told my staff that when reasonable people decide to have a responsible dialogue, you can solve anything. I always believed in listening to people who had a point of view different from mine. I got to know the pro-choice people and those who were adamantly opposed to gambling, for instance, even though I was pro-life and often had a hand in helping the horse racing industry. I believe that if you discount anyone or anyone's views from the very beginning, you lose all chance of a rational, reasonable conversation.

Third, I always thought it was important to remind people that government is not self-executing.[1] Somebody has to make it work for the people for whom it is supposed to work. That means government and public officials have to be accessible. It's why I made it a Senate rule that if someone came to Springfield to talk to a committee about an issue, that person should not be sent away without being heard. It's also why I made it possible for members to have district offices and staff support—so they could be more accessible to the constituents they were elected to serve.

Fourth, I tried to show by example that it was not productive to be vindictive. I admit that there were indeed many times that someone angered me or frustrated me and I wanted to lash out. I can't say I never did, but it's fair to say that wasn't my style. *Chicago Tribune* writer Tom Hardy once said that I had a "disciplined silence," and I think that's right.[2] I didn't speak just because somebody thought I should say something. I spoke when I had something to say, and I often stayed quiet when others thought I should lash out. I suppose that felt awkward for those waiting for me to say something, but it was my way of being disciplined internally.

So in short, here are the principles I espoused as a legislative leader:

- Be fair and evenhanded.
- Care about what you're doing and the people you serve.

- Remember that effective change can take years. If you don't accomplish something this year, usually you can try again later.
- Choose to have a responsible and reasonable dialogue, especially with people with whom you disagree.
- Take action to make government work for the people for whom it is supposed to work. Government is not self-executing.
- Give everyone a chance to be heard.
- Don't be vindictive. No retaliation allowed.

On that last point, I want to explain that I had to be practical because I usually had just barely more than the constitutional majority of thirty members. I needed all the votes that were on the floor, and I didn't want to antagonize anybody. Some members would deliberately goad me from time to time because, I guess, they wanted to see me in full flower, but I just wouldn't give them the opportunity. I would call some members aside and try to persuade them of the errors of their ways, and if it didn't work, it didn't work. I let people have their say.

Vindictiveness borders on pettiness most of the time. It sours the whole punch bowl and doesn't accomplish its purpose. My members were aware that I had the capacity to make their lives miserable if I had to. I just chose not to do so. It takes personal discipline not to be vindictive. There are other ways to make a point besides plotting vengeance. To me, it would have bordered on weakness to resort to that kind of activity to get something done. I didn't have to, and I didn't do it.

For years, I had a paperweight on my desk with the inscription "Nobody calls to say hello." Back in 1970, when I first ran for office, I learned that once you put your name on the Democratic ballot, you're fair game. Seldom, if ever, did anyone call—I am talking about friends, supporters, supplicants—just to say hello or inquire about my health. One wanted a job for his cousin, another a license plate for her father-in-law, and another a garbage can for the lady next door. Other times the topic at hand was a bit loftier, some policy issue. It never stopped. You name it, and people would ask for it. What was important was their cause above all else. And I'm not talking just about phone calls. There were also many visitors to my office and thousands upon thousands of impromptu conversations as I ran into people. But I learned that it was important always to listen.

My district staff, my Springfield staff, or I would follow up by making a lot of calls in response to these inquiries. That is part and parcel of the job of state senator or state representative, as well as of alderman. You were intended to be the person between the government and the world out there. Many times, people didn't understand if their issue was a state issue or a local issue or a federal issue. They just knew they wanted help from the government. You quickly realize that you can't spend a lot of time saying it's someone else's problem; you just help if you can. That is still true today for elected officials who really understand what the job is. If that changes too radically, we will impede an important function of government. We seem to be heading in a direction where good government groups or the media complain about officials making a call or trying to help someone, as if the mere fact of making a call is providing unfair influence on behalf of someone. That's unfortunate for the official and for the citizens. If officials back off from providing constituent services, they take the risk of putting too much distance between them and the citizens who need the help of government. That contradicts my own view, mentioned earlier, that the number one function of government is to help people.

Kathy McDonnell of my staff gave me that paperweight with the seal of the state of Illinois and the inscription. Kathy had worked for U.S. senator Alan Dixon, and after assisting me in my U.S. Senate campaign in 1984 and then helping with my Illinois Senate Democratic staff, she went to work for Dorothy Brown, the Cook County circuit clerk. I always appreciated that paperweight. It's why I kept it on my desk and still have it today. I didn't mind that people would call or drop by with their request of the day. Frankly, though, it also helps me remember to pick up the phone once in a while and call colleagues, current and past, to ask how they're doing. I call just to say hello.

I recognize that other officials will have their own perspectives on the years and issues that I write about. I'm thinking of prominent Republicans such as Governors Thompson and Jim Edgar and Senator James "Pate" Philip as well as important Democrats such as Speaker Madigan, Chicago mayors Richard J. Daley, Harold Washington, and Richard M. Daley, Senator Paul Simon, and Illinois state senator Dawn Clark Netsch.

You might be surprised to know that Senator Philip, whose view of government is very different from mine, was and is my good friend. We got along very well, irrespective of his political views, irrespective of the fact that he had little use for the city of Chicago, irrespective of the fact that he was the leader from the seat of Republican power in the state, DuPage County. When the DuPage Republicans held a Lincoln Day dinner to honor Philip, I was the only Democrat at the head table. He and I frequently sat together at Cubs games at Wrigley Field and would go across the street to Bernie's Saloon and have a beer or two. We liked to share a beer in Springfield, too. I would call him almost every morning to give him a heads-up on what we, the Democrats, were going to do in the Senate that day. Even if I might tell him that we were going to beat him on a number of issues, I thought it was courteous just to let him know, because both of us had the highest regard for the institution of the Illinois Senate.

Governor Thompson and I also were friends. He was governor for twelve of the fourteen years that I served as Senate president. Edgar then became governor in my final two years. Few people know that when I lost the U.S. Senate primary election in 1984 to Paul Simon—a bitter time for me—Thompson and Philip hosted a fund-raiser, held in a private residence in Oak Park, my hometown, in order to retire my debt from that campaign. I was very grateful. That says a lot about our relationships and how Republicans and Democrats could interact in those days.

Even today when people ask me what it takes to make a legislature work effectively, I always start by advising them to try to be fair and to give everyone a chance, and everything else comes after that.

1. They Told Me It Wasn't My Turn

*I didn't know how lucky I was, as a political
novice, to be living in the Thirty-Seventh Ward
along with Bill Clark and Art McGloon.*

M Y MOTHER AND DAD WERE DILIGENT ABOUT VOTING but never actively engaged in politics. Nobody in my extended family got involved in politics, either, nor did we know anybody politically involved. When I was growing up, I didn't even know what ward I lived in—which is not good if you want to be involved.

People have said, rightly so, that I was born a Catholic, a Democrat, and a Cubs fan, though not necessarily in that order. When I was in high school and college, I thought I had a vocation to be a Catholic priest. I spent ten years in the seminary in Chicago, first as a high school student at Archbishop Quigley Preparatory Seminary and later as an undergraduate and theology student at St. Mary of the Lake Seminary in Mundelein, Illinois. I needed only two more years of training and education before I would have been ordained a diocesan priest for the Archdiocese of Chicago. I was living and studying in Mundelein, in my early twenties, when I told the Jesuit fathers that I was going to leave the seminary. I came to the realization that the lifestyle of a cleric was not for me—the whole package of what it means to be a full-time priest for the rest of my life. I was not cut out for it, nor it for me, although I wasn't quite sure what I was going to do. I considered some possibilities—medical school, for one thing, or a master's degree in business. I discarded both of those options.

Upon brief reflection, I decided I wanted to go to law school. So one of the priests at the seminary picked up the phone and called the Loyola University School of Law in Chicago and recommended me for admission. I left the seminary on a Thursday night in 1961 and started law school the next Monday. At the end of the week, the dean whistled me into his office and said, "I hate to tell you this, but at some point you're going to have to take an entrance exam." So he set up a special test for me a couple weeks later, and fortunately, I passed it. I think I made the right choice. I decided to pursue law for a lot of the same reasons that I had entered the seminary. I felt that as an attorney, I could be of service to people. My seminary training—my predisposition to be of service, if you will—led logically to law school and then to politics.

In May 1964, I graduated from law school and married Sheila Graber the same month. We settled on the West Side of Chicago, not far from where I grew up. I was actively looking for a permanent job. A couple of large law firms approached me, but I wasn't interested in megafirm practice, holding somebody else's briefcase for ten years before finally getting into court. That didn't interest me.

Some law school friends were working for Illinois attorney general William Clark, a Democrat. They spoke highly of him and suggested that I talk to him. Clark had been attorney general since 1961 and had served in the state legislature before that. I called and made an appointment to see him. We had a good conversation in his office in the old State of Illinois Building at 160 North LaSalle in downtown Chicago. Near the conclusion of the interview, he asked, "Who's your ward committeeman?"

I had to tell him I honestly didn't know. Then he asked what ward I lived in, and again I told him I did not know.

He just looked at me with a smile and said, "Well, do you at least know where you live?" That one I could answer, and I gave him my address in Austin, on the western edge of the city.

Clark looked at me and said, "You live in the Thirty-Seventh Ward. Your committeeman is an old friend of mine; he's the Illinois Senate minority leader, and his name is Art McGloon." At the time, the Republicans controlled the Illinois Senate. My political education was beginning, and I didn't know how lucky I was to live where I did. Clark himself was a former state senator and a renowned Chicago Democrat, and his father had been a ward committeeman. Clark knew more about me than I realized. He proceeded to get McGloon on the phone and said, "I'd like to send this young man in to see you at the ward office, and I'm interested in hiring him. If you give me your blessing, it's done." So I made an appointment to go to the Thirty-Seventh Ward office to see Senator McGloon and Alderman Tom Casey. Both were impressed that Clark himself had called. They explained that they would dearly love to have me as a member of the organization and yes, I could have the job with the attorney general. That's how it started.

With my new job in the attorney general's office, I got the message quickly for the first time in my life: I would become actively involved in politics, in the Thirty-Seventh Ward. I had voted Democratic previously. I think like everybody else in my generation, I was overwhelmed and moved by John F. Kennedy's election and assassination, and I felt attracted to Democratic politics. I had no compunction about that. We had a big organization. Because of my enthusiasm and work ethic, it wasn't long before I wound up in the ward's inner circle of ten to twelve people—what we used to call the "backroom boys." We would do more than set up and take down chairs. We were in on the political conversation about what was going on in the ward, in Cook County, and in the city of Chicago. I was the youngest one. I'm not sure that I was consulted much, but at least I was in on the conversation.

I wasn't a very good precinct captain myself. But going door to door was a critical part of the job, so I did it, canvassing the precinct in my little area of the world. If you were to ask me for a grade on my prowess as a precinct captain, I'd say at best a C+ or possibly a B. Certainly, I wasn't one of the A-class guys. I think lawyers make lousy precinct captains. You've got to be more of a salesperson, not an analyst or strategist. A precinct captain's job is to sell a candidate or a ticket. I learned that with some people, you can't sell an entire ticket—some people don't like to hear "Vote straight Democratic." I learned how to ask for support for just one or two candidates on the ballot, the big hitters. For instance, when McGloon was on the ticket, we wanted to get a big vote for him. When the mayor was on the ticket, we wanted to get a good vote for him. Frankly, we considered most of the other offices of lesser importance.

What I enjoyed more than being a precinct captain was being in the ward office, on the receiving end of information, and motivating the precinct captains. Being in the ward office was much different from going door to door. All year long we had office hours in the evening, usually once a week, then twice a week as an election neared. I would have mass meetings with the precinct captains, where the candidates would come in and make their pitch, and then we'd have meetings on Saturdays or Sunday mornings for the captains so they could tell us what was on their minds. It was local politics at its best. One captain would come in and say the city had to get a tree cut down; they could get six votes for the House candidate if a certain resident's tree came down. I used to do a lot of that. I'd call up the forestry department and say, "You've got to get that damned tree down by Tuesday; let's get going here." It was a lot of fun. There was and still is an expression used by the Democratic believers: "You carry your precinct, you carry the world!"

Meanwhile, my day job was in the attorney general's office. I was fortunate to work for Bill Clark, a man of great integrity. I mostly worked in the State of Illinois Building in Chicago in the appeals division. The only time we traveled downstate to Springfield was when the Illinois Supreme Court was in session. We always had a case or two on the docket. So we'd go down to Springfield for the argument, but we didn't spend a lot of time there. My first impression of the capital city was how small it was, almost quaint. It was like a time warp, like Mayberry RFD, the fictional small town in the old television show. Springfield certainly wasn't a bustling metropolis, but it was the home of the government, and I respected that.

Early in his first term, Clark helped to pass what I would describe as a series of "pushing the envelope" consumer protection laws. They came in a package and were nationally recognized because of the tremendous boost they gave to consumer protection. Then in 1967, Clark asked me to take over as the chief of the Bureau of Consumer Fraud. It was housed in Chicago, with additional staff in Springfield. I readily accepted, and this appointment eventually would lead me to the next chapter of my political education, the Illinois Senate. One of the persons I worked closely with was Jane Byrne, who was appointed by Mayor Richard J. Daley to be the consumer protection commissioner for the city. The city had its own ordinances, mirroring some of the state laws. It's worth noting that Byrne's enforcement often generated complaints from business owners to Daley's office, and she had a rocky relationship with him. But she and I spent a good deal of time together, trying to coordinate our consumer protection efforts, and she became a close friend.

Working in consumer fraud, I traveled to Springfield more frequently. I had a distinct advantage because my ward committeeman, Senator McGloon, was also the minority leader of the Illinois Senate. Early on, I was mightily impressed with the operation of the General Assembly. The Senate chamber itself inspired awe. I sat with McGloon and watched and listened to the proceedings, and I wandered around and talked to some of the members. I determined at that point that someday I would be a member of the Senate. I didn't know when, because I was sitting with the guy who was representing my own district, and he was our party's leader in the chamber. I would have to wait for my turn.

My career was progressing nicely, and so was that of Attorney General Clark. With Democratic governor Otto Kerner nearing the end of his second term, Clark was the odds-on favorite to be our party's candidate for governor in 1968. But Kerner stunned everyone by announcing his resignation in February and then becoming a federal judge in the U.S.

Court of Appeals in Chicago in May 1968. That meant Lieutenant Governor Samuel H. Shapiro of Kankakee became not only the state's thirty-third governor but also the Democratic nominee for governor in 1968. The party could have made Clark our nominee, but the downstate county chairmen wanted the incumbent Shapiro, even though Clark had been groomed for the job and was highly regarded, especially by the Chicago Democrats. Instead, Clark got the Democratic nod to run for the U.S. Senate against a very popular incumbent Republican, U.S. senator Everett McKinley Dirksen.

Before the campaigns got going, though, something of major significance happened in August 1968: the Democratic National Convention in Chicago, held in the International Amphitheater at the stockyards. What everybody remembers about that convention is the national coverage of the demonstrations by antiwar protesters. I did not attend the convention, but I had a minor role in writing one of its most controversial documents—the minority "peace plank." It was introduced as a substitute for the official Vietnam War platform document supported by our eventual nominee, Hubert Humphrey.

I was involved in writing the peace plank because Attorney General Clark drafted it, along with some of former President Kennedy's top aides: Theodore Sorenson, Pierre Salinger, and Richard Goodwin. A few people in the attorney general's office still supported the war—hawks, as we called them—and that basically was Hubert Humphrey's position. But the majority of us favored the proposal to get us out of Vietnam.

Almost every lawyer in our office assisted Clark in writing the peace plank. He was supposed to make a speech in prime time—a time when the national viewing audience would be highly engaged. But convention leaders changed the schedule. The peace platform, also called the "minority plank," was presented the afternoon of Wednesday, August 28, 1968, by Congressman Phillip Burton of California, when there was virtually no one around.[1] That was a disappointment for all of us. We were young and idealistic and thought they pulled a dirty trick on Clark, who was called to the dais along with eight others who supported the minority plank; Clark never did get to speak. But his support for the minority plank appeared to cost him significant political support in Illinois.

One backlash was that Clark got less than Mayor Daley's and the party's full support in his quest for the U.S. Senate in the fall of 1968. Running against Dirksen was like running against Santa Claus, honest to goodness. It was not an easy pull for Clark, but he managed to get 47 percent of the vote in losing to Dirksen. It was a bad year for many Democrats.

Incumbent governor Samuel H. Shapiro lost the governor's office to Richard B. Ogilvie, and Vice President Hubert Humphrey lost to Richard Nixon, who regained the White House for the Republicans.

My own career in the attorney general's office would soon be coming to an end because a Republican, William Scott, was elected attorney general of Illinois. I was still leading the consumer fraud bureau. Scott asked me if I would stay. I liked Bill Scott but told him he ought to have his own person in there. I warned him, "You're going to take some political flak for some of the things you do—when you pick on a car dealer or the Fred Astaire dance studios, that kind of stuff—so you've got to have somebody in there who you're comfortable with. I suppose we could learn to be comfortable, but I'm a Democrat and you ought to have a Republican in there." I stayed only a brief time after Scott became the attorney general in January 1969, and I got a job in Cook County, in traffic court, working for State's Attorney Ed Hanrahan.

As my career shifted, I maintained my interest in politics. Two big opportunities emerged in 1969. I thought I might have the good fortune of being appointed to the U.S. House of Representatives in the Sixth Congressional District of Illinois after Congressman Daniel J. Ronan died on August 13, 1969. The timing seemed perfect to me, and I was indeed under consideration to take his seat. But there was a big brouhaha and turmoil on Chicago's West Side, where I lived. The ward organization considered that seat its entitlement, but Jesse Jackson and some others were saying that the seat should go to an African American. So the debate went back and forth. Mayor Daley, who also was the Cook County Democratic chairman, called a few of us to his big office at the Sherman House Hotel. I remember George Collins, a black ward committeeman from the West Side, being there. It so happens that at the same time, another congressional seat was opening up on the South Side of Chicago because William T. Murphy of the Third District was not going to run for reelection in 1970. The African Americans made the same pitch for the South Side seat. They were going after both seats. The mayor was more interested in the South Side district. He wanted a white person to get that one. The Third District was 80 percent white, and my West Side Sixth District was about 70 percent white. So the mayor literally made a deal with the minorities, Jesse Jackson, and the *Chicago Defender*, to allow Morgan Murphy, a white Irishman and a friend of mine, to run for the South Side seat in 1970. That meant our district would go to an African American, who turned out to be George Collins. So Murphy and Collins would be slated for the congressional seats, as if they and the party were saying: "We're a pair here. If you don't like to deal, that's something else, but if you like to deal, keep your mouth shut." I was left hanging. I didn't like it. I thought it was a lousy way of doing business. I was young and full of piss and vinegar, and I thought it was terrible. But I was out, and that was the end of it.

Also in 1969 came the call for a state constitutional convention (con-con). I wanted to be a delegate. Each of the fifty-eight senatorial districts in Illinois would send two delegates to Springfield to write a new constitution for Illinois. Everyone understood that it was political, but they didn't run on party labels; they ran as individuals. I had my heart set on being one of the two from McGloon's district. I thought it would be a great thing to deliberate and write a new constitution. Both the primary and general elections for con-con delegates would be held in the fall of 1969, with the slating much earlier. Even though it was nonpartisan, the Democratic Party was going to decide which two people would represent our district. I recognized that one of them would be white and the other would be African American. I thought I had a good shot at the white seat.

I lived near the city limit on the West Side of Chicago, near Austin Boulevard. In those days, those Senate district lines stopped at the suburban line, at Austin, which runs north and south. The legislative districts didn't go beyond the Chicago city limits into other parts of Cook County. Our Senate district was about 30 percent minority; the mayor in his wisdom had determined that virtually every legislative district in the city would have that kind of ratio. I was one of the finalists, but first it was showtime. The ward leaders called a committee meeting and met with the finalists. It was kind of like, "Let's hear from the troops. Let's have participatory democracy here before we make up our minds."

I thought I was the front-runner. About five or six of us presented our credentials and let the committee know of our interest. The chairman was Bernard Neistein, a state senator and a legendary ward committeeman. He ran the Twenty-Ninth Ward, which had a nearly 100 percent minority population. Bernie was an old-style, cigar-chomping politician, a wonderful guy, who had a great saying: "I got two rules: Don't make no waves and don't back no losers." That inspired the title of one of Milton L. Rakove's books about Chicago politics.[2] Bernie was a little guy and a concert violinist, a great musician who sometimes played at Mayor Daley's victory celebrations. I didn't know Bernie that well then. Subsequently, though, as the years went on, if Bernie would say, "Jump out the window," I would just say, "Which one? It doesn't make any difference how high up or whether it's open or closed." He was an amazing guy and became a great friend, a mentor of sorts.

Neistein held the slate-making meeting for con-con at his ward office, at Madison and Laramie, next door to Mother McKenna's saloon. I showed up bright and early on a Saturday morning, suit and tie and all set. Bernie was sitting there with a couple of other committee members. McGloon was in Springfield, so my main supporter was not there. I presented my credentials, and Neistein said, "You are really overqualified for this job."

And I said, "Oh, really? And what, may I ask, does that mean?"

He said, "It's not your turn."

He said it just like that. "It's not your turn. I'd love to help you, but we don't have enough room, and it's not your turn. Nothing personal, kid. That's the way this game plays. Just bide your time. Something will happen."

The white con-con delegate from our district turned out to be Eddie Rosewell, who later became the Cook County treasurer and was indicted in 1983 on charges of bank fraud. Rosewell was Neistein's top precinct captain. His precinct would come in with vote totals of 600–3, or something that outrageous. Eddie had to have at least three Republican votes because there were three Republican poll judges, but sometimes, according to legend, he wouldn't even let them vote. He got into trouble a couple of times because he wouldn't let the Republican judges vote Republican. As a precinct captain, Eddie was an icon. He eventually got himself into financial trouble, though, and his political career was over.

Then, in addition to Eddie, Neistein and the slate-makers picked a black candidate, Leonard Foster, from the Twenty-Eighth Ward. Foster was an assistant corporation counsel. He also was a rabble-rouser. In my opinion and that of many others, there is no way Foster should have gone to that convention. But he did, and once again, for the second time in 1969, I literally got confronted with the black-and-white issue—first regarding the congressional seat and now this—and was left on the sidelines.

I thought I had gotten the short shrift. I tried to call McGloon in Springfield, where legislators were in an overtime session. They gave me the old razzle-dazzle: "He's on the Senate floor. He can't come to the phone." I learned that trick pretty well later on when I was in the Senate. I finally did talk to him, and McGloon said, "What did Bernie say?"

I said, "Well, he said it's not my turn."

And McGloon said, "Oh, hell. It's not your turn."

I got the message. Neither Neistein nor McGloon was going to back me. And that was it. The conversation was over.

2. Getting My Opportunity in Springfield

Many observers say there are three [new senators] who
stand out above the rest: Terry Bruce of Olney, Thomas
Hynes of Chicago, and Philip Rock of Chicago.
—Illinois State Register

I N 1970, WHEN THERE WAS AN OPENING ON the Democratic State
Central Committee from the Sixth Congressional District, the lineup
worked in my favor. The Sixth District included parts of several wards.
In two other wards, about ten candidates each wanted to be on the state
central committee. But in my ward, the Thirty-Seventh, there was only
one candidate—me. The leaders of the other two wards did not want any
fighting over this state central committee seat, and I was acceptable to
all of them. So once they got their intramural fires put out in those other
two wards, I was selected as the candidate, was elected, and became the
youngest member of the Democratic State Central Committee. What a
great opportunity so early in my career.

Illinois then had twenty-four members in the U.S. Congress, and every
congressional district had a state central committee person. I was one of
twenty-four in 1970 elected or reelected to the state central committee, which
was equivalent to the board of directors of the Democratic Party statewide.

The role of the state party was very different in those days. It was more
influential than it is today. One reason is that we had the phenomenon of
Mayor Richard J. Daley as chairman of the Cook County organization.
Everybody understood that he was the leader of the Democratic Party not
only in his ward but also in his city, in his county, and in his state. Daley
had been mayor since 1955, for fifteen years. State chairman Jim Ronan—
"Mr. Ronan" to everybody—had no trouble with that. Mr. Ronan was an
old-timer; it seemed like he had been around for a hundred years and
reminded me of everybody's grandfather. He was easygoing, laid-back,
soft-spoken, very shrewd, and just a font of wisdom. The party faithful

sought him out for advice and counsel. He had a remarkable institutional memory and knew all about the politics of the state and every county. He also knew individuals and those who wanted to run for office. I never saw him get angry. He was just a steady hand on the tiller of government. Mr. Ronan was one of the most patient and tolerant leaders I ever met, especially in the face of adversity.

All of the state central committee meetings were open. Mr. Ronan would invite people to express their views. He liked to have the meetings in Springfield, where the state party had a small office in a building behind the St. Nicholas Hotel. His rationale for meeting in Springfield was good: he told people in Chicago that if they wanted to get involved in the state party, they needed to go to Springfield, where there aren't any of the Chicago ward distractions. When I first started, Mr. Ronan told me to keep my mouth shut until he needed me. Every once in awhile, he would tell me ahead of time he would appreciate my support on something during the meeting, and so I would be ready.

Those meetings were wide open, with people really speaking their minds. Some members would be less than temperate. Their remarks were badly made and badly received. In response, Mr. Ronan was just as patient as could be. He heard everybody, explained his point of view, clarified what he thought was wrong about other points of view, and was just extremely professional. All of us on the committee picked up on his sense that there was a right way and a wrong way to listen to criticism, to listen to somebody's off-the-wall views and deal with them. The right way was to be fair and respectful. I never forgot Mr. Ronan's ability not to take criticism personally and to respect whatever someone had to say. I tried to follow his example the rest of my career. Looking back, I'm pleased that I took advantage of opportunities to sit with Mr. Ronan and talk with him whenever I had the chance.

Something else began to line up in my favor in 1970. State representative John "Jack" Touhy, the former Democratic Speaker of the House and current minority leader, decided he was going to get out of state government. Touhy was one of those typical Chicago guys; he didn't like going to Springfield. The first question his Chicago members asked when they arrived in Springfield was, "When are we going home?" Touhy, being the leader, was always thinking, "When am I going to turn these guys loose?" He and Art McGloon were very close. Touhy confided to McGloon, "I'm going to retire. I'm getting out of here. I'm taking a seat on the Cook County board. I won't have to travel; I don't like it." So McGloon fell in line, saying, "Well, I'm not staying down here if you're not." He didn't like traveling to Springfield, either. They drafted legislation to create a few new appellate court positions, which were needed in Cook County. "One of those seats is mine, or the bill isn't going to pass," McGloon said. Everybody bought in, including Mayor Daley.

With McGloon lined up for the appellate court, a Senate seat would open up, and I happened to live in McGloon's district. He suggested that I run for his seat.

So I said to him, as my commander in chief, "I'd really like to go after this one. The last two times, for the congressional seat and the con-con seat, I got the razzle-dazzle that you're not black enough or old enough or something, and I'd really like to do this."

"OK, let's do it," McGloon said. He indicated I should do whatever Mr. Ronan told me to do and took me downtown to see Mayor Daley. As we entered the mayor's office in city hall, I noticed that Michael J. Madigan was there as well. Madigan, twenty-eight years old at the time, was politically active on the South Side. We were both there by invitation only. Madigan was running for the House of Representatives for the first time. I think the state representative in his area, the Thirteenth Ward, had died, and it was his turn to go to Springfield, too.

"What nationality are you?" the mayor asked me.

"Mr. Mayor, my father emigrated from Luxembourg when he was fifteen; I'm Luxembourg, and my mother, of course, is Irish." That's when the mayor learned my heritage; I guess he thought I was all Irish.

"You know who else is Luxembourg?" he asked.

"No, sir."

"Well, I think Tom Keane is, and I think Jerry Huppert is; there's not very many of you guys around." He was referring to Thomas E. Keane, the Thirty-First Ward alderman, and Jerome Huppert, the Fiftieth Ward committeeman.

We had a nice chat, and I told him I was very interested in going to Springfield. "This would be a perfect opportunity," I said, "and I would appreciate your support." He said OK, and the deal was made. But first I had to go through another one of those razzle-dazzle committee meetings where there must have been twenty-five hopefuls applying for the Senate vacancy, because they knew the seat was not going to open up again for quite a while. This time, I drew everyone's support. Back then, if you didn't have the support of the mayor, you need not apply. Or, you could apply, but you shouldn't count on anything. He had appointed McGloon and Touhy as a committee of two to screen all the candidates for all House and Senate districts, not just mine.

McGloon went to bat for me. A couple of other candidates from his ward were a little older, and they thought it was their time. Everybody said my closest competitor was state representative Robert McPartlin. Another was Eddie Rosewell, who had won the con-con seat I had wanted. In many instances in the city of Chicago, a seat in the General Assembly was a reward for a job well done. A ward leader would say, "You're a helluva precinct captain; you've done this; you go to Springfield for two years or four years or six." It was a gift that they would hand out. We went through the motions in front of McGloon, and I was indeed slated for the Senate seat. McPartlin was told to stay put, and he ended up easily winning reelection as a state representative.

The idea that I would become a state senator was exciting for me. It trickled into the news that I was taking McGloon's place, McGloon was going to the appellate court, and Touhy was leaving. My West Side saloonkeeper had a news clipping enlarged, which he put on the back wall of the saloon.

So I was the slated Democratic candidate for the Eighteenth Senate District of Illinois in the 1970 election. I had Republican opposition: a woman who looked like everybody's grandmother, Marie Pedersen. I figured that as long as I was in this thing, I was going to do it right. So we did it all, the whole nine yards. I was the first guy to run for office out of my group of up-and-comers. I contacted my whole law school bunch and a lot of the young lawyers from downtown. They would come out on a Saturday and blitz the neighborhood; we'd have fifty guys out there. I had signs in every saloon on the West Side. I received the endorsements of the *Chicago Tribune*, the old *Chicago Today*, the *Sun-Times*, and the *Austinite*, my neighborhood paper circulated on the city's West Side. That recognition was a big thrill.

I was still living in the city on a little street called Midway Park, just east of Austin Boulevard, where the Chicago city limits stopped. Rags Flanagan, one of the old-timers from farther east, into the city down near Holman Avenue, said, "Send me a hundred signs, but nothing with a picture on it." I didn't understand why he said that. I had already sent a bunch of signs, and he had returned them. Rags's entire area was African American. They didn't want any white man's picture in their windows. "No pictures," Rags said. "If you want me handling signs, no pictures." I did what he said because Rags was a legendary precinct captain—another one who would bring in vote totals of 600–1 or 500–2. Whatever it took, he delivered.

The issues in that first Senate race were not a big deal, to be honest. I campaigned on such issues as removing the sales tax on food and

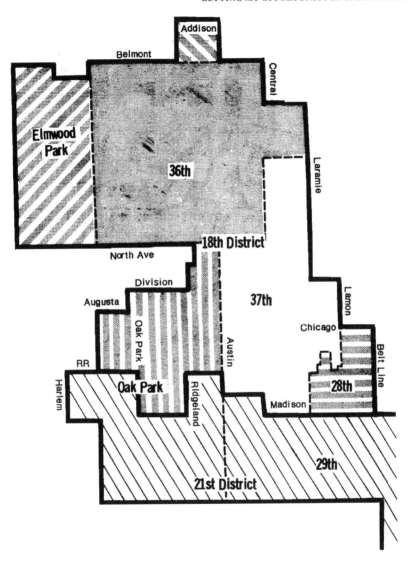

The Eighteenth Senate District, which Rock represented from 1971 to 1982.

medicine, better pollution controls for air and water, stronger consumer protection laws, reforms on individuals' credit reports, aid for nonpublic schools, and opposing abortion (three years before the landmark *Roe v. Wade* decision). The local papers mentioned that I was active in St. Lucy's parish in my neighborhood—activity that was viewed positively by a lot of voters. I never was confronted with what I was going to do substantively.

It was just Marie Pedersen and me, going block to block. Marie was a nice lady but didn't have a clue about running a campaign. In fact, a picture of the two of us was on the cover of the *Austinite* one week, and it looked like some nice young fellow and his grandmother.[1] If you didn't know it was about politics, you'd say that was a nice picture, like at Easter time.

My friends and colleagues and I opened a campaign office and mounted the charge. We didn't need a great deal of money because we had so many volunteers. Some of my pals had never worked for a candidate or for a ward organization. They thought it was fun, because we'd start out on a Saturday morning, gather a pile of signs or bumper stickers or brochures, and hit the street. "Be back at 1:00 or 1:30 and we're going to have some sandwiches and beer and then everybody go home, go watch the ballgame, or go do something else," I would tell them.

Thanks to 33,001 voters in my Eighteenth District, I won 82 percent of the vote in the November general election. It was an amazing, incredible day for the Illinois Senate Democrats—shocking, really. We gained nine seats by defeating a few incumbents and winning some open seats, and we won control of the Illinois Senate for the first time since 1941. The other new Democratic senators from Chicago who entered when I did were Daniel P. O'Brien Jr., Robert Egan, Norb Kosinski, Frank Savickas, and Thomas Hynes. Other Democratic newcomers were John Knuppel of Petersburg, Sam Vadalabene of Edwardsville, Kenneth Hall of East St. Louis, Terry Bruce of Olney, and Gene Johns of Marion. There was no single reason for all those victories—just different circumstances in different parts of the state that added up to a remarkable day for us.

We Democrats did not literally have a majority of the Senate seats. As a result of the 1970 elections, the Senate was evenly split, with twenty-nine Democrats and twenty-nine Republicans, compared to thirty-eight Republicans and only twenty Democrats in the previous session. (When the new constitution was written, the number of Illinois senators increased from fifty-eight to fifty-nine so that this even split would not happen again.) But in 1971, by virtue of the fact that Democrat Paul Simon was the lieutenant governor and would preside over the Senate, Democrats could count on his tie-breaking vote whenever it might be needed. So we had majority control of the Senate when we were all seated in January 1971, and we were able to elect the Senate president, replacing the legendary Republican W. Russell Arrington. (A bit later into the session, one of our members died—downstate senator Bill Lyons of Eagerville—and we were again in a stalemate.)

What a thrill it was to travel to Springfield for that first swearing-in session! The whole family went. By then, Sheila and I had four children:

Jay was in diapers, Colleen was two, Meghan was four, and Kathleen was five. It was common then, and still is, for members to bring their families to see them take the oath of office on the second Wednesday of January. We had been alerted that the formal organization of the Senate and the ceremony would go rather quickly. Cardinal John Cody of Chicago came down, adding solemnity to the occasion, along with his chief of staff, Monsignor Francis A. Brackin, vicar general of the archdiocese. Brackin had taught both Tom Hynes and me at Quigley North, and we walked him and the cardinal around the floor, introducing them to everybody.

McGloon, of course, had been our chamber's leader—the Senate minority leader—in previous sessions, so the Senate Democrats, now in the majority, had to pick a new leader. We settled on Senator Cecil Partee of Chicago as the Senate president, the first Democrat in that role in thirty years and the first African American ever to be Senate president. It was a sign of the growing importance of blacks in the Illinois General Assembly and in the city of Chicago.

Putting Partee into the position was Mayor Daley's call. Robert Cherry wanted to be the Senate president; so did Dan Daugherty. Both were from Chicago—one from the South Side, the other from the North Side. But the mayor was going to be running for reelection himself. He didn't want any fuss from the black community, so he gladly backed Partee. It was all calculated. Cherry became one of Partee's assistants on the leadership team.

In those first years as a senator, I used to take the convenient and reliable Gulf Mobile & Ohio train—the GM&O—to and from Chicago and Springfield, along with ten or fifteen other legislators from Chicago. There was no Amtrak in those days. The GM&O always had a dining car and a club car, where we would gather and get ourselves a couple of beers. Then the train would stop in Joliet, and a few more legislators would get on. I used to talk a lot with George O'Brien, the Yale-trained lawyer and state representative from Joliet, and to Robert McPartlin, the representative from my own area of Chicago. O'Brien and I were freshmen at the same time. I would bring a stack of bills and sit there and read them the whole trip while having a beer with the others. Not many other legislators were as interested as I was in the language of all the bills. When I started in the Senate, we would have the bill books on our desks. By the end of the session, they would be twelve inches high. There were no computers, so these were just paper copies. We didn't even have telephones on our desks at first. There were phone booths in the back of the chamber, and everyone was always running to a phone booth.

In Springfield, many legislators looked for an inexpensive apartment so they didn't have to check in and out of hotels and lug clothes back and forth every week. I asked my former colleagues at the attorney general's office in Springfield to keep an eye out for an apartment when I became a senator. One of the assistant attorneys general, Jerry Mayberry from Murphysboro in southern Illinois, lived at College and Capitol Streets—close to the Capitol, near the location where the Stratton Building currently stands. The house was across the street from a church, but the church and our building are both gone now. It was an old Victorian house that was converted to a two-flat, owned by a Decatur man not in the best of health. He didn't want to do any work on the place; he just wanted his rent check every month. He left us alone. Mayberry had the first floor, and I had the second floor. There were three or four bedrooms and the kitchen. Subsequently, I acquired two roommates—state representative Daniel J. O'Brien (different from Daniel P. O'Brien, mentioned earlier), who later became a judge, and Robert McPartlin. We lived there for a few years. We didn't cook much, but Mayberry used to grill in the backyard once in a while.

The legislative schedule seemed erratic. In order to arrive for the start of business on Monday, I'd get the late afternoon train on Sunday in Chicago after Sheila and the kids and I had dinner. We would stay in session until Wednesday or Thursday. That was something the leaders had to work out with the membership, what days they didn't want to be there. When I returned to Chicago, I would usually go to my law firm at 29 South LaSalle, not far from the train station, and then Sheila and I would meet a little later and she would drive me home. When I say "my law firm," I'm referring to the law partnership I had with Daniel R. Fusco. We went to law school together; a few years later he started a private practice, and I agreed to join him in 1970. We're still in practice together, forty years later, and we're proud of the fact that the successor to our firm, known as Rock Fusco, LLC, is flourishing.

At any rate, in that first session in 1971, with ten of the twenty-nine Democrats being freshmen, we were aggressive, yet we all got along. There was a little bit of competition but not a great deal. Republicans had had it their way for three decades. They were shell-shocked that the Democrats had taken over. In addition, early in that session, the Republicans' longtime powerful Senate leader, Russell Arrington, suffered a stroke, and that threw their caucus into greater turmoil. Arrington survived the stroke but never was the same. Over in the House, the Republicans took control from the Democrats and installed W. Robert Blair as Speaker. So in terms of legislative control, we had the Senate, but the Republicans had the House. And there was still a Republican governor, Richard Ogilvie, halfway through his term.

The first piece of legislation that I carried had nothing to do with any of the major issues on my campaign list. Nor was it of great importance, such as implementing the new Illinois Constitution or working on the budget. It actually amused some of my colleagues from Cook County when I became the Senate sponsor of House Bill 756, a farm bill introduced by Representative Clarence Neff, a Republican from Henderson County in rural western Illinois. I had met Clarence at the new members' conference when I first arrived in Springfield. At that conference we learned how the system works, what was available in terms of insurance, how we would be paid, and that kind of business. It was more social than anything. I decided not to sit with people I already knew from Cook County, and I wound up at lunch and dinner with downstate legislators, including Neff and Representative Tom McMaster, another rural Republican from western Illinois. My friendship with Neff and McMaster lasted until they retired. They would come over and visit me, or I'd visit them in the House and find out what the heck was going on, because they had a whole different sphere of interest, namely agriculture. I knew nothing about agriculture.

At any rate, Neff's bill was going to save farmers money. Farmers use a lot of heavy equipment and occasionally have to drive it on state, county, and township roads, and so the equipment had to be licensed. Neff's bill was written to exempt water trucks—those very large tanks of water on trailers—from the need for license plates, because they didn't go anywhere except on the farm. The only problem was that some legislators never wanted to deprive the state of any revenue, and they didn't want to exempt the water trucks. Neff already had a commitment from Governor Ogilvie to sign it, but he was concerned that the Cook County contingent wouldn't care at all about helping the farmers and so they might oppose his bill. He appealed to me, saying, "None of you guys from Cook County knows anything about agriculture, and so you can get them to support it if you ask them to." When the bill came to the Senate floor on May 5, 1971, I stood up and spoke in favor of it. My Cook County colleagues were overwhelmed. They couldn't believe that I was handling a farm bill and could speak eloquently about it. They razzed me a little, but the bill passed, 55–0, and was signed into law a month later. I think it was due to the odd couple of Neff and me that the bill sailed out of the Senate. It also became my first opportunity to have my picture taken with the governor. The photo appeared on the cover of a newsletter of the Land

Improvement Contractors of America, a group dedicated to soil and water conservation. The group's president, Don Hurst, was also in the picture, along with lobbyist Randy Richter, Governor Ogilvie, Neff, and me. It was a great thrill to get that first bill enacted.

One of our big jobs in 1971 was to implement the new Illinois Constitution, which the voters had approved in 1970. It would take effect on July 1, 1971. Another item of huge importance was the budget, because this was the first shot any of the current Democratic senators had at crafting the budget after thirty years of being in the minority. Tom Hynes, Terry Bruce, and I—all freshmen—used to sit there until ten or eleven at night and go over countless details. We talked to agency directors and their staffs to find out what they wanted. It got to be a little tedious, but the fact is we were very successful in changing a number of things, including the priorities. Hynes, Bruce, and I were able to make a major contribution to the process by learning everything we could and then sharing the information with the other members. Some of the others would have considered it a burden, but I loved it.

I remember Governor Ogilvie giving a major address about the importance of public transportation and a newly created Illinois Department of Transportation. That was big stuff in those days, and I spent the rest of my Senate career working with people on funding for various transportation authorities in the state and in the Chicago region. In that first year, we also passed the state's first minimum-wage bill, which I voted for. It set the Illinois minimum wage at $1.60 an hour for most workers and $1.25 an hour for persons under the age of nineteen.

I also supported a bill to provide some state funding for parochial schoolchildren, which was one of my campaign issues. The approach was and still is controversial. We managed to get $4.5 million that year to help finance low-income children in nonpublic schools. We wrote the law so that parents of parochial school students would receive vouchers or reimbursements for services such as transportation, textbooks, and health care. My theory was that all children deserved the same opportunity for a safe ride to school, for example, regardless of whether they were going to a private school or public school. We won thirty-two votes for the bill, just barely enough to pass. People might be surprised to know that twenty-five of those votes were from Democratic senators. We did have three heavy hitters as supporters—Mayor Daley, Governor Ogilvie, and Cardinal Cody of Chicago.

In that session, I also had my first inside look at how singularly important the subject of education is for the state's public schools and universities. Some members wanted to approve a bill that would have increased tuition for students in public universities by up to 50 percent. I said it would be wrong to increase tuition so much that large numbers of students would be forced out of college because they couldn't afford to pay. I became a strong supporter of public higher education in my first year and did my best to carry water for the state's universities for the next two decades.

When the session ended, the *Illinois Political Reporter* newsletter, edited by Richard Lockhart, named Tom Hynes and me the "co-freshmen of the year" in the Illinois Senate. That was a nice honor. Terry Bruce, another freshman, should have received more accolades, but he was from Olney in southern Illinois, which is really a different part of the world. It's so far down south that nobody in Chicago or Springfield cared about Bruce as much as they should have.

I really enjoyed the experience of the first session. I was actively involved in the operation of the General Assembly. President Partee gave me a lot of responsibilities, many more than a freshman should have been given. I presided at the podium a lot, which I loved. That allowed me to learn the details of the legislative process right away. Perhaps an *Illinois State Register* columnist summed it up as well as anyone in explaining what was on people's minds: "Many observers say there are three [new senators] who stand out above the rest: Terry Bruce of Olney, Thomas Hynes of Chicago and Philip Rock of Chicago. The trio has unusual intellect and courage."[2]

In that first year, we created new legislative districts under the rules of the new state constitution. It's something we were required to do every ten years. The way it worked was that the Democrats drew their maps and the Republicans drew theirs. Of course, the parties did not agree on what the districts should look like. This time, because of the new constitution, the Senate districts for the first time did not stop at the Chicago city limits but extended into the suburbs. The South Side districts encroached into suburbia, as did the West Side districts. I was still living on the western edge of the Chicago city limits at the time. The idea of expanding legislative districts beyond the city border was intended to help the Democrats so that our districts would take in a little suburban territory—not enough to hurt us but maybe enough to keep some Republicans out. The two Republican senators on the eight-member redistricting commission that voted on the maps strongly objected, but the House Republicans for some unknown reason sided with the four Democrats, and so the special redistricting panel approved the new Democratic map by a 6–2 vote.

It proved to be the only time the eight-member bipartisan commission would not end up in a 4–4 deadlock along partisan lines. The 4–4 stalemate occurred in 1981, 1991, and 2001, when there was a Republican governor and at least one of the legislative chambers was controlled by the Democrats. But in 2011, the Democrats had majorities in both chambers and also had the governor's office, so the Democrats controlled that remapping process entirely.

The 1971 map was supposed to help the Democrats, but it gave me the toughest reelection battle I would ever experience. When I ran for reelection for the first time, in 1972, I was opposed by Elmer Conti, the Republican mayor of Elmwood Park. That village had only about thirty precincts but was very powerful. Conti had half a dozen workers in every precinct and had the place covered.

Conti had served in the Illinois House from 1956 to 1962 and was the village president for life in Elmwood Park, eventually serving thirty-two years, from 1953 to 1985. There wasn't any question that he was going to be a very tough opponent. He was a recognized Republican who had run countywide and had a strong political organization. He was quite formidable, and the district was new, including all of Elmwood Park and about three-quarters of Oak Park, which was new territory for me. It was about 60 percent city and 40 percent suburban and still included my neighborhood on the West Side of Chicago. Suburbia, frankly, traditionally had better voter turnout than the Chicago precincts, which would have been identified as Democratic.

We worked long and hard. I opened an office in Elmwood Park, right under the village mayor's nose, just to keep Conti on his toes. Our campaign office had an enormous number of volunteers. We canvassed all the precincts, putting particular emphasis on the thirty precincts in Elmwood Park. We constantly sent campaign volunteers in there with literature, knowing full well it was going to be a close election.

Then on election night, as the results came in, the *Chicago Tribune* and others declared me a loser. With just a few precincts remaining to be counted, I was down about a hundred votes. We were in the ward office and doing the tally for the whole ticket, as usual, and there was overwhelming interest in my survival among the Democrats in the ward and my constituents. Those last eight to ten precincts didn't trickle in until the wee hours of the morning. I was so darned tired and felt terrible; I thought I was a one-termer. About five o'clock in the morning, I sent my brother, Mike, who was a Chicago policeman, and a couple of volunteers from the ward into the West Side, and I said, "Find these precinct captains. Find out what happened to them, to the votes." They did, and they reported that Conti's numbers weren't correct and that I should be declared the winner. We went downtown without going to bed and showed up at the Sherman Hotel, at the office of the Cook County Democratic organization. We walked in, and who was standing there but Mayor Richard J. Daley. He had a small office in the hotel for conducting the Cook County political business.

"Congratulations, I think you won," he said.

And I replied, "I hope you're right, Mr. Mayor."

He had received the official copy of all the votes. The Republican chairman and the Democratic chairman both received the election authorities' copies. Those day-after-election returns showed that I had won by 366 votes. Conti couldn't believe it. He claimed that the Democrats had stolen the election, and he formally challenged the outcome with the secretary of state. He alleged vote fraud in 51 precincts in Chicago—one-fourth of the district's 206 precincts. The discovery recount actually came out in my favor, giving me 122 more votes than we had in the preliminary tally. Part of Conti's complaint had to do with the timing of the canvass in some of the precincts, which would suggest that the last precincts altered their numbers in my favor. But I don't think that happened. It was a hard-fought victory. I did extremely well in the black precincts, which helped me achieve the final official tally of 40,509 to Conti's 40,021.[3] With 50.3 percent of the vote, I never came any closer to losing than I did that year.

That wasn't the only trouble the Democrats had in that 1972 election. We lost control of the Senate by a narrow one-vote margin and would be in the minority again for a number of reasons, not the least of which was the divisiveness of Dan Walker's campaign for governor. Walker was a Democrat and won, but he didn't seem to be on our side. His election was bad for the Democrats and bad for Illinois. We were stuck with him, and he was stuck with us. He didn't want reconciliation; he didn't want cooperation. He wanted confrontation.

3. Battling Walker and Fighting for Children

We came to the unmistakable conclusion
that child abuse was vastly underreported in
Illinois. We had to do something about it.

WHEN I PREPARED FOR MY SECOND TERM IN 1973, I wanted to get more involved. I wanted to be named an assistant leader under Senator Cecil Partee, the leader of the Senate Democrats. So I asked my mentor, former senator Art McGloon, "How does one go about getting into leadership?"

"The same way you got into the Senate," he said. "Go to see the mayor."

So I made the appointment, went to see Mayor Daley, and indicated that I was interested in becoming an assistant leader when the Senate organized itself in January 1973. He did not make a commitment one way or the other. After all, the Democrats had not done well in the 1972 elections. Dan Walker had campaigned as a big anti-Daley reformer and defeated the then lieutenant governor Paul Simon in the Democratic primary, and that changed everything. Under Walker, if you were a "Daley Democrat"— a member of the Cook County Democratic organization—you need not apply for anything. Walker was going to confront the mayor and showcase his independence with the hope, I suppose, of becoming a candidate for president of the United States. He miscalculated badly. Had he been a little conciliatory and a little cooperative, I think the mayor gladly would have sponsored him for president, if only to get him out of Illinois. It could have happened. Another little-known governor, Jimmy Carter of Georgia, did arise out of nowhere in 1976. Being governor of Illinois, not Georgia, could have put Walker in a much stronger position than the one Carter was in. As things turned out, Walker fought the legislature too much, and we were all glad to get rid of him after only one term. A little later he went to prison for crimes unrelated to his term as governor, but he's still known as another Illinois governor who went to jail.

At any rate, when we went to Springfield to organize the Senate in January 1973, the Republicans had thirty senators and we Democrats had twenty-nine, and so they got to pick the Senate president. They chose William Harris of Pontiac. We kept Partee as our leader. In my freshman term, Partee appointed Senators Jim Donnewald of downstate Breese and Bob Cherry of Chicago as his assistants. Then Cherry withdrew as a Senate candidate in 1972 because he said he couldn't handle the longer sessions that the new constitution would require. The legendary Bernard Neistein, a state senator as well as a ward boss back home, also stepped down from the Senate that year, which was significant because he might have risen to the leadership slot. Things were changing with the departures of Cherry and Neistein. In addition to me, there were some other possibilities from Chicago for leadership positions, some of whom had more seniority and thought they deserved consideration. Everyone assumed the popular Donnewald would stay in leadership and represent the downstaters. Partee, I suppose, had conferred with Mayor Daley and decided that I would be the other assistant leader. I approached some other members and told them I would appreciate their support, asking them to put in a word for me with Partee if the opportunity arose. Partee, the mayor, and the other members must have felt that some new, young, aggressive blood would be good, and I was the logical candidate. So Partee added me to his team, along with Donnewald.

It's ironic that on that day of great satisfaction for me, Elmer Conti filed yet another challenge to my election, contesting my right to be seated in the Illinois Senate. Conti's challenge went to the Senate Elections Committee, which heard witnesses and ordered an independent discovery recount. Those on the committee looked over the ballots and totals to make sure there was no obvious discrepancy. About a year later, the committee, under the aegis of the Republican chairman, issued its report denying Conti's challenge. I think the Republicans dragged it out to keep a threat hanging over my head: "Stay in line, kid, or we're going to have a report that bumps you out of here." I was confident all along that justice would prevail. Our case was solid. There was no chicanery, as Conti had claimed. I just kept working, knowing full well that at some point the Republicans would get tired of this and let it drop. It finally came out in my favor, as I knew it would.

Being in leadership after only two years in the Senate was exciting despite the problems that Governor Walker caused. Walker and his staff didn't work well with the legislature or the leaders. It didn't help Walker that Republicans controlled both chambers of the General Assembly, with

Harris the new Senate president and Blair starting his second term as Speaker of the House. On the Democratic side, we had Partee as minority leader in the Senate, and the House had Representative Clyde Choate of southern Illinois as its minority leader.

The Democratic leaders met during session about once a week at the Governor's Mansion, which covers a large city block just two blocks east and one block south of the Capitol. Victor de Grazia, the governor's point person with the legislature, used to meet with us weekly, either at the beginning of the week or at the end of the week. We would talk about where we were going, where we should be going, what the governor's office wanted, and what it didn't want. When Walker attended the meetings, he would put Partee on one side of him and Choate on the other. Then it was Representative Gerald Shea of Riverside and then me. Shea was there representing Mayor Daley's interests. Walker would always put de Grazia next to me, his theory being that I was the only guy who was going to tell the truth. So when push came to shove, de Grazia could find out from me what was really going on. The only guy Walker got to talk to was Choate, and Choate would bullshit the governor around the block. It was comical. Choate would give Walker all kinds of puff about the House membership's concerns. But Choate did not give a darn what the membership wanted, and some of us knew it. He was a showman. He would spin around de Grazia and the governor. Then Choate and Partee sometimes would go at it. Although both were Democrats, they did not like each other. It was actually kind of funny. None of us trusted the governor or liked what he was doing as a Democrat. We weren't quite sure most of the time where he stood. And Walker was not comfortable with us; rather, he was confrontational.

It did not take long before relations became especially strained between Partee and the governor, and also between Choate and the governor, all Democrats. So the governor wasn't always there, and he would deal with Shea and me through de Grazia. I became the middleman. Walker didn't feel it was appropriate to meet with Shea or me because our leaders weren't there—we were only assistants—so de Grazia would visit with us from time to time, and we would give him our assessment about where the governor's program was going, if anywhere, and what he had to do to pass his program. This governor's staff was not used to dealing with anybody. They thought Walker was the king, and the king doesn't have to answer to anybody. The legislature doesn't work that way, though, so we had a bumpy ride the first session. Some unhappy Democrats accused Walker of getting along better with Bill Harris, the Republican Senate president, than he did with the Democratic leaders, and that was accurate. He was giving Harris jobs and consideration of public works projects to the detriment of the Democrats. So the tension became worse, especially between Partee and Choate. They did not care for one another, and they started engaging in a personal contest about who would have the upper hand with the governor and his people.

Shea and I were the two top-level Democratic leaders who got along. Toward the end of the session, he and I would meet almost every morning at seven o'clock in one of our offices in the Capitol. We compared House and Senate calendars and compared all the bills in play. If one of them had slipped out of the House against Shea's will or out of the Senate against our will, we would plan to make the appropriate disposition. Usually we would let those bills die a quiet death in our chambers. Shea and I worked together well because we weren't arbitrary, and neither one of us had a personal agenda. Members knew if they wanted to have a bill passed, they had to go with the Democratic program—go with the flow of the leadership. No solo flights were allowed.

That spring, the silver lining for me was working with Jim Donnewald. Partee's appointment of Donnewald and me as assistant leaders was the start of a lifelong friendship. Donnewald was a lawyer from the small central Illinois town of Breese. He and I had the two desks in the Senate chamber next to Partee's. That was traditional. All the leadership sat in a row in proximity to one another. When a person is your seatmate in Springfield, given the fact that you spend so much time on the floor—including, at times, late evenings and early mornings—you certainly get to know the measure of a man. I had the good fortune to work with Donnewald for fourteen years in the Senate, and then a while longer after he was elected state treasurer in 1982. Donnewald made things happen. He would suggest to Governor Walker what should be done for southern Illinois, and Walker would listen. Donnewald was one of the few guys Walker would listen to, because he also had a reputation of having no personal agenda. He didn't need one. He was a wealthy, successful businessman and lawyer who aided people who couldn't do it for themselves. He really cared about all of southern Illinois and the people of his district. You probably couldn't find a project or bill for southern Illinois in those days that Donnewald wasn't involved in; he was just terrific. Before my time, however, he had one major disappointment. He wanted Interstate 64, an east-west highway that started in St. Louis and went to Louisville, Kentucky, and then on to the Atlantic coast, to go past his hometown of Breese, along U.S. Route 50. But the governor of Indiana wanted it to go through Evansville, Indiana, and so I-64 skipped Breese. It went instead through Mt. Vernon, Illinois, on its way to Evansville and Louisville.[1]

Donnewald got along with everybody. He acted as a mediator in settling disputes among General Assembly members, particularly Democratic members who managed to get crosswise with one another. Donnewald calmed members down so that the disputes didn't get away from us. He was a great leader and had basic common sense. One of the pitfalls of any legislative effort is that there is always the law of unintended consequences—a surprise that happens after you pass a bill. Donnewald had the uncanny ability to foresee what others couldn't in terms of future consequences, and he would point it out. He had great insights and horse sense.

Developing such relationships is one of the great benefits of public service. On my list of friends in the Senate, Donnewald would be right at the top. In my career, I had the opportunity to work with a whole host of genuinely compassionate, giving, caring people. Donnewald would be at the top of that list, too. His decency helped me understand as a young senator the merit of treating others with respect.

Meanwhile, in the summer of 1972, a tragic incident on Chicago's West Side captured the attention of the entire General Assembly. It became the catalyst for one of the most important pieces of legislation I ever sponsored. On July 28, a six-year-old boy named Johnny Lindquist was badly beaten by his father, William Lindquist. The story is that little Johnny was screaming and crying at home, so his father dragged him to the bathroom and started fisting him. He knocked the boy unconscious and kicked him, then an ambulance was called when the boy failed to respond. Johnny went to St. Anne's Hospital with a fractured skull and many bruises. The case attracted statewide attention when authorities learned that Johnny had been returned to his natural parents earlier in the year. He had been living rather happily in a foster home in Wisconsin, according to all reports, and it was unclear whether the state or an agency or a social worker had recommended that he be returned to his parents.[2] One newspaper headline described the nurses' "vigil of love" in the hospital two weeks after the incident.[3] Johnny never did recover, and he died August 31, three days after his seventh birthday. Both parents were charged with murder.

Partee appointed me to conduct an investigation into why Johnny had been allowed to return home to his abusive parents. Partee thought the legislature needed to do something to address child abuse. At the time, public sentiment favored keeping children with their natural parents.

Two days after Johnny died, even the *Chicago Tribune* ran an editorial warning against making it "legally easier for social agencies, the state, or the courts to take away children from their natural parents . . . because of an isolated tragedy."[4] Johnny had been living for three years with some good foster parents, and during that time they moved to a Wisconsin farm. But on March 28 he had been returned to his natural parents, despite the fact that there were earlier indications of abuse in their home. Evidently, the parents had heard they would get a larger welfare check if Johnny was back in their custody.

In my attempt to make some sense of it and to make the Department of Children and Family Services (DCFS) explain its action, I convened a subcommittee of the Senate Judiciary Committee. Then I was asked to cochair a special Legislative Investigating Commission along with a Republican senator, Jim Soper. At one of the hearings, we learned a lot about the cooperation of Catholic Charities with DCFS on foster child cases. Monsignor Thomas Holbrook of Catholic Charities told our subcommittee that the intention was to get Johnny back to his biological parents on a trial basis, and if that worked out, the agency would have sought a court order to return Johnny to his natural parents permanently. Monsignor Holbrook also urged us to pass a law to limit the amount of time a child could stay in foster homes.

The real tragedy was that we learned that the breadth of the child abuse problem was much greater than anyone had imagined. While Johnny was still in the hospital, for instance, a judge removed Johnny's two brothers and two sisters from the family home because his two-year-old sister inexplicably fell from a second-story window and was treated for several cuts and bruises. She was treated at St. Anne's Hospital while Johnny was still there in a coma. When police investigated the family home, they discovered that ketchup had been splattered around the kitchen, apparently by the children who had been playing, and dog waste from their two dogs had not been picked up for days. So the kids were taken away.

At that time, we didn't have a system for getting to these kids early enough. It became clear that we needed to change the legal system and the juvenile code. This was a situation where, sadly enough, it took a few high-profile cases to get something onto the agenda in Springfield. We knew we had to make significant changes in the 1973 session, but such major social and legal changes were difficult to pass. The *Tribune* and many others feared an invasion of family rights. We attempted to remove "the presumption of custody" for biological parents who were known to have abused their children in some way and wanted such parents to have to prove they were fit to regain custody. That would indeed weaken the biological parents' rights to raise their own children. I knew that; we all knew that. It was a tough sell, and we didn't sell it at first. I took the position that once children had been removed, the presumption of custody would switch in favor of the foster parents if there was no contact or very little contact from the biological parents for a period of up to eighteen months. If the biological parents for eighteen months to two years didn't have any contact with their child and made no effort at rehabilitation through the ordinary means of medicine or consultation or psychiatric help, I believed that DCFS ought to be able to go into court and say the foster parents should maintain custody.

Our investigation and some more highly publicized cases gave everybody some idea of the scope of the problem of abused and neglected children. As the debate continued in the spring of 1973, the story of a young girl named Adrianne Sandoval received a great deal of attention.[5] When Adrianne was four months old in 1971, her mother told relatives that her husband had abused the baby. So the mother, Lily Gallagher, gave the baby to another couple, Juan and Elsie Carrizales. When the Carrizales family decided to adopt Adrianne two years later, the natural mother took the toddler back home. Juan and Elsie Carrizales took the case to court, where they provided evidence that the father was a drug addict and had indeed abused the baby. But the court decided in favor of the natural parents, and Adrianne went home. Tragedy struck again when two-year-old Adrianne was taken to Ravenswood Hospital, where she was treated for many bruises and scratches; she also had patches of hair torn out. The state placed Adrianne in a temporary foster home, and another court battle was waged to determine who would get custody of the girl. The natural parents still wanted her, and so did her new foster parents. There were many headlines and lots of news coverage.

It was the kind of story we heard time and again during our hearings. We came to the unmistakable conclusion that child abuse was vastly underreported in Illinois. We had to do something about it.

By the time little Adrianne left Ravenswood Hospital on June 7, 1973—following Johnny Lindquist's death the previous year—we already had passed four bills in the Senate to provide more protection for children. Illinois's first child abuse reporting law had been enacted in 1965, but we learned that it didn't have nearly enough teeth. One of my bills significantly enlarged the scope of individuals who would have to report a case of child abuse. Previously, only physicians did. What we tried to do was put that reporting obligation on virtually anyone who came into daily contact with young kids. We tried to become more inclusive, so we added teachers, school administrators, truant officers, law enforcement officers, social workers, nurses, directors and staff assistants of nursery schools and day care centers, and field personnel of the Illinois Department of Public Aid. We also included staff working for Cook County agencies because the county had field personnel working with children. We also found out that state social workers did not always respond promptly enough, and so we changed the law to require the state to begin an investigation within twenty-four hours after getting a report of child abuse. Our bills passed easily and became the new law of Illinois. The momentum on this issue continued, leading eventually to a total overhaul of the 1965 law in the Abused and Neglected Child Reporting Act of 1975. The new law also allowed physicians to retain temporary protective custody of children who might be in imminent danger if returned to their homes. What we did became a national model. In subsequent years, we tightened restrictions even more as new situations arose.

The law dramatically increased the number of reported cases of abuse. In 1966, the first year that Illinoisans had to report child abuse cases, DCFS officially heard about 483 cases. In 1973, the figure more than doubled, to 1,160 cases, and two years later, the number more than doubled again, to 2,801. After we passed the 1975 law, the number of reported cases soared to 6,748 in 1976.[6] The idea was to protect more children, and I think we did. A few senators thought we were giving too much discretion to the doctors, and some were concerned that we were cutting into the rights of families. But we just couldn't ignore what we learned at those hearings—that children were being beaten and neglected—and believed the government had to step in to help them. DCFS now has much more sophisticated reporting and investigating procedures. Starting in fiscal year 1989, the number of reported cases in Illinois exceeded 100,000 every year except for fiscal years 2002 and 2003, with the peak of 139,720 occurring in fiscal year 1995.[7] We still have a long way to go to truly protect all of these endangered kids, but at least we are responding to many more cases; three decades ago, such cases were hardly reported at all.

Another issue that unexpectedly arose in Illinois and every other state legislature early in 1973 was abortion. On January 22, the U.S. Supreme Court narrowly approved the historic *Roe v. Wade* decision, which gave women a constitutional right to an abortion under certain conditions.

The decision caught all the public health officials and legislative leaders in Illinois by surprise. They didn't expect it to happen, nor did they expect that kind of usurpation of states' rights. Leaders in the Illinois

Department of Public Health appealed to the legislature to respond to the Court decision. They said if we didn't pass something, there would be nothing to regulate this procedure in Illinois. I introduced three bills at their request, and then because of the press of business, I gave them over to Senator Don Wooten of Rock Island. He was interested in this subject and was prepared to sit down and work through it. Nobody quite knew what to make of the Court's decision or how to respond to it. So the Department of Public Health took the lead and set up the right of the state to regulate abortions after the first trimester. According to the Supreme Court's decision, for the first trimester, there could be virtually no state regulation of abortions. Back then, the term "back-alley abortion" had become the phrase everybody used for women getting abortions in their homes or in other places that were quite likely unsanitary. The Court made some attempt at regulation during the second trimester, in that an abortion had to be performed in a hospital, in pristine sanitary conditions, with life-support systems available. In the third trimester, abortions were nearly outlawed except to preserve the physical or mental health of the mother. That language about the health of the mother became more controversial over the years.

We were working on this rather quickly and reached a compromise with the Department of Public Health, the Illinois State Medical Society, and the Illinois Hospital Association. Senator Wooten explained the bills during the emotional debate on the Senate floor. He was especially concerned about defining the end of the second trimester of a pregnancy as the twenty-fourth or twenty-fifth week of pregnancy and that it would be permissible up to that time to have an abortion. He thought that was a bad definition and a bad cutoff point for abortions. "Twenty weeks is more nearly the accurate figure," he said. "I know because I have a son who was born at about that period of time [of his mother's pregnancy], and he is a healthy youngster today, so I know. . . . But I would point out, that in that case as in so many others, we are absolutely caught on the Supreme Court decision."[8]

In 1973, a majority of the senators, including the Senate Democrats, and a majority of the House members would have been labeled pro-life. I was certainly among the legislators who was, and is, pro-life. The "choice" movement, consisting of people who preferred or demanded choice or defended the right to an abortion, which is what they did (and do), weren't in ascendancy. They weren't even around, or if they were, they were very quiet or they weren't organized. There was virtually no debate. There was some haranguing on the floor regarding the Court and its decision, but on any given pro-life issue, we had a dramatic majority in favor of the pro-life position. Interestingly, those first three bills to regulate abortion received only thirty, thirty-two, and thirty votes out of fifty-nine senators, just enough to get a majority in the Senate. There were not many votes against those bills; rather, nearly everybody else was silent when it came to voting. For example, I was among the twenty-eight senators, many of them Democrats, who did not vote at all on SB 1050, one of the three bills we passed to regulate abortion in Illinois, because I did not approve of making abortions legal in the first two trimesters of a woman's pregnancy. To make sure it was clear that many did not vote at all, the presider took a formal poll of these twenty-eight "absentees."[9]

One of the big issues during the abortion debate was whether doctors, nurses, and hospitals would be required to perform an abortion if they had a moral objection to it. Some medical practitioners didn't want to be involved in the procedure at all because of their beliefs. Representative Edmund Kucharski, a Chicago Republican, introduced a "conscience bill" in the House and got it passed, and I readily sponsored it in the Senate.[10] I wanted the doctors, nurses, and hospitals to be held harmless if they remained steadfast in their beliefs. Under this bill, medical personnel could not be fired, demoted, or reprimanded if they refused to participate in the procedure. A number of senators complained to me privately and on the Senate floor about the bill, with some saying that doctors might refuse to treat women who were having acute medical emergencies related to their pregnancy. But that was not the point of my bill. "What the bill does say," I said during the final debate, "is that if in fact a physician or a hospital through its board of directors decides that human life should not be terminated except and only to save the life of the mother . . . if they so decide, they shall not be answerable in damages for that decision. That's all it says. It in no way impinges upon or circumscribes an otherwise medical judgment."[11] We won with thirty-seven votes on this bill, with only four voting no. It's interesting that two of the most vocal opponents, Senators Harris Fawell and Hudson Sours, were Republicans. The bill was signed into law; it is still in existence, and it should be.

It's fair to say that times obviously have changed, because many Republicans, except for the moderate Republicans, are pro-life today, and many Democrats, if not most, are pro-choice. It is unfortunate that many groups and the two major parties have become so polarized over the abortion issue. It has become a political lightning rod in the past four decades. Over the years, I had many conversations about the issue, and some of my best staff members strongly disagreed with me and were unqualifiedly pro-choice. But I am not defensive about my pro-life position. I believe that we should not end human life prematurely in the womb. I agree with the pro-choice people who say that this is indeed an issue about women and children, but we obviously come to different conclusions about whether that means a woman should have a right to choose abortion on demand. I devoted my entire Senate career to helping women and children get more services and more protection from the state of Illinois, and I helped to establish many support services for disadvantaged and disabled people. My record on those issues is clear. But the pro-choice advocates today have made it quite clear that if you're not pro-choice, don't even bother to run, especially as a Democrat. They don't mind telling you, "We'll run you out of town," which is truly unfortunate.

4. My Finest Accomplishment

I felt strongly that too many people believed it was reasonable to warehouse these youngsters.

RICHARD M. DALEY, THE SON OF MAYOR RICHARD J. DALEY, arrived in Springfield as a state senator in 1973. He was thirty-one then, five years younger than I. The Illinois Senate was his first legislative office, although he had been elected a delegate to the 1970 constitutional convention. Everybody assumed he had a political future ahead of him; a lot of us thought it would be in Chicago or Cook County. Referred to privately either as "the kid" or "Richie" when he first arrived, he ended up staying in the Senate for eight years, until 1981, when he left Springfield after winning election as Cook County state's attorney.

Daley was rather quiet in his first Senate term. But he started to challenge the Senate Democratic leadership in 1975. Thanks to successes in the 1974 elections, we took control of the Senate again with a comfortable 34–25 margin. The House Democrats, meanwhile, had a whopping 101–76 edge. Even with a difficult Democratic governor in Dan Walker, it was the first time the Democrats controlled both chambers and the Governor's Mansion in thirty-eight years, since 1937, when Henry Horner was governor. So 1975 should have been a great year for Democrats. But right out of the gate, the House had all kinds of problems, needing ninety-three ballots to elect William Redmond—who had no previous leadership experience—as Speaker as a compromise candidate. Representative Gerald Shea, Mayor Daley's House floor leader, was viewed by many as the House's actual Democratic leader. As the House remained unsettled, Shea had to deliver the word to Clyde Choate of Anna, the popular southern Illinois Democratic representative, that he no longer would have the support of the mayor to become Speaker. In the previous two years, Choate had been the top Democrat in the Illinois House, and many assumed he would become Speaker. But Redmond got the nod in a House divided.

In the Senate, we also began to see some unraveling among the troops. We reinstalled Cecil Partee as Senate president after Bill Harris's one term as the Republican Senate president, and Partee relied on me to be his floor leader. But starting this year, we couldn't always get Senator Daley and a few of his Chicago allies on board. Daley would tell reporters that he respected Partee and that I was one of his best friends in the Senate. The truth is, there was some competition between Daley and me most of the time we were in the Senate. The *Chicago Tribune* reported in 1975 that "Daley and his allies made life miserable for Rock and Partee" by joining forces with independent senators such as Dawn Clark Netsch and Richard Newhouse, two Chicago Democrats. The *Tribune* also credited Daley with dividing the Senate Democrats in 1975 by challenging Senate president Partee and threatening to kill bills that were popular with the liberals in our caucus. Meanwhile, Netsch grew so frustrated with him that she called him "dirty little Richie."[1]

When Daley first arrived in the Senate and talked about anything, a lot of people thought, "This is what the mayor, his father, thinks." I never put as much stock in that as the other Cook County legislators did. Maybe part of Senator Daley's attitude toward me stemmed from the fact that before he got there, I was the Senate's leader for bills of interest to the city of Chicago. His father, Mayor Daley, kept me in that role, and I think the younger Daley was surprised at that, which he expressed to some other members. I took great pride in representing the interests of the city of Chicago and the Cook County Democratic organization. Working with those in my party as well as downstaters on both sides of the aisle were among the keys to my early success in the Senate.

A particular issue that damaged the relationship between Senator Daley and all of us in leadership in 1975 was education funding. Governor Walker had vetoed two major education bills—$81 million in general school funds and $36 million for specific education programs. That meant a loss of millions of dollars for the Chicago schools, a move that irritated Mayor Daley. So in a spectacular power play, the mayor decided to make a rare trip to Springfield during the veto session in October and testify before the House in support of overriding the governor's vetoes. The mayor received some advice about that from his son and from Mike Madigan, who, as the assistant majority leader, suggested the mayor's trek to Springfield. The mayor did not consult with Partee, Shea, or me. We would have advised him not to come because nobody was certain he had the votes in the House for an override. It didn't bother me that the mayor did not ask for my opinion or Shea's opinion, but it is fair to say that Senator Daley's attempt to demonstrate his power by getting his dad to Springfield without our advice further strained Senator Daley's relationship with those of us in Senate leadership.

Madigan's role in bringing the mayor to Springfield added to the tension; the mayor evidently was grooming Madigan to replace Shea as Chicago's floor leader in the other chamber. Part of that had to do with the mayor looking ahead to the 1976 elections. For a while, the mayor publicly supported Shea to be the Democratic organization's candidate for state's attorney in Cook County, and he publicly floated my name to be the party's nominee for Illinois attorney general. But the truth is, Shea never did have the Cook County organization's support, or the mayor's.[2] Neither one of us ended up being candidates for those positions, and Shea just retired from the House at the end of 1976. There was also speculation that Mayor Daley wanted both Partee and me to run for Cook County or statewide offices in 1976 to clear the way for the younger Daley to become Senate president, but that was more talk than anything.[3]

I loved serving in the Senate and being in leadership when the Democrats had the majority, which we would not relinquish for the remainder of my eighteen years as a senator. I was forging alliances with some downstaters so that I could be of help not only to Cook County but also to agriculture and coal mining. The downstaters never were all that organized as a bloc, but they all had interests, and they all had constituencies with one common attitude: a politically anti-Chicago attitude. One time when I took my family to the DuQuoin State Fair in southern Illinois, we saw candidates' billboards declaring how awful it would be to support anything the "northern bosses" wanted. My kids asked me who those northern bosses were, and I had to laugh and tell them, "Well, I guess I'm one of them."

We took advantage of our new majority in 1975. The previous year, we had passed some modest sales tax rebates for senior citizens who had less than $10,000 in income, but Governor Walker vetoed them. He said we couldn't afford it, but frankly, I don't know what he was thinking or why he would say that. The national economy was in bad shape then, and senior citizens groups, especially those on fixed incomes, were telling us that any kind of tax relief would help. The governor's veto irritated us. Even worse, his very late timing of the veto did not allow the General Assembly time to reconvene to override it in the fall of 1974. The press got all over this issue, putting senior citizens on television to give them a chance to say how insensitive state government was. We looked bad, but it wasn't the legislature's fault.

Lieutenant Governor Neil Hartigan and a few of us in leadership led the charge to resurrect the rebates early in 1975. Shea handled the bill in the House, and I sponsored it in the Senate. We wanted to provide tax rebates of $50 to $100 a year to persons over the age of sixty-five and to permanently disabled people with less than $10,000 a year in income. I pulled a parliamentary move to dispense with our normal procedures early in the 1975 session to sail this bill back to the governor very quickly. It was unusual to move major legislation that early in a session, but we needed to send the governor a message and let the people of the state know we cared. A few of my colleagues thought we were moving too fast and wanted the bill referred to a committee, which is the normal process. But I believed there was nothing new to be learned in committees. We had heard testimony the previous year, and just about everybody in the General Assembly had voted for this legislation. It was Walker who put on the brakes. So my friend on the other side of the aisle, Bill Harris of Pontiac, who was still the Republican leader, stood up and asked for a special Committee of the Whole to move things along. I immediately replied on the floor that I thought it was a great suggestion. Having a Committee of the Whole—which means the entire Senate gathers as a "committee" to discuss a topic or bill—would serve two purposes. First, assigning the bills to the Committee of the Whole would allow us to bypass all other committees. It also would give the Senate a chance to bring in people to speak favorably and very publicly on this topic and send a message to the citizens of the state and to the governor that we wanted sales tax relief for senior citizens as soon as possible. We knew the press would cover the issue extensively.

President Partee scheduled the Committee of the Whole almost immediately; it was set to begin two hours before the regular session on February 4, 1975. It was a brilliant move, and we did indeed hear a couple of hours of testimony. Ken Johnston of the Senior Action Coalition thanked us for "trying to help the elderly, the poor of Illinois, put another meal on their table a week, fill another prescription or to pay a fuel bill."[4] The hearing also gave Hartigan a chance to distance himself from the governor by making an eloquent speech about the many needs of senior citizens and recognizing how they have worked so long and paid so many taxes over the years; the least we could do would be to give them a little relief. Everyone was speculating that Hartigan would challenge Walker in the Democratic primary for governor the next year, because the regular Democrats were looking for a new direction and Walker was vetoing our bills. Hartigan pointed out that probably not enough of the eligible seniors were taking advantage of some of the programs we already had, such as the property tax benefit commonly called the "circuit breaker," and so this was one more way to help—at a cost of only $34 million, which was money we had in surplus at the time. I'm sure Governor Walker saw the writing on the wall about the foolishness of his veto when the House approved it by a 162–0 vote and the Senate gave final approval, 47–2.

Overall, 1975 wasn't a good year for the governor. Many of us grew frustrated with him because he wasn't giving a lot of consideration to our bills. What he mostly talked about was a 6 percent across-the-board cut in funding for state agencies. That was Walker being "Walker the great reformer." But he didn't understand the process or how government worked. His handling of the session started a lot of talk about which Democrat was going to run against him in the primary the following year. Hartigan's name was frequently mentioned. We all knew that we had to run somebody against Walker; it was just a matter of who was going to do it.

On the other hand, it also proved to be the year of what I consider my finest legislative accomplishment. I first got interested in a new issue a couple of years earlier when an acquaintance of mine had a son who became blind and deaf at the age of two, the result of a childhood disease. Her son was the same age as my son, Jay. She asked that I meet with a number of other parents whose children were both blind and deaf. There was little to nothing going on in the state of Illinois to help what I called these "dually afflicted" children. A private facility, the Hope School, was located in Springfield, and there were state facilities in downstate Jacksonville assisting deaf and blind children separately, but it was very expensive to provide round-the-clock care. For the most part, the deaf and blind children were being what I called "warehoused." Plus, both Jacksonville and Springfield were too far for Chicago parents, and the special education districts could not handle the children who were dually afflicted.

The parents came to me for help. We all thought it made sense to establish a school and center in the Chicago area. I had eighteen months of intense discussions and negotiations with the Office of Illinois Education, the Office of the Superintendent of Public Instruction, and the Departments of Mental Health and Children and Family Services. I found the state superintendent of public instruction, Michael Bakalis, to be sympathetic but not altogether enthusiastic. In March 1975, I drafted a bill to create and operate a service center for deaf and blind individuals. The House had drafted a similar bill the previous year, but it was buried in a committee. My bill, Senate Bill 379 in the Seventy-Ninth General Assembly, was cosponsored by President Partee as well as by Senators Tom Hynes and Bob Egan, another great friend from Chicago.

As my bill was going through the Senate, Bakalis testified against it on the basis that he didn't think that the Illinois school superintendent's office ought to operate that type of school. I took the other position. I did not want the facility to be under the auspices of the Department of Mental Health or DCFS or the Department of Public Aid or any other such agency. We had identified 123 children in the state who were deaf and blind and needed educational services. I felt strongly that too many people believed it was reasonable to warehouse these youngsters. That is, the state would take care of their physical needs, but there would be no attempt to educate them or open up the world to them as we know it. We stood firm. The bill eventually passed, virtually unanimously, in both the House and Senate.

Actually, one vote against it did show up on the Senate board on May 21, 1975, the day of final passage in the Senate. It came from my good Democratic friend Sam Vadalabene of Madison County. After the tally, Sam immediately asked to speak. He declared that he had voted aye, but the light on the board was red, indicating a nay vote. "Something is wrong with my switch," he said for the record. "Somebody worked on it over the night so that when I vote yes, it [shows up as] no. . . . There's been a sabotage at my desk."[5] So in deference to Sam's objection, we took another vote, and the Senate approved this new center and school by a 56–0 margin.

Unfortunately, it wasn't smooth sailing for the school and center even after that. Governor Walker signed the bill but failed to sign the appropriation to pay for the services. We estimated that we needed $800,000 to get the center and school up and running. The parents became frustrated because their advisory committee was meeting with some regularity, but nobody seemed to be paying attention to either the parents or the committee. We had to keep fighting for the money, and we finally got some of it after a year or so. For our first location, I went to the Archdiocese of Chicago, which gave us a vacant school building. But we didn't have any money to make it a fully accessible building, and the state wasn't prepared to commit to it fully.

We did have some operating money and hired some extraordinarily dedicated teachers and staff members. As I had hoped, it was operated by the state school superintendent's office. The problem was that the facility itself was in a bad, run-down neighborhood that was not particularly safe. The staff was there on a twenty-four-hour basis, so we had to move it out of that area if it was going to succeed. We were losing too many workers.

We found a new location in Glen Ellyn. The building had been a nursing home or a motel at one point, or maybe both. It was a small facility with substantial property around it and was at a tremendous location, near the intersection of Roosevelt Road and Highway 53. It has proved to be a tremendous success and quite inspirational, when you realize what can be done to educate these youngsters. It is no easy task, but the results are remarkable. Some of the first group of students eventually "aged out." Most of them, I would say, are in independent living and frankly are doing quite well. The last time I checked, the center was serving more than 500 children a year—truly a testament to its need.

I have always considered the establishment of this school as my finest legislative accomplishment because over the years I fought over it with two governors (Walker and James R. Thompson), the state superintendent, and the State Board of Education. We wound up winning the funding battle and the philosophical battle over what it should be, and we helped many disadvantaged Illinoisans and their families. Getting the school established and fighting for all of the funding took quite a bit of time, twelve or thirteen years.

5. A Scandal I Didn't Deserve

Those ERA demonstrators must have thought I had
some magical power to change everyone's minds.

M Y DAD, A BARBER BY TRADE, was an avid horse player. When I was
a kid, he took me to the track, usually Arlington Park. Once or
twice we went way south to a track called Washington Park; it was like the
South Side's Arlington Park. Over time, I enjoyed the races more and more
and started following the horses. I still do. Sometimes when I worked
in my Chicago law office, I would go to Arlington Park just for a break.
I've been to the Kentucky Derby a half-dozen times but not the other two
races in the famous Triple Crown, the Belmont or the Preakness, and I've
been to the Breeders' Cup—the annual season-ending championship of
thoroughbred racing—and to Saratoga in New York.

Over the years, I made it my business to learn how to read and study
the forms. When you get into it over the course of a season, you start
recognizing the names, the jockeys, the trainers, and the owners. I got
to know many of the track owners and some of the horsemen and horse
owners from downstate Illinois. When I became a senator, someone told
me that the Illinois Department of Agriculture had a legislative liaison
by the name of Dick Davidson. Everybody knew him; he was a fixture.
He had been there for years and years and knew a great deal about the
operation of the Department of Agriculture and the Illinois State Fair and
all things agrarian. So I got to know him and learned from him about the
state's interest in the regulation of breeding and racing horses.

Historically, Illinois had a problem with the quality of its horses in the
big races. At the Hambletonian in southern Illinois, which people called
the Kentucky Derby of harness racing, horses from Illinois didn't have a
real shot at winning. It doesn't sound good to say that, but everybody knew
it was true. Illinois-bred horses could not be competitive on the track
with horses from other states such as Kentucky. The horses in Kentucky,

frankly, were a little higher class for the most part, and they would march into Ohio and Illinois and New Jersey and go away with the big purses.

So the Illinois breeders wanted some additional incentives. Richard Duchossois, the founder and chairman of Duchossois Industries, headquartered in Elmhurst, had a big breeding farm. He wanted to have races and purses specifically earmarked for Illinois-conceived and Illinois-foaled horses. Illinois laws needed some changes to make these things happen. I had been around the tracks, and Duchossois and others knew of my big interest in horses.

Unfortunately, the industry's image was tarnished by a big scandal when the federal government indicted former Illinois governor Otto Kerner in 1971 for buying racetrack stock at a huge discount from Marjorie Everett, the former owner of the Arlington Park, Washington Park, and Balmoral racetracks in the Chicago area. *Sports Illustrated* once called Everett "the racing lady of Chicago."[1] Kerner was accused of paying Everett the small amount of $50,000 for $300,000 worth of stock in exchange for giving her favorable racing dates. Setting the dates was Kerner's prerogative at the time of the purchase. James R. Thompson, at that time the U.S. attorney, and his chief assistant, Sam Skinner, prosecuted Kerner. Thompson claimed that Everett gave Kerner a $45,000 campaign contribution in 1960—big money in those days and 10 percent of Kerner's entire campaign fund that year. It wasn't illegal, just a lot of money, and it bolstered the implication that Kerner was beholden to the track owner and might have purchased the stock at a deep discount. But Kerner denied knowing the contribution was that large and denied accepting any bribe. The case just dragged on. Kerner, five years out of office and by then a sitting federal judge, was finally convicted in 1973 and went to prison in July 1974. So it was a black eye on the horse racing industry that stayed in the headlines.

There was another scandal, too—depicted as a scandal, anyway—when word got out that a New Jersey businessman with an interest in horses had given $100,000 to Illinois Republicans in 1970. The publicity led the legislature in 1972 to ban political contributions from people in the horse racing industry. It was a big mess, and it was big news over a period of years.

I became the cochair of the Legislative Investigative Commission that was charged with looking into these scandals. We took testimony ad nauseam from breeders, owners, jockeys, and everyone involved. It's what the government often does in response to a scandal: create a special committee or commission and hold public hearings. We listened to everyone and ultimately started down the path of rewriting the state's entire horse racing laws. The last one had been enacted sometime in the early 1940s; it was thirty years old and not up-to-date.

I learned along the way that whenever we considered serious horse racing legislation, the horse owners would accuse the track owners of taking advantage of them. To some extent, they were right. The track owners didn't give the horse owners much in terms of concessions. That fight has been going on forever and still is—the track owners versus the rest of the world. Not only that, but some of the churches were opposed to gambling in any form. We would always hear from the reverends who opposed gambling and alcohol, and they were lining up against us big time.

I gave everyone a chance to provide input, and then I drafted a long, complicated, comprehensive bill to overhaul the industry. We called it the Horse Racing Act of 1975 to replace the old Horse Racing Act, the Harness Racing Act, and the Quarter Horse Racing Act.

It turned out that there was a great deal of interest in this bill, which ended up with a lot of amendments. My biggest fight was with Anthony Scariano, the head of the Illinois Racing Board and a reformer. He was on the other side of almost everything I ever sponsored. Scariano found a crook under every rock, under every stairwell; to him, just about everyone was crooked except him. He was the shining star of the reformers; all you had to do was ask him. He scorched me many times about the bill, saying it was tilted too much toward the track owners and racing associations.

He wanted to continue the prohibition against political donations from anyone with ownership interest in horses, racetracks, or the industry. I told him that was silly. "Why are you going to shut off their First Amendment rights and not everybody else's?" I asked him. "What in the world are you doing? We already have a disclosure law, the one that was passed last year." Illinois had passed a campaign reform act in 1974 in response to all the Watergate issues as well as to the Illinois scandals. The major parts of our new campaign finance law required candidates to file reports disclosing who gave campaign contributions and how much they gave. I reminded Scariano that if Duchossois wanted to give me a million bucks—which he never did—I had to report it and show the world.

But Scariano fought me in the House, he fought me in the conference committee, and he fought me on the floor of the Senate. His theory was that the horse owners and track owners were regulated by the state, so they should not be giving money to state candidates. "So why don't you take on the insurance companies?" I asked, knowing that he had received some of W. Clement Stone's money. Stone was a successful insurance magnate from Chicago's South Side who reportedly gave $2 million to

Richard Nixon in 1968 and 1972. Former senator Russell Arrington, a Republican, also passed around money from the insurance companies, even though Illinois law since at least 1937 had prohibited insurance companies from making direct political contributions in Illinois. I had to laugh that the fakers and hypocrites who wanted to regulate the track owners didn't want to touch the insurance industry.

Despite my objections, the continued prohibition against the horse industry making campaign contributions prevailed. Scariano, Walker, and other reformers took a lot of credit for that. The *Chicago Sun-Times* opposed my bill, too, primarily because of the campaign finance issue. I said to Scariano and others, "If you get money, you have to report it under current law. Disclosure is enough. So why are we shutting people off? If we do that, we're going to make this a playground for the rich, in which only the rich guys can get elected because they've got their own money. It's not the kind of General Assembly we want." We got beat on the issue but eventually got rid of the prohibition several years later.[2]

Despite that controversy, it was a great deal of fun to put the final touches on the Horse Racing Act of 1975. I tried to keep it fair, and just about everyone was happy with the end product except for Scariano, Walker, some of their friends, and the church people. We ended up with a law that really helped Illinois. We added races in which only Illinois horses would compete and changed the tax structure to generate millions of new dollars for Illinois. The law also increased revenue for those engaged in the business of breeding and racing horses, added a substantial number of racing dates, and helped the downstate tracks. It made us much more competitive with Kentucky, Indiana, and Ohio, and it set the stage for what we now enjoy in terms of simulcasting races in different places. It's a big-money business, and the state relies on it.

As important as that bill was to me, it wasn't the biggest issue we took up in 1975 or the most publicized. For one, the proposed Equal Rights Amendment to the U.S. Constitution had been bouncing around the Illinois General Assembly for three years. This very short amendment that said, "Equality of rights under the law shall not be denied or abridged by the United States or by any state on account of sex," was a big deal nationwide. Congress approved it and sent it to the states for ratification in 1972. Like any proposed constitutional amendment, it needed ratification from thirty-eight states. I supported the ERA from the beginning, but in the early going, we could not get the Illinois Senate and House on the same page in the same year. Both chambers needed to vote in favor of ratification in the same session of the General Assembly for the amendment to be ratified by the state of Illinois. The media were saying there might be a more difficult time in the Senate.[3] We had become a national focal point because thirty-four other states had ratified the ERA rather quickly after Congress sent it out, but then the momentum stalled. With four more states needed for ratification, Illinois, along with Florida, North Carolina, and Indiana, became the center of attention for the amendment's proponents. It was such a hot issue that opponents also showed up en masse every time it came up. In 1975, the Illinois House passed it, so we in the Senate felt the eyes of the nation upon us, some hoping for our support and others wanting us to reject the ERA.

Our Senate president, Cecil Partee, kept holding off a floor vote because he knew we didn't have enough votes in support of the ERA. One of the big arguments was whether we needed a simple majority of thirty votes or a three-fifths majority, thirty-six votes, for official ratification in each chamber. Four House members took this issue to federal court in 1973, challenging the Illinois Constitution and the House rule that said a three-fifths vote was required in that chamber. A federal court ruled in 1975 that the General Assembly could decide for itself how large a majority was needed to ratify a federal constitutional amendment. Since the Senate also set a three-fifths rule, from then on we were certain we needed thirty-six votes.[4]

The trouble was, we never had thirty-six votes lined up. We let the issue lie for almost eighteen months; Partee refused to call a vote. Then Jimmy Carter was elected president in November 1976, defeating Gerald Ford. Before he was sworn in, Carter called Partee to encourage him and Illinois to make a strong push for the ERA. This was in December 1976, when only one month remained in that session. I ended up presiding over a long and contentious debate on December 16. It was Illinois's best chance in years to ratify the ERA. Carter's phone call convinced Partee to give it a shot, up or down. It took a bit of wrangling on my part to deal with Bill Harris, the Republican minority leader. He opposed the ERA and challenged from a parliamentary perspective how we could get the tabled amendment onto the Senate floor for a vote. It was really something, and the debate got heated. Senator Charlie Chew of Chicago really got carried away. Chew was for the amendment, but some of his arguments were, as usual, a bit different. He ended up talking about his mother's and his wife's driving habits—raising old, negative stereotypes about women—and whether the amendment meant that men and women would start using the same bathrooms.[5] Chew was passionate but not helpful. The vote was 29–22 in favor of the ERA, with three voting present. So we fell seven votes short in that session.

After that, the issue came up every year for six years. But we never took it to the Senate floor because we still didn't have the votes. Indiana ratified the ERA in 1977, and Congress extended the ratification deadline from 1979 to 1982. I talked to President Carter about it a couple of times on the phone because it remained a hot topic in Springfield, even though we couldn't get the votes.

Then in 1980, President Carter invited a few leaders of the General Assembly and some Chicago leaders to the White House. The pressure was on Illinois big time. Quite a few of us went, including Senators Emil Jones and Dawn Clark Netsch and Barbara Flynn Currie from the House. James Taylor also went because he was Chicago mayor Jane Byrne's deputy. We were cordially received and almost immediately ushered into the cabinet room. It was impressive. A few minutes later, President Carter and a few of his people entered. He had a previous Illinois Senate roll call in his hand and asked about different members on the roll. He wanted to know how close we were to passage and what, if anything, he could do to help. We told him how we had been trying to get enough votes, but our opponents felt safe. The three-fifths rule really hurt our chances. I told the president that the ERA might come up for a vote in just a few days, and if he wanted to make some calls, I would surely welcome that. I also suggested that he send some telegrams. If nothing else, the members would have a telegram from the president of the United States asking for a vote. So he did send everybody a telegram. It's a great story except for the ending: we didn't pass the ERA that year. We didn't even get enough votes to pass it out of committee. It just went away after a lot of tumult and shouting by some of the opponents. But we still had two more years to try to get it passed.

Even though I strongly supported the ERA, I took some heat for not doing enough, especially from the demonstrators who came from all over the country. It was a raucous time in the Capitol. Those demonstrators must have thought I had some magical power to change everyone's minds. I had to explain that this was a high-visibility issue on which members had taken positions publicly back home in their districts, and they weren't going to change their minds. Even some great friends like Jim Donnewald never voted for it because, first of all, he did not support it and, second, the people of his southern Illinois district wouldn't stand for it.

It was all theatrics in those final couple of years. I knew we never had enough votes, and so we usually held the resolution in committee. By keeping it there, at least we weren't defeating it one more time. With the national 1982 deadline for ratification, even then I tried to stop it from coming to the floor. But there was a big outcry, and I decided to allow the members to have their say, up or down, a few days before the end of the 1982 session. We called the resolution for a short floor debate and a vote on June 25. Six or seven people spoke up, with nothing new being offered. Then we took the vote, 31 in favor and 27 against. We had a majority but fell five votes short of the thirty-six. So Illinois never ratified the ERA—and by the way, the House never passed it after 1975, either. The ERA never became part of the U.S. Constitution because it fell three states short, Illinois being one of fifteen states not to ratify it. After that, it seemed that Senator Netsch never missed a chance to remind everyone that Illinois was the only northern industrial state not to ratify it.

In telling that story about the final failure of the ERA in 1982, I'm a little ahead of myself, but I thought it made sense to carry that story through. It had the same ending in 1982 that it had in 1976: we lost.

I was up for reelection in 1976, seeking my third term. I was hoping for something a little easier than my last election, the close one against Elmer Conti. I had no opposition from the Democrats. My Republican opponent was Ronald Stolle, a twenty-seven-year-old man whose father, Helmutt Stolle, had served in the Illinois House of Representatives. Stolle harassed me during the campaign, accusing me of some illegal or quasi-illegal activity. Then my picture was on the front page of the *Chicago Sun-Times* on June 2, 1976, along with fifteen other legislators. Our individual pictures appeared in two rows, eight head shots across, filling the top half of the front page. The headline said, "16 Legislators Got Cash Gifts, Bribery Trial Told." In those days, you could always get the next day's paper the night before; they called it the early edition. There was a big paper stand at Madison and Austin and another big one at Madison and Des Plaines. When the *Sun-Times* hit the street, somebody called me and asked what the hell was going on. I didn't know it was coming out, and it was very disconcerting.

What was happening was a big trial that everyone was calling the "cement bribery trial," which was in its fifth week.[6] At issue was a piece of legislation from 1972, when the concrete industry wanted its mixer trucks to be allowed to carry heavier loads on state highways. Every time the bill came up, we said, "Here comes the 'higher and wider' one," because the bill would have allowed the use of bigger cement trucks. Supposedly, the ready-mix concrete industry created a $30,000 cash fund to be distributed to legislators as the bill went through the House and Senate. So the federal government was going after legislators who took those bribes in exchange for supporting the bill. Two Republican legislators, Representative Pete Pappas of Rock Island and former senator Donald Carpentier of East Moline, pled guilty early to lesser charges and became government witnesses in the federal courthouse in the summer of 1976.

It got sensational. When that paper came out and showed all of our pictures, it appeared we were all guilty of receiving some cash for supporting the "higher and wider" bill. But although the paper had sixteen pictures, including mine, only eight people were on trial—Senator Kenneth W. Course (D-Chicago); former senator Jack E. Walker (R-Lansing), a one-time House Speaker; ex-representative Frank P. North (R-Rockford); Representatives John F. Wall and Louis F. Capuzi (both R-Chicago); Representative Robert Craig (D-Danville); a lobbyist from Lake Bluff; and a cement executive from Highland Park. I guess the paper assumed a few more of us got a piece of the action from the concrete industry.

Course's defense was that he did not get all the money; he had to spread it out. What he meant was that he did not get to keep all of the money that he was given but had to share it with other like-minded legislators. He ended up committing suicide later. I guess he saw the writing on the wall and knew he was headed for prison, so he jacked up his car, took the tire off, laid under the car, and kicked the jack out. It was terrible. A few of my colleagues did get convicted and were sent to prison. Carpentier was one of them, and Jack Walker, too. A number of them pled guilty, and life went on. Of the eight people on trial, only Wall and the cement executive were found not guilty.

It wasn't funny then, and it isn't funny now. It's a terrible thing to find yourself against all of those barrels of ink. My kids were small enough that they did not understand what was going on, but their daddy was on the front page of the *Sun-Times* and other kids were saying bad things about him in the schoolyard. I felt awful; this had never happened to me before. I suppose I was dragged into the proceedings because I had been the presiding officer in the Senate when the bill was being considered, during my freshman term. I had not accepted any money or done anything wrong. To this day, I don't know for sure why my picture was there with all the others.

That's why I went to see Sam Skinner, U.S. attorney for the Northern District of Illinois, during all of this. He had been an assistant U.S. attorney for seven years until President Ford gave him the top prosecutor's job in 1975. I told him, "First of all, all of this stuff in the grand jury is supposed to be a secret, so how did it all leak out? It's not fair." He, of course, didn't have an answer for that. Then I said, "Sam, this is absolute bullshit. I was surprised to hear you talking on the Sunday morning talk shows about these sixteen legislators. Sam, you know me better than that. I didn't take any money." So he did a public apology on the radio, clearing me totally of any hint of illegal action. He didn't have to do that, and I appreciated it, but the front page of that *Sun-Times* will be out there forever for people to see if they want to.

Despite Skinner's public exoneration of me and the fact that I was never charged with anything because I didn't do anything illegal, Stolle wouldn't let it go during the fall campaign. He kept claiming, wrongly, that I refused to say whether I had any role in the cement bribery case. I couldn't get him to stop. I had stated repeatedly in public forums and in the newspapers, "I can unequivocally say I have not taken a bribe from anyone for any reason." It was 100 percent true. It was especially troubling to see my local community papers like the *Austinite* and the *World* continue to repeat what Stolle was saying.

The problem with such accusations is that they become a big distraction. When I was at a ward meeting or neighborhood association meeting, I was spending fifteen or twenty minutes responding to questions about the trial, or at least providing my point of view. I finally got a little short with Stolle, and I told him if he kept it up, I would sue him. I know that's unusual in a campaign, but I had had enough. Even Jim Thompson, who was running for governor for the first time and had been the U.S. attorney for the Northern District, came to my defense after Stolle distributed two pieces of negative campaign literature that attacked me. The letter from Thompson, through his campaign manager James Fletcher, assured me that they did not approve of the mailing that trashed me. I copied that letter and sent it out to residents of my district.

Despite feeling so harassed, I got the endorsements of my local papers as well as those of the *Sun-Times*, the *Tribune*, and the *Daily News* in Chicago. Also, for the first time in a campaign, I disclosed my income, assets, and net worth in a press release. I think an individual's financial matters are private, but this was four years after the Watergate break-in and two years after President Nixon resigned in disgrace. There was a lot of cynicism about public officials, and I decided to disclose this kind of information: my house on Midway Park on the West Side of Chicago was valued at $35,000. I had $3,000 in savings accounts and forty shares of stock worth $100. I also had a $20,000 mortgage on my house and was liable for $4,000 for my share of the partnership in the law firm with Dan Fusco. That was big stuff at the time, but it doesn't seem like much today.

I won the general election with 62.5 percent of the vote. Overall, the campaign went well. The local newspapers reminded people that I had sponsored a senior citizens tax relief bill, the new child abuse laws, and insurance protection for newborns. They also seemed pleased that I had pushed branch banking legislation, favored handgun control on the national level, and supported the ERA. I had helped on local issues, too, sponsoring legislation to get the Oak Park Village Mall built, for instance—and that was before I moved to Oak Park—and mandating a study of local grade railroad crossings. I remained visible in the district, and the voters rewarded me with a third term.

6. The Crazy Eight Emerge

*The Senate was starting to look silly. One day we even got
into a contentious debate about the opening prayer.*

I WAS AT MY LAW OFFICE CHRISTMAS PARTY on December 20, 1976,
at a place called the Junk in Chicago's Chinatown. We took the staff
there and had lunch and a few drinks, the typical Christmas party. The
Junk's owner, George Chung, a big-time Democrat, came running out of
the kitchen and said, "Turn the TV on; turn the TV on!" It was all over
the news that Mayor Richard J. Daley had died of a heart attack at the
age of seventy-four. As his health had been declining, his family had been
keeping him at their house on Lake Michigan. Thomas R. Donovan, one
of the mayor's closest advisors as well as his patronage chief, actually had
been running city hall for a while. (Donovan later became the nationally
acclaimed president and CEO of the Chicago Board of Trade.)[1] News
of Daley's death stunned us because the mayor had been such a force, a
legendary power, since the 1950s, certainly for my entire political career.

Nobody was prepared, politically, for the mayor's death. It was another
blow that rocked the status quo and meant that enormous changes were
looming at the beginning of 1977. Because of the November election results, we were already going to have a new governor, a new U.S. president,
and, for us, a new Senate president. So it was more than just the mayor's
death. Political life as we knew it in the city and the county would be
forever different.

Republican James R. Thompson won his first of four terms as governor,
defeating our party's candidate, Michael Howlett Sr., after Howlett had
upended the incumbent, Governor Dan Walker, in the primary back in
March. Howlett had won four consecutive statewide general elections
before that—three as auditor of public accounts (a predecessor to the
comptroller position) and one as secretary of state. At least we got rid
of Walker—something we were all happy about. Thompson's first term

was a two-year term, mandated by the 1970 Illinois Constitution so that all future gubernatorial elections, starting in 1978, would not be held the same year as a presidential election. Jimmy Carter, meanwhile, ousted incumbent president Gerald R. Ford at the national level, so there were changes everywhere at the top—Thompson the Republican governor, Carter the Democratic president.

Our leader, Cecil Partee, gave up his Senate seat and the Senate presidency to be the Democratic nominee for attorney general. But he lost in the general election to incumbent Republican William Scott, who won his third term as attorney general. With Partee's return to Chicago, there was a lot of speculation that I would become the new Senate president, a position I indeed wanted. It's fair to say many considered me the front-runner.

I had indicated to Mayor Daley right after the November election that I was interested in becoming Senate president. Daley seemed receptive. He didn't say no, but he didn't say yes, either. He was usually more direct. If he didn't like something, you knew about it. I was enthused by the fact that he did not say no and considered myself a contender. So after the mayor died, I went to see George Dunne, committeeman of the Forty-Second Ward and a former state representative. I also went to see Parky Cullerton, the Thirty-Eighth Ward committeeman and influential member of the late mayor's inner circle, and Chicago alderman Michael Bilandic.

After Daley died, of course, the big question became who was going to take over for the mayor. The city council voted to make Bilandic the acting mayor, pending a special election. The powers also settled on Dunne as the Cook County board president and leader of the Democratic Party in Cook County. Dunne apparently did not get the reception he wanted in order for him to become a future candidate for mayor. More than a few people thought that Alderman Wilson Frost, an African American from the South Side, had a good shot at becoming acting mayor. Frost was the head of the finance committee and was Emil Jones's Thirty-Fourth Ward committeeman. He was highly regarded but didn't get the mayoral nod; he later became a member of the Cook County Board of Tax Appeals.

Even though people in Springfield considered me the front-runner, I went to all the major elected officials in Cook County about the Senate presidency and, frankly, didn't get much encouragement from any of them. Dunne wanted to be the county chairman and was more concerned about lining up his political support for that. The Daleys and those who had been loyal to the late mayor were still a force to be reckoned with. My troubles got bigger with the mayor's passing, and I wasn't getting the support I should have gotten to be the Senate president. Had the mayor lived, I think I would have had that support, but I wasn't getting it from his son, Senator Daley. He was much more comfortable with Senator Thomas Hynes. So Hynes was viewed as more pro-Daley and I was viewed as a bit more independent but still a loyal member of the party. I recognized that. I talked to Hynes about it. He indicated that he was going to be a candidate for Senate president and that he thought he had the support of the Daleys. Some of the politicians from Cook County who were close to Senator Daley decided not to back me. Senators such as Frank Savickas and Howard Carroll and some others were very tied to Senator Daley and didn't have use for me particularly. Finally, Dunne told me directly that Hynes was the Cook County Democratic Party's choice to be the Senate president. I didn't like it, but I told Hynes, who was my friend, that I would support him as long as he had the support of the Democratic organization of Cook County.

It turned out not to be so cut and dried once we got to Springfield for our biennial organization in the second week of January. Hynes was our party's choice, and I announced three days before our day of organization that I was dropping out of contention for the good of the party. I meant it. I said I would support Hynes, and I did. Carroll had promoted himself as a candidate, but he also backed off in favor of Hynes. That should have paved the way for Hynes, but we also knew that Senators Harold Washington of Chicago and Terry Bruce of downstate Olney remained in the running. We assumed that Washington and Bruce would work things out with Hynes before Wednesday.

No question about it, Hynes was highly respected. The year after we were jointly recognized as the top two freshmen senators in 1971, the Federation of Independent Illinois Colleges and Universities singled out Hynes as the best legislator, period, in either the House or Senate. Then he accomplished a lot in the next six years. So on the constitutionally mandated day of organization in 1977, we arranged for Senator Fred Smith, an African American from Chicago, to put Hynes's name into nomination for the Senate presidency, as he had done for Partee two years earlier. I seconded the motion, just as I had done for Partee two years earlier. There is a prearranged formality to all of this. It's the kind of protocol in the Senate that I respected and really loved. I wanted to send the clear message that the party needed unity and that I backed Hynes. "Tom's commitment to excellence is obvious to all who know him," I said from the floor. "His competency and integrity are unquestioned, and . . . additionally and more importantly, he is and will forever remain my friend. I am pleased to second his nomination."[2]

With the leading Democrat nominated, we then followed the custom of having the opposition party nominate its candidate for Senate president. That person, of course, would never win, but he would become the minority leader in the chamber. That's how it worked. So the Republicans nominated Senator David Shapiro of Amboy. They had only twenty-five members and we had thirty-four. We should have elected Hynes as our president in the next few minutes, but we didn't.

Little did we know how determined some of our Democratic members were to flex some political muscle. Of greatest significance was the rise of the so-called Crazy Eight, a group of eight mostly downstate senators who saw Mayor Daley's death as an opportunity, I guess, to further their independence. They wanted to be independent of the Democratic Party regulars and structure. They considered themselves Democrats and got elected as Democrats, but they didn't want to be part of the program. I was among those whom the press began to call one of twenty-one "regular Democrats" in the Senate, to differentiate us from the Crazy Eight and the black caucus.

The formation of the Crazy Eight is an interesting story in itself. It started as a smaller group of independents who called themselves the Democratic Study Group. Back in 1973–74, there were five so-called independents among the Democrats: Terry Bruce, Ken Buzbee of Carbondale, Betty Ann Keegan of Rockford, Don Wooten of Rock Island, and Dawn Clark Netsch of Chicago, who beat a regular Democrat, Daniel O'Brien, to win her seat initially. They used to meet and discuss issues, but they weren't a true voting bloc and weren't much of a force in what we did. They were loosely organized. In 1975, they were joined by three new independent-thinking members of the Senate—Vince Demuzio of Carlinville, Jerome Joyce of Reddick, and William Morris of Waukegan— and that's how they became the Crazy Eight.

Back in 1975, when the Democrats regained control of the Illinois Senate, most of us were set to elect Partee as Senate president, but we didn't get it done on the first ballot because of the Crazy Eight. On the first roll call in January 1975, eight Democrats did not vote yes or no but rather voted present, and so Partee did not get the required thirty votes. Sending a message by voting present were Netsch, Wooten, Buzbee, Joyce, Morris, Bruce, Demuzio, and Vivian Hickey, who took over the Rockford seat after Betty Ann Keegan died in April 1974. (A number of women senators represented that Rockford district over the years, and so back then it was called the "woman's seat.") After the Crazy Eight voted present, we immediately called for a recess. Somebody explained to them that we had to put in Partee as Senate president because he was our choice. We returned, and on the next roll call Partee received all thirty-five Democratic votes. The eight independents got their moment in the sun when they were polled individually and each said, "I would like to change my vote from present to Partee." They changed their minds because during the recess, Partee agreed to give the independents an official voice on the leadership team. That spot went to Terry Bruce, who joined Jim Donnewald and me as assistant leaders. So the Crazy Eight got some visibility. Of those eight, Morris was the primary activist. Netsch was always her usual independent self. She did not like being referred to in the same sentence with regular organization members from Cook County. That was anathema to her, and that's why she joined the Crazy Eight, which was otherwise a downstate group. Later on, I heard that some of Daley's allies promised to back her for Senate president, or to make her an assistant leader at least. I told her not to take a run at me while I was Senate president. "We don't need that kind of fight, and it won't do you any good," I told her. Thankfully, she never did try to oust me once I became the president of the Illinois Senate.

When we were getting organized in 1977, the memory of the little show of independence by the Crazy Eight two years earlier was not forgotten. The Crazy Eight took it upon themselves to boycott the Senate president's election altogether when we met to organize in January 1977. They withheld their votes from our party candidate, Tom Hynes.

It was the tradition of Senate Democrats at that time to have a dinner caucus the night before the day of organization. So on that Tuesday night, we would gather as a group in a locked-door facility and have dinner and then have a caucus and decide on the leadership. In 1977 on Tuesday night, there was significant support for Hynes, but there were not thirty votes that we needed for a constitutional majority.

When we got to the Senate the next day to organize, Bruce, the choice of the Crazy Eight, got nine votes on the first ballot for Senate president, including that of George Sangmeister of Mokena, who then became identified with the Crazy Eight. The name Crazy Eight stuck, but the group was also called the Nutty Nine and other things from time to time. Harold Washington got four votes, meanwhile, with the blacks positioning themselves for more influence. Netsch, who voted for Bruce, gave a long speech about the importance of "participatory democracy." She called the four-way battle for Senate president "possibly the first contest on our side of the aisle for that position in recorded history, at least in my recorded history, and I think the fact of that contest may well be more important than . . . the virtues of the individual candidates."[3]

If nobody gets elected on the first ballot, the presider, who by virtue of the Illinois Constitution is the Illinois governor, immediately calls for another vote, because the Senate can't do any business until it has a president, a minority leader, leadership teams, and committee chairs. "No candidate having received a constitutional majority of thirty votes, I will direct the [Senate] secretary to call the roll again," said newly installed governor James R. Thompson, who was presiding over our chamber for the first time.[4] Having the governor there adds formality and solemnity to the process. In the Illinois House of Representatives, the secretary of state presides when the House elects a Speaker. In 1977, the House elected Bill Redmond on the first ballot after going through ninety-three ballots and an ugly fight two years earlier. In both chambers, it is usually a ceremony without any rancor.

"Call the roll" or "Call the roll again" was a statement Thompson would repeat, with some variations, more than 180 times in the next five weeks. We took two more votes on the first afternoon of the session. The results were identical, with Hynes getting the most votes but Bruce getting nine and Washington four, despite recesses and lively private discussions. Shapiro always won all twenty-four Republican votes, also not enough to make him Senate president. After the third unsuccessful vote, I asked for adjournment until the next morning. Many of us had family and friends in town for the swearing-in and organization, and it was clear that the three Democrats in contention were in a deadlock.

We went into session again the next morning, unsure whether we were going to be able to organize. It turns out we didn't even take a roll call vote. We convened in the morning, took a break for lunch, and then called it quits until the following week. We had not resolved anything.

Over the weekend, with the Senate entrenched in gridlock, my name popped up again as a possible compromise candidate. I considered it briefly, but publicly and privately I still supported Hynes all the way. We convened again on January 17 and went through three more unsuccessful roll call votes. It didn't go well. The totals didn't change much, except that on the second and third roll calls of the second week, Senator John Knuppel of Petersburg cast his vote for Winnie the Pooh and Alice in Wonderland, respectively, with Hynes, Bruce, and Washington remaining in gridlock. There was some objection to Knuppel's silly votes, but the chair properly ruled that Knuppel could vote for whomever he wished. It was my job to declare us at an impasse. We adjourned again until the next day.

The independent whites kept voting for Bruce, and Washington brought part of the black caucus with him. I guess he figured if Bruce could do it, he could buck the party, too. Washington complained that Hynes had reneged on a promise to let the black senators put their own choice into yet another assistant leader's spot. They said they wanted Kenneth Hall of East St. Louis, but Hynes had let it be known that his choice was Charlie Chew of Chicago. So the blacks were holding out to have their own voice. It was obvious we weren't going anywhere.

The Senate was starting to look silly. One day we even got into a contentious debate about the opening prayer. Republican senator John Grotberg of St. Charles, anticipating another unsuccessful round of roll calls for the Senate presidency on January 27, began by inserting the names of various senators into generally recognized parts of a familiar prayer: "Our Father, who art in heaven, *Vadalabene* thy name, we Re*Joyce* in thy presence. . . ." On and on and on he went: "May we *Daley* find *Moore* spring flowers in *Bloom* in thy heavenly *Bowers* than the *Sommers'* weeds we have known amid the *Netsches, Rocks, Glass* and *Berning* bushes of the past few weeks."[5] It got worse, and afterward, Ken Buzbee stood up and told Grotberg that he deeply resented what was purported to be the prayer of the Senate when they were trying to solve the serious problem of electing a Senate president. We then took another roll call without progress, and after listening to some more clamoring from the floor, I also rose to express my strong objection to the opening "prayer."

It's not a good day in the Senate when even the prayer goes badly.

If anything, it set an adversarial tone for the whole day. The floor debate also went sour. People were testy, and the weather forecast called for a terrible blizzard to arrive by the next morning. Knuppel made a strange comment about the small group of black senators who kept voting for Washington; he said if the leadership slots were based on "pigmentation," then Chew "deserves to be in leadership; he's the blackest." One of the Chicago African Americans, Richard Newhouse, took offense to that, saying, "I find this session getting less funny as the time goes along and [with] the remarks a moment ago that suggested that Charlie Chew should be the leader because he's the blackest; I found [that] condescending to no end, and I'm personally offended by it."[6] Several of the blacks and members of the Crazy Eight took the floor, making long speeches, with no resolution in sight. We finally took another roll call vote with a few senators missing, and it was Hynes with nineteen, Bruce with seven, and Washington with two. By then, Thompson had learned to "call the roll" and do other work from the presider's podium, making phone calls and reading his mail while the secretary called each senator's name. Republican senator Prescott Bloom of Peoria, mindful of the approaching snowstorm and members' eagerness to get out of town, asked for a rare roll call vote on a motion to adjourn, saying, "There's some of us who are here prepared to wait till hell freezes over to get this resolved." Thompson responded by saying he joined those who would wait "till hell freezes over," but thirty-one members voted to adjourn and only nineteen voted to stay. We voted not to return for five days, but it was late enough that we couldn't get out of town that day. It was a strange, strange day that had started and ended with great tension, with objections to the prayer and a close vote on adjourning—two very unusual occurrences and signs of just how acidic the atmosphere had become.

It didn't help that the blizzard arrived with a vengeance overnight. In Chicago, the temperature dropped from 19 degrees above zero to 13 below by daybreak, aided by 50 miles-per-hour winds. Many of us were still in Springfield the next morning, and the temperature was 11 below. The snow was blowing and drifting up to twelve feet high. That was just one storm in what proved to be a terrible winter, making matters even worse when we could not get a Senate president elected. We scheduled a couple of days where half the troops couldn't make it because of snow and bitter cold. The airports sometimes shut down. By then we usually were flying back and forth, not taking the train. There were a couple of periods where we couldn't get together for several days, and the longer it went on, strangely enough, the more comfortable some members became with the status quo. "What's the harm? We don't really have to organize; there's no urgency for it," a few folks mumbled.

Some members also were taken with Bruce's analysis that we usually didn't meet all that often in January or February anyway, so what was the rush? Bruce did the math and informed us that we were formally in session only nine hours and fifty minutes during all of January. That didn't count, of course, all the time we spent in small caucuses and talking to one another about how to resolve our dispute. One time after spending three or four days arguing with one another in Springfield, our flight to Chicago got diverted to Peoria because of the weather, which made for some unhappy campers. We could do nothing except wait, and we all headed for the bar. We were about ready to go to war with one another. Everybody started pontificating. It wasn't the friendliest of gatherings, because we had just spent a few days together in Springfield not getting along, and then we were forced to socialize when all we wanted to do was get home. The weather did indeed make a bad situation worse.

When we returned February 2, the first roll call was symptomatic of what was happening. Hynes received his customary nineteen votes (a number that would top at twenty-one, depending upon how many members were in the chamber), but for the first time, there were no votes for Bruce and none for Washington, either. Buzbee, one of the Crazy Eight, soon showed up and told the chamber: "I would like the record to show I just ran up three flights of stairs. . . . Thirteen of us were having a meeting. That's why the lack of votes for Senator Bruce and Senator Washington."[7] What was happening was that the Crazy Eight, the four blacks, and Sangmeister would meet among themselves and not in a caucus with the other twenty-one Democrats. So we couldn't get anywhere. The thirteen were still holding out.

In four weeks, we kept taking votes, but there was not a lot of jockeying going on, except that every once in a while somebody would surface and say, "If you could move off Hynes and elect me, then I'll do this and this and this and this." The Crazy Eight stayed with Bruce all the way. The blacks were on again, off again, depending on what Washington was doing. Over time, I quietly started some negotiations. Hynes kept himself pretty well locked in the office; he wasn't comfortable with what was going on. I started to negotiate with the black members and some of Hynes's supporters. I asked moderates like Buzbee, Joyce, and Sangmeister, "What will it take? Do you want more to say? Do you want committee chairs? Tell me what is going to help put this thing together." There had to be some serious concessions, and the concessions had to be matters of substance. They weren't going to settle for a pat on the head or something as simple as saying the party would handle their next campaign.

The press gave some attention to how much it was costing to keep us in Springfield when we weren't getting any work done. At that time, members received $36 a day in expense allowances, plus travel expenses. So it was adding up. A Republican state representative, Tim Simms of Rockford, floated a bill to prohibit legislators from collecting their daily expense allowance until they elected a presiding officer. It didn't go anywhere, but we were all very frustrated.

It began to come together, finally, about the second week of February. After the 182nd unsuccessful vote, on February 10, Sangmeister broke from the Crazy Eight. He rose and asked if nominations could be reopened. Everyone knew what he was doing—he put my name into nomination as a compromise candidate. This was a Thursday, and Donnewald immediately got up and asked for a recess after Sangmeister nominated me. Then we adjourned for the Lincoln's Birthday weekend. There was speculation in the newspapers that the Cook County leaders were going to George Dunne and saying he should switch his support to me because

Hynes couldn't get it done after so many roll call votes. I was viewed as more independent of Daley than Hynes, and so I might get the backing of enough independents to get the regular twenty-one votes and nine independent votes.

When we came back Tuesday, February 15, everybody knew that Sangmeister might start pushing me for the presidency. We went into session as usual, with Thompson threatening to keep us there until we finished the job, and then we recessed for a caucus until late afternoon. Sangmeister was declaring, "The time has come; let's quit fooling around." The whole place just kind of stopped, because I think people realized that I had a fair chance of getting elected. They were so disgusted at that point. Sangmeister was telling people on the floor that they should vote for me, but I begged off. Dunne and the Cook County Democrats had not changed their allegiance from Hynes, and neither did I. "Look," I told everybody, "we are at the point of no return here. If you're going to elect a president, you better be prepared to make some concessions." I went around and put together a written agreement. After many discussions and private negotiations, I showed everybody what we were going to do: Hynes would be the Senate president, Bruce would be an assistant leader, and the blacks would get an assistant leader of their choice—who did not turn out to be Chew or Washington but Kenneth Hall of East St. Louis. We also agreed on committee chairmen and important committee assignments for various members. We created a second appropriations committee and a second judiciary committee so that people such as Daley, Netsch, Buzbee, and Howard Carroll could get some major committee chairmanships. And for the first time, we named a Democratic caucus chair, which was different from an assistant leader, and gave that to Gene Johns of southern Illinois. I handled all the nitty-gritty stuff, including who was going to get what office space. That was and is a big deal—the assignment of offices in the Capitol. With all the deals made, everything was supposed to be happiness and light by the time we cast the next ballot.

When we returned to the floor late in the afternoon and prepared for our next vote, I paused to respond to Sangmeister's nomination of me. "I want it well understood that the nomination was, in fact, unsolicited," I said. "I am overtly and forever grateful for the thought on his part. I think more than that, it was and is a legitimate means of moving the factions within our ranks to a decision. I think we are awfully close. I vote for Hynes." That was our 183rd ballot, but not the last. Bruce and Washington were still getting votes. We also took the 184th and 185th roll calls that day, with the results changing very little, except that Sangmeister did indeed vote for me all three times. Knowing we were very close, I called for yet another recess, and some of us thought we should adjourn because it was well past midnight. But the motion to adjourn failed overwhelmingly, and we went into recess yet again. I frankly can't recall why we didn't resolve it at that point; everything dragged on.

We had one last meeting where we reached the final agreements on how we would proceed and who would get what. When we got back to the floor in the early hours of the morning—still before sunrise, and nobody had gone to bed—Bruce was the first to speak. He said he was withdrawing as a candidate and wanted his supporters to vote for Hynes. Then Washington followed suit and gave an impassioned speech of his own. Washington commended Bruce, other members of the Crazy Eight, and the black senators for being persistent in demanding their right to have a greater voice. "I think what has happened here will breed new vitality in the party structure of this state," he said. "It is without a doubt that systems, institutions, as they grow and develop, become more rigid, and periodically it's necessary to shake them up, traumatically, if necessary, but shake them up, you must."[8] He also indicated that he and the three blacks who had been supporting him would vote for Hynes on the next roll call. So on the 186th ballot, at about 5:30 A.M. on February 16, Hynes got thirty-three votes, Shapiro the Republican got twenty-five, and Knuppel voted present for some strange reason after being with us, for Hynes, all along. Hynes voted for Shapiro—a customary courteous tradition for the incoming Senate president to vote for the person who will become the minority leader.

Although the whole ordeal was grueling and uncomfortable, it might have helped Thompson, who had to spend so much time so close to the legislature during those five weeks. He replaced a governor who had been very unpopular with the legislature on both sides of the aisle. "I have learned a good deal from this process," Thompson said from the podium after Hynes was elected. "I shall take it back with me to the second floor [of the Capitol, where the governor's office is], where I more properly belong, and I hope that at all times within the next two years, all of you, Republicans and Democrats alike, can feel that the state of Illinois has a governor who is ready, willing and able to work with all members of the General Assembly for the benefit of the people of this state."[9] Then Hynes delivered his own gracious acceptance speech, announced his leadership team, and implored the Democrats to work together. We had to do a little more routine business and finally adjourned about 6:00 A.M. on February 16, with plans to go into session that afternoon.

"Henry Kissinger would be proud of state Sen. Philip J. Rock," wrote political columnists Edward S. Gilbreth and Robert G. Schultz in the *Chicago Daily News* the next day. "It was Rock who emerged as Illinois' statesman of the year in breaking the five-week-old deadlock over electing a president of the state Senate."[10] Schultz, who lived in Oak Park just across the Chicago border from me, appreciated the fact that I put together such a comprehensive political package for somebody else, for Hynes. Another columnist, Bill O'Connell, wrote in the *Peoria Journal-Star* that I deserved to be the Senate president, but absent that, I was the sensible choice to work out the settlement in a deeply divided Democratic caucus.[11] Indeed, I had spent the better part of two days as the chief negotiator, putting all of the deals together and paving the way for Hynes. He accepted the job as the decision of the party organization, and he kept the presidency for only one term before leaving the Senate and winning election to a Cook County office two years later.

Both O'Connell and Gilbreth and Schultz quoted something I was overheard saying after those five long weeks of bitter conversations. "It's a helluva of a deal," I said. "I got to engineer my own demise."[12] For many years, I had a framed copy of that *Daily News* article hanging in my office. The columnists were right, but it wasn't a total political loss for me. Dealing with the black caucus, the Crazy Eight, and the white ethnics that year helped the Democratic members see that I could orchestrate compromises for our caucus and the party, even though it meant a political sacrifice on my part. I am convinced that showing all the members that my word was good by sticking with Hynes, even as I was "engineering my own demise," later helped me handle a fractured, sensitive, and unruly caucus the entire time I was Senate president.

7. A Move to Oak Park

A law about mandatory seat belts got enacted,
in part, because a busy doctor took the time to
visit my district office and get my attention.

I N 1977, SHEILA AND I DECIDED TO MOVE from our house on the West Side of Chicago just over the city border into Oak Park. What surprised me was that the move aroused such great suspicion. Some of the independents in Oak Park and the West Side publicly cast aspersions and placed an unfair, devious political slant on the family move.[1] Around the same time, circuit court clerk Morgan Finley, who was part of the mayor's Eleventh Ward organization, was also moving out of the city, to Burr Ridge, to run for Lyons Township committeeman. So the reporters played it like we were two Daley Democrats encroaching on the suburbs, grabbing a lot of new territory. Gerald Shea, meanwhile, who already lived in Riverside, made it clear that he would try to win a different suburban committeeman position, thereby expanding on the Daley conspiracy theory.[2] In Oak Park, they got quite a campaign going—a scare campaign that the Chicago Democrats were going to take over Oak Park, where the Republicans enjoyed a majority, by the way, by about a four-to-one margin.

The fact is, my family moved to Oak Park for personal reasons, not political reasons. We had a large, beautiful house one block east of Austin Boulevard, which is the street that separates the Chicago city limits from Oak Park. We lived on Midway Park, which was only three blocks long. The house had many rooms, a finished basement, the whole nine yards. If you picked it up and put it in Oak Park, it would have been worth a million and a half dollars. On the block where we lived, we were the only white family, and I was the only white precinct captain south of Chicago Avenue. The house had been burglarized three times, I think. Fortunately, no one was home any of those times. My kids were young—preschoolers and in the early grades—and they also had their tricycles and bikes and scooters stolen, just taken away from them after being pushed off. Sheila and I thought of ourselves as urban pioneers. We were going to be the diversity in this neighborhood. That's nice and laudable, but the reality was the crime rate wasn't so good for my kids. Even our kind African American neighbors suggested that it was no longer safe for our children.

I was in line to become the Thirty-Seventh Ward committeeman in a part of Chicago from North Avenue south to Cicero. It was a strong Democratic ward. The southern part of it was mostly black, and the northern part was all white. I went to see Alderman Tom Casey and Judge Art McGloon, and I said, "I appreciate everything you've done for me politically, and I'll never walk away from you, but I want to be taken out of consideration for committeeman, because I can't live there anymore. I have to move." They were very nice about it, fortunately.

We moved two miles west to a house on North Oak Park Avenue in Oak Park. Politically, it seemed that all of a sudden the whole world was crashing on my head, with people saying I was trying to take over Oak Park. An Oak Park schoolteacher, Andrew Prinz, was an independent and the committeeman. He had beaten Ray Welch, the regular Democrat in Oak Park. Prinz considered himself the reformer, and so did a lot of other people. I initially tried to get along with Prinz. No chance of that, though. I would tell him that as a senator, I was trying to get jobs for specific people, and he said, "I wish you wouldn't do that; I'm trying to get a job myself." Here was this reformer, trying to get a political job. So I said, "I can help you, too, if you want my help." It turns out he wanted to be the king of the universe; he didn't want some penny-ante job. Enough people just got tired of him, and some of us decided to try to replace him. I announced my intention to run for Oak Park committeeman in March 1978, and Prinz decided not to run. Some reformers and the League of Women Voters got a little uptight about my race. Elaine "Toddy" Van Wieren ran against me, saying I was bringing the Chicago machine to Oak Park and the village should not allow that.[3] She ranted when I got the endorsement of the Chicago Teachers Union. But a lot of teachers in Oak Park belonged to the American Federation of Teachers, and they appreciated my strong support for education. Also, my opponent had no answer for why I received the endorsement of two other Chicago groups: the Chicago Women's Political Caucus and the Independent Voters of Illinois. Van Wieren also had a rough time because many of those reformers didn't vote in the primaries; they did not want to be identified as either a Democrat or a Republican. I won handily as the Oak Park committeeman, and over time, people got the idea that I was actually good for Oak Park.

I set up a district office in a storefront at 306 Madison. I used it as both my Senate office and my committeeman office. I worked hard for Oak Park, but I give a lot of credit to my first and only office manager, Pat Arman. Pat had no political experience in 1978 when she started. I knew her and her husband, Ed, very well, and she did a fabulous job. When she agreed to run the office, I didn't give a lot of direction, but I advised her to help everyone who came in or called. I also said never to ask if the person lived in the district or whether he or she voted; she should just try to help.

I would go to the district office almost every Saturday morning and would see anyone who wanted to talk. Most visitors were not looking for a Nobel Prize–type answer to some important philosophical question. Some were looking for jobs. Some had a serious issue. Some felt they were wrongfully denied a state service they were entitled to. Some would come with social security issues, even though that's a federal issue, or maybe their public aid was denied or their kid's was denied, and pretty soon they're frustrated as hell and don't know where to turn. That's the beauty of public office, really. Constituents can pick up the phone and say, "Hey, I want some answers, and if I don't get them, you'll hear some more from me."

One day, Pat quietly complained to me about a man who appeared regularly on Saturday mornings but would never tell her why he wanted to see me. He came so often that Pat finally told him he didn't have to visit every week. After he died, Pat revealed how much it bugged her that the guy came in so frequently.

"Well, he couldn't read," I said, "and so he would bring me some papers or documents to read to him and explain what they were about." He wanted to see me, and so he did. That's the way it worked. He needed some help, and so I helped him.

Another time, I admitted to Pat that I wasn't too crazy about seeing a group of kids—they must have been ten to twelve years old—at the district office, so I told her I'd give them four minutes. They were Boy Scouts working on a badge, and they had to seek information about state government. I started explaining to them what it was like to be in Springfield. I got out a map of Illinois with outlines of the Illinois Senate districts and put it on the floor, pointing out where my Senate colleagues lived and what they needed. One senator needed more money for "L" trains, and one downstate member (I pointed to the district because suburban kids knew very little about downstate) needed a road for the farmers in his district, and this guy over here needed a water tower. I said, "Each of them thinks his thing is the most important, and I think mine is the most important. There is not enough money for all of us, so what should we do?"

One of the little guys looked up and said, "Compromise."

"You got it," I said. I was really tickled that they were catching on. So I kept going: "You know, three of us might argue about our projects on the floor of the Senate down in Springfield, or in a meeting before we put a bill together, and we would all talk about how important our project is, and then we would go out to dinner and not have any animosity at all toward one another. Here is what I want you to know: that in government, we can be respectful toward one another, disagree without being disagreeable, and not be derogatory or mean at any time." I really felt great when I went home that day. I think Sheila called Pat to tell her that whatever happened that morning, she should try to make it happen again because I was in such a great mood.[4]

Later on, when I became Senate president, more high-powered leaders from organizations would show up at the district office. Some lobbyists would make it their business to find my office in Oak Park, knowing full well that I would be there. Dr. Henry Betts from the world-famous Chicago Institute of Rehabilitation was one of my Saturday morning regulars. He was a physician who spent his illustrious career trying to improve the lives of people with disabilities. Betts was renowned for what he accomplished with medical treatments, and it's fair to call him one of the biggest advocates for people with disabilities in American history. He was a leader in getting the Americans with Disabilities Act passed in 1990, for instance. Betts also was an early promoter of a state law to make sure that all cars had seat belts, and he believed people should be required to wear them. He had some sayings that got everybody's attention, such as, "If you think seat belts are confining, you should try a wheelchair." New York was the first state to require seat belts, in 1984. Dr. Betts wasn't far behind, leading an essentially one-man push in Illinois for seat belts. He would come to my office and patiently take a seat and wait his turn to talk to me, deferring to the people ahead of him—he was very gracious that way. Then he would visit with me and talk about seat belts, and afterward I think he would go over to Representative James DeLeo's office. He made the rounds. I suggested to him that he do that.

One time in Springfield, he asked me what he could do to get a mandatory seat belt law. "The best thing to do," I told him, "is to talk to as many people as you can and tell them that in your opinion, seat belts can save lives, and certainly can cut down on your clientele, the ones who have frozen limbs and that sort of thing." I warned him that it wouldn't be easy to catch some of the legislators in Springfield, where things move fast with committees, appointments, and phone calls. I advised him to go to various district offices, just as he came to mine, and told him I would help him get a roll call on a bill and also get the votes. He was persistent and persuasive, and I did indeed help him when the legislation came to the floor in 1984 during the veto session. It wasn't easy. A number of opponents said that mandatory seat belts needlessly invade our privacy. I thought they were wrong.

When the final debate for a mandatory seat belt law occurred on the Senate floor, Charlie Chew was the first one up, passionately supportive; he was the Senate sponsor. Dawn Clark Netsch made a particularly emotional pitch: "My [Chicago] office is across the street from the rehabilitation institute," she said. "I see with my own eyes [every day] a reminder of why seat belts are absolutely critical. . . . If any of you would like to have a reminder of why seat belts should be used and even mandated, please come visit me in my office, look out on those who are at the rehabilitation institute, and you will have reminder enough."[5] The bill passed with two votes to spare and became Illinois law in 1985. It's interesting that such a critical policy got enacted, in part, because a busy doctor who was a strong advocate took the time to visit my district office and get my attention.

Being in the district office and working in the city of Chicago gave me a perspective on state government that was very different from the view I had in Springfield. It was fascinating that people in the Chicago area knew or cared very little about what was happening in Springfield. When I would return to Chicago from the capital city and land at Meigs Field downtown, I would tell my state government colleagues to go to the nearest corner and ask people if they knew that we weren't in session in Springfield any more. A couple of colleagues got out of the car and actually did it. Nobody they asked ever had a clue. There we were in Springfield all week, beating our brains out working on legislation, and none of these people knew that we were even there, and frankly, they never give a damn until it had an impact on their lives.

One reason for that, I always thought, was that we did not get as much coverage in the Chicago newspapers as I thought we should get. In retrospect, though, the amount of coverage actually got smaller after I left. There were fewer newspapers, as one daily newspaper after another shut down, and the ones still alive seemed to cut back on their state coverage. To be fair, I will say there were some reporters whom I spent a lot of time with and respected. It helped immensely that I had a press secretary, Judy Erwin, who had a terrific relationship with reporters and could explain what we were trying to do. But I was never all that satisfied that the people of Illinois could learn through the media all the important things that were happening in Springfield. Even more certainly, not enough people in the Chicago area cared.

At any rate, after I became the Oak Park committeeman, the Democratic organization in Oak Park grew quite a bit in the next two decades. We became very formidable. When I first moved there, we used to have a lousy turnout in the primaries. Many Oak Park residents consider themselves independents. But we were able to increase the registration significantly. The organization did pretty well once voters got over the fear that someone was going to punish them for voting Democratic.

One big issue on which Oak Park became a national leader was in the restriction of gun ownership. Morton Grove was first, and we were second. We had a big public discussion in Oak Park about a village prohibition on handguns. The village board initially rejected a call for a handgun ban in 1982, but the issue did not die. After a local attorney named James Piszczor was shot and killed in Cook County divorce court in October 1983, the Oak Park Citizens Committee for Handgun Control launched a petition drive to ban handguns in honor of Piszczor's widow, Maureen.[6] Committee members presented their petitions to the village board, which voted 4–3 to pass it on April 16, 1984. There was a great deal of controversy about it, with opponents calling for a local advisory referendum to repeal the handgun ban that had just been passed. I certainly supported the handgun ban, and I turned my organization loose to oppose the referendum. We won that one, too, because 56 percent voted in April 1985 not to repeal the handgun ban. Once we had our ordinance, every year in Springfield the gun people would try to put in a preemption bill, saying a municipality can't have those kinds of laws because it's a state issue. I killed it every year. I didn't make a big fanfare of it, but the gun groups and the other senators knew where I stood. It's still a controversial issue today. The U.S. Supreme Court issued rulings in 2008 and 2010 saying it was a violation of the Second Amendment for a municipality to have its own sweeping prohibition against handguns. The 2008 case dealt with the District of Columbia, and the 2010 case gutted Chicago's handgun ban. That effectively outlawed the Oak Park ban as well. But I have no regrets about supporting it, and I still think it's a good idea. I'm certain that local and national conversations about the issue will continue.

Some people picketed my house and my office over the gun issue. There was considerable opposition to the gun control law, and since I was a leader in supporting it, we were picketed. It wasn't the first time it had happened, though—when we lived on Midway Park, there was some kind of budget crisis, and public aid advocates carried signs at our house then, too. Some citizens weren't getting their public aid checks, and their supporters publicized the legislators' home phone numbers and addresses, saying, "Call right away!" Much of that grassroots effort happened when I was in Springfield. Back home, Sheila was getting calls by the dozen, so she phoned me in Springfield and said, "Whatever it is that these people are calling about, please pass it!" And we did—but not because of the demonstrators. When people picketed my house over the gun issue in Oak Park, I took it in stride. As long as they weren't nutty or carrying a weapon or something like that, I didn't mind.

Another issue that really stirred people up in Oak Park was abortion. I was pro-life my entire career, and I had a number of pro-choice people in my district. They used to come to my district office with some regularity. Even though I disagreed with them, I always took the time to listen to them, thank them for coming in, and remind them that I felt it was OK to disagree without being disagreeable. I told anybody who asked that I was not changing my mind about being pro-life. I didn't wear it on my sleeve or tattoo it on my chest; it was just the way I was, and still am, on this issue.

8. Finally, the Senate Presidency

I realized that if Jane Byrne became mayor of
Chicago, she was going to be looking for friends,
and I was going to be one of them for sure.

W HEN I MOVED TO OAK PARK, TOM HYNES was in his first and only
two-year term as Senate president. He wasn't in the job very long
before he decided to run for Cook County assessor in 1978. He wanted
out of Springfield.

Legislative cycles being what they are, it seemed that in 1977 and 1978
we dealt with some high-profile issues that had been around for a while
and kept coming back. That's the way it works. If you don't get your idea
passed one year, you can bring it back another year. I think people forget,
when their issue fails in Springfield or Washington, that persistence over
years can pay off on controversial issues. One such issue in this session
was off-track betting (OTB), which had the strong support of Chicago
mayor Michael Bilandic and Governor Thompson. Chicago really wanted
the $21 million it would generate for the city. To make it politically and
geographically more palatable, we added to the bill OTB sites for Decatur,
Rockford, Peoria, Springfield, and East St. Louis. The House passed the
bill after a hot debate on the floor. Thompson took a lot of blows for his
early support of OTB because he had said during his campaign that he
would oppose any new form of legalized gambling; he specifically said that
he would oppose OTB run by municipalities.[1] Thompson insisted that
he had not changed his position, but the OTB opponents wore everyone
down. By the time the bill reached the Senate, it didn't have much of a
chance, and we could not muster the votes for OTB. Not yet, anyway.

Another issue we discussed again this session was branch banking. During the 1970s, branch banking, interstate banking, and regional banking
were hot topics, with the big banks wanting branches and many community banks not wanting competition from the big national or state banks.

I sponsored the bill for branch banking, which was limited. For example, Chicago banks would not be able to open branches outside of Cook County. Also, banks could open one branch per year in 1978 and 1979 and two annually after that. I thought it was a reasonable consumer issue, because we could identify 1,500 municipalities in the state without any banking facilities at all. I thought some of these communities would appreciate having a branch of a larger bank. But some of the downstate members would not support it, and a few of the members said they had conflicts of interest because of associations with hometown banks. Then there was Harold Washington, who voiced his opposition by saying that big banks would set up "collection houses" in African American neighborhoods in his district and then use the money to lend to people elsewhere. He thought it was bad for the blacks and the minority communities. Toward the end of the session, we were still five votes short in the Senate, so I had to let it go.

This was also the first session that I tried to move the primary date from March to September. I believed this would reduce campaign expenditures and the amount of time that candidates would have to spend campaigning. It also would eliminate that long lag between March and the November general elections. In addition, having a September primary would give candidates an opportunity to circulate petitions and do some door-to-door canvassing while there was decent weather. I thought my arguments were compelling, but I believe it's fair to say that a majority of the Democratic organization did not wish to move the primary. Their motives were not so noble. They thought they would be better protected from the independent candidates if the competition had to go out in the worst possible weather. This also meant, however, that our loyal precinct captains would have to trudge through the snow and ice to get signatures and spread the gospel about our candidates.

I tried two or three times in different years to move the primary to September, but opponents would throw all kinds of arguments at me, like we're interfering with the Jewish holidays in September or interfering with farmers taking the crops from the fields. Opponents also said the general election season would not be long enough between September and November. I countered by advising them to look at the most important race in Illinois: the one for mayor of Chicago. From the time a candidate files petitions until the election, only two or three months pass. That's plenty of time for that campaign, and so it would be enough time for all campaigns in the state.

The majority of the opposition was from the regular Democratic organization in Cook County. I talked to George Dunne, the county chairman, and he wasn't prepared to take that kind of step. I did have a couple of the good government types on my side. Dawn Clark Netsch was one of my stalwarts. I used to kid her: "Would you please not say anything about wanting to change the primary date? You're scaring people off. If you and your independent friends are for it, there's got to be something wrong with it." I had no help from the Republicans, either, even though in my opinion, they should have supported the good-weather election season for the same reason that it was good for the Democrats. But they didn't. I still think the September primary would be better for the Democratic organization, but I never got enough support on this one, ever.

By most accounts, the 1977–78 session was not all that eventful. There was a great deal of talk about who was going to run for various statewide offices, especially who would take a run at Thompson in 1978. It turned out to be Michael Bakalis, who didn't do well. My name was out there as a possible candidate for state treasurer, but I really wanted to be Senate president. I said publicly I would stay in the Senate until I became president. It was fortuitous for me that Hynes went back to Cook County to run for county assessor; he was another in a long line of people who gave up a legislative seat in Springfield for some position in Cook County. That's just home to a lot of Illinois politicians. And Thompson won reelection to his second term rather easily.

Going into the new General Assembly in 1979, Democrats had thirty-two seats and the Republicans twenty-seven. Over in the House, there were eighty-eight Democrats, eighty-eight Republicans, and one independent. When we were getting ready to organize another session of the General Assembly in January 1979, I think everyone understood that I would be the first candidate out of the box for Senate president.

Two years earlier, when I was also the early favorite, I had learned a good political lesson: you can't take anything for granted. Back then, I expected George Dunne and Parky Cullerton to rally around my desire to be Senate president, but they didn't. Part of Cullerton's ward was in my legislative district, and I had helped him with a number of issues. It was mainly due to the influence of Senator Richard M. Daley, though, that Cullerton wasn't there for me. So in 1979, I went around and tried to get every member's support long before our day of organization. I told them this was an important vote and they needed to make up their minds.

They were indeed lining up for me on the day of organization, the second Wednesday in January 1979. Senator Jim Donnewald formally placed my name into nomination. The fact that Senators Daley and Frank Savickas seconded the motion and gave speeches for me to be Senate president is one of the ironies of this business. I think Daley figured out that if he caused me any more trouble, he had nowhere to go. He also didn't want to be viewed as an obstructionist, because he was already planning to run for mayor of Chicago. He wound up leaving the Senate and being a candidate for Cook County state's attorney the next year, in 1980, as a stepping-stone to getting back into Chicago politics full time. It seems he didn't want to fight anybody in Springfield any more, and I was the guy he always had been targeting. So he made a speech in support of me, and he also prevailed on me to install Savickas as one of the leaders, predicated on the notion that Savickas was the choice of the white ethnics. I said fine. That was one of the ways I tried to hold the caucus together—allowing the groups like the white ethnics and the Crazy Eight and the black caucus to designate their own person to be on my leadership team.

Most years, there isn't a real contest about who will be Senate president, and there wasn't in 1979. It was all predetermined and ceremonial—the first of seven times I would be elected Senate president. For the installation, my good friend Father John Smyth from Maryville City of Youth (also known as Maryville Academy) gave the opening prayer. My mom, Kathryn Rock, was there; she attended all of my installations before she died in 1991. Sheila and the kids were, of course, present, as were Danny Fusco, my law partner, his wife, Dorothy, and their kids. I asked Art McGloon, my mentor, to attend, too, because it was such a special occasion. He was by this point an appellate court judge and had the honor of swearing in all the senators for their new terms, and then he personally performed the ceremony in which I was sworn in as Senate president. It was a great thrill for both of us.

Thompson congratulated me on becoming Senate president, and then it was my turn. I did not give what would be called an "inaugural address" or even a lengthy speech, as sometimes happens on these occasions. Instead, I was brief. I spoke barely more than one hundred words, saying in part, "I am truly overwhelmed. I will promise you and pledge to you my best effort as the presiding officer of this body, and I will, in the Eighty-First General Assembly, work with you to bring to the people of Illinois responsible and accountable government—a government in this body that we can all be proud of, whether we're Democrat or Republican. I pledge to you that I will do my very best, and I deeply appreciate your support."[2]

We all went to Baur's restaurant afterward, just south of the Capitol. That's when the kids were introduced to bananas flambé. I used to call them barbecued bananas. Everybody ordered them, and I think we almost set fire to the back of the restaurant. We stayed at a hotel, and the kids loved it. What a great celebration it was, and I had the position I wanted.

Then it was time for me to get to work, and I asked Bob O'Keefe to stay as chief of staff to the Senate president. That's an important position because the chief of staff runs a lot of the day-to-day operations. I never considered anybody else. He had been McGloon's chief of staff; I also knew him from my days in the attorney general's office a decade earlier. Also giving me great advice from the get-go was an attorney, Pat Cadigan, and a budget expert, Francis Whitney. Everybody in the Capitol wanted to talk to Francis because he knew more about the state budget than anybody—including anybody in the governor's Bureau of the Budget. He had worked for McGloon, too.

My routine in those first few months was pretty standard. I would see some members on a daily basis, some on a weekly basis. I did let them know that contrary to what was going on in other parts of the building or in the other chamber, I would see any of my members who wanted to see me. My style from the beginning was to let any of them come in, with any gripe they had, with any slight, real or imagined, and let them speak their peace. If I could help them, I certainly tried to do it. Bill Redmond, a Democrat, was Speaker of the House then, and my first term as Senate president turned out to be Redmond's final term as Speaker. Michael Madigan was on the House Democratic leadership team but would not become Speaker for another four years.

Redmond didn't like Governor Thompson very much, but Thompson and I got along great. He sought my advice, and I gave it to him. He had been governor for two years when I became Senate president, and we would hold those respective positions simultaneously for the next twelve years. He would call me and bounce ideas off of me, including those that came from his chief policy person, Paula Wolff. Sometimes I would tell him candidly that he would get murdered politically if he proposed a certain policy.

My Senate presidency got its first big jolt a few months into 1979. Chicago had had a terrible snowstorm during the winter, and everybody was blaming incumbent mayor Michael Bilandic for not getting the snow removed from the city streets. It was a terrible mess and was all over the news. That fiasco propelled Jane Byrne, whom Bilandic had fired from her city commissioner job, into a primary battle against Bilandic. I was in Florida with my family on Easter break or spring break and flew home for the election. I spent all day in the ward and the precincts and rode around with McGloon, something we were accustomed to doing together on election day. As the votes were being tallied, it looked more and more like Bilandic was getting his butt kicked and Byrne would become the city's first woman mayor. Bilandic and McGloon were very close friends, and McGloon felt terrible. The mood was very somber, but my perspective was not the same as McGloon's.

We stayed out late as usual on election night. I never did leave the ward office. I just went to the airport in the morning so I could get back to Florida and my family. A precinct captain named Dominic gave me a ride.

"Dominic, do you see what's going on here?" I asked him. "The buses are still running. The police are still directing traffic. The airport is still full. I guess people don't know that Jane Byrne got elected mayor. It's not the end of the world." Dominic felt sure that he was going to get fired from his city job. I said, "You're not going to get fired. Jane Byrne is not the enemy. She's not my enemy." I was in a no-lose situation. If Bilandic won, he was McGloon's pal and so that was good for me, but if Byrne won, she was going to be looking for friends, and I was going to be one of them for sure.

I had gone to school with Jane Byrne's brother, Ed Burke, who was a great lawyer—not the longtime Fourteenth Ward alderman Edward M. Burke but a different Ed Burke. Burke called me after his sister got elected mayor and said that she wanted to assure me of her help in Springfield. I said, "Ed, that's great. Tell her the same thing. There's always a lot going on in Springfield, and if I can help, just pick up the phone and let me know."

Byrne's victory was an upset, and it had the organization people dancing around. But I was confident it would be all right because I knew Byrne personally and knew how to work with her. We had become friends when both of us were in consumer fraud work. Bilandic had fired her from her consumer sales commissioner's job after she blew up and accused him of "greasing" the city's approval of a taxi fare increase that she said was illegal.[3] It's never a good idea for a city commissioner to attack the mayor publicly, and so the mayor was right to toss her out. Then she came back and beat him. I was pleased that I had a good relationship with her.

One time, though, while she was mayor, she became upset with me after telling me that she wanted me to run for state's attorney against Richard M. Daley in 1980. I said, "Jane, I don't want to be the state's attorney. I was in the state's attorney's office when Ed Hanrahan was there, and at some point I would have had a chance to run for the position myself. But I don't want the position, and I don't want to be a U.S. attorney, either. Those people are prosecutors. I don't think that way. I don't act that way." So she talked Alderman Edward M. Burke into running against Daley. But Daley easily beat Burke in the primary, and then Daley ousted incumbent Republican Bernard Carey in the general election to become the state's attorney in 1981.

One of my best Springfield stories is from the time Byrne was mayor. She had irritated enough people that Harold Washington was leading the charge for her recall. He wanted to change the law so that voters could recall a public official, like the mayor of Chicago, before his or her term ended. Illinois did not have a recall statute of any kind; I never allowed it. I don't think you should ever give the voters a chance to undo an election. They make up their minds and it's over. But on the floor of the Senate, Washington was ripping into Byrne, declaring that he was doing so much more for the good of the people of Chicago—the downtrodden, the homeless, the helpless. He was going on and on and was joined by Senator Richard Newhouse. They were convinced that voters would get rid of Byrne quickly if given the chance.

I was at my seat on the Senate floor, not presiding, so I could keep track of what the troops were thinking. All of a sudden I got a phone call. Everyone knew I seldom took calls on the floor. I didn't want to be interrupted.

The operator said, "It's your wife."

The only phones we had were in the back of the chamber in those days. There were no phones at the desks, and certainly no cell phones. So I went back and took the call.

"Are you having a good day?" Sheila asked. She was at home in Oak Park.

"Not particularly. I've had better ones."

"Well, I just want you to know," she said, "that I just dropped the air conditioner out of the third-floor window of our house. I couldn't hold on. Nobody was down below or in the gangway, so nobody was hurt." We had a small window on the third floor, and it didn't have a substantial window sill, and so it would be very easy for an air conditioner to topple over and fall. We had a little chuckle about it, and I just said go on and enjoy the rest of your day. It also changed my opinion about what was happening on the Senate floor at that moment. I decided to shut down the debate. I asked Senator Newhouse if he would yield the floor, and I said: "I just want you to know that life goes on. My wife just dropped an air conditioner out of a third-floor window while we were debating this highly important provision." Everybody started to laugh, and it kind of broke the ice. Until that point, everybody was uptight, given the rhetoric that was floating around about Byrne being recalled.

About eighteen months later, the Republican minority leader, Senator James "Pate" Philip, was on the floor arguing for the recall of Harold Washington, who had become the mayor of Chicago. Washington called me from Chicago and complained, and I just said, "Harold, what goes around comes around. I warned you about trying to pass a recall law back when Jane Byrne was mayor."

"What's going to happen?" he asked.

"The same thing that happened to your bill," I said. "I'm going to kill it. So go back to work and don't even worry about it."

9. Choosing Leaders and Saving Chrysler

This is probably a very bad idea, and we may
rue the day we ever started down this path.
                                              —Dawn Clark Netsch

I KEPT THE SENATE DEMOCRATIC LEADERSHIP TEAM IN PLACE in my
first term as Senate president: Jim Donnewald, Kenny Hall, Frank
Savickas, and Terry Bruce. Donnewald was from the downstate town of
Breese and was a steady presence and somebody I could always count
on. Hall, of East St. Louis, represented the choice of the black caucus,
and Terry Bruce, of Olney, was there for the independents and the Crazy
Eight. I would put the various groups in a room and say, "You tell me who
you want to be your leader. If you want my opinion, I'll certainly give it
to you, but you pick whoever you want and I'll live with it." That's how
Savickas, who wasn't my favorite person, stayed on the leadership team,
as the choice of the white ethnics.

When I arrived in the Senate in 1971, there were only three leaders in
our caucus: the Senate president and his two assistant leaders, one for
Chicago and one for downstate. On two or three occasions, I was in touch
with Alan Rosenthal, a political scientist from Rutgers. His specialty was
state legislatures. He asked me at some meeting if I ever thought about
rewarding members who had extra work as a committee chair or as an assistant leader by giving them additional pay. I told him that we had talked
about it, and I said I could see it coming as the demand for additional
leadership positions grew because of the diversity of our caucus and the
divisions within it. We did indeed expand the leadership team to meet
different wishes of the members. They liked it when I started attaching a
$6,000 stipend to leadership positions. We also started paying an extra
$5,000 to each of the four caucus chairs, and later, additional money was
given to committee chairs as well. That bumped up the pension base
for all these legislators, so it was popular. We created the caucus chair

position for two reasons: to designate someone to have documents and logistics ready for a caucus meeting, and to have one more person who would get an extra stipend and, presumably, be more loyal to the head of the caucus. It was a make-work position. Not long afterward, the House picked up on it and started doing the same thing.

Savickas was presiding when we had one of our most contentious debates in 1979; it was about tax relief. Illinois still had a five-cent sales tax on food and drugs and was said to be the only industrial state with this tax still on the books. It had been a controversial issue for decades. Doug Whitley of the Taxpayers Federation of Illinois reported there had been at least thirty-one attempts to remove the tax since it went into effect some forty-six years earlier.[1] Around the country, tax revolts of all kinds were in the air. In 1978, California voters overwhelmingly approved Proposition 13, which limited property tax increases to 2 percent a year for homeowners at a time that property values and property taxes were increasing significantly. The voters loved it, but California cities and counties that relied on property tax revenues were going to be choked for a while. Politicians everywhere felt a lot of pressure to provide tax relief. Governor Thompson had his proposal, too. In his 1978 reelection campaign against Democrat Mike Bakalis, he got the so-called Thompson Proposition on the ballot. It was an advisory vote but got a lot of press because it called for a tax and spending ceiling. It asked, "Shall legislation be enacted and the Illinois Constitution be amended to impose ceilings on taxes and spending by the state of Illinois, units of local government, and school districts?" Thompson pushed really hard to get that question onto the November ballot, the same ballot on which he was up for reelection. His proposition was nonbinding and advisory, and so it didn't mean anything. But the carefully crafted language sounded as if action would be taken if it passed, so it got voters excited.[2] Thompson received a great deal of heat and was charged with impropriety in the collection of more than 600,000 signatures to get the proposition on the ballot. He withstood that challenge before the State Board of Elections, though, and 83 percent of Illinois voters said yes to the wildly popular idea. It scored political points for Thompson. That was the context of the election in 1978—tremendous political pressure to provide tax relief.

Representative Clarence Darrow of Rock Island sponsored a bill in 1979 to get rid of the sales tax on groceries and prescription medicine over a four-year period, starting in 1980. Republicans and Thompson had their own tax relief packages, but we were able to quash all of those Republican alternatives and move ahead with a bill to eliminate just that portion of the sales tax that Darrow had stipulated. Thompson warned us that he would veto Darrow's bill, and that's exactly what he did after both the Democratically controlled Senate and House overwhelmingly passed the bill to eliminate the sales tax on food and medicine.

Thompson's veto led to a showdown in the 1979 fall veto session. Would we be able to override the veto and give the people of Illinois this sales tax relief? Bill Redmond was the House Speaker, but it was House majority leader Mike Madigan and I, along with Senator Richard M. Daley, who vowed to override Thompson's veto. Then everything got more complicated when Mayor Jane Byrne unexpectedly came out in support of Thompson's alternate plan, which was to enact a one-cent reduction in the sales tax instead of all five cents. The mayor was concerned about revenue for the city, which would drop significantly if the state stopped returning millions of dollars in sales tax revenue to local governments. Not only that, but Byrne and Thompson were also working together on a billion-dollar road program.

That moved the mayor toward favoring Thompson's one-penny decrease in the sales tax. So we Chicago Democrats were caught between our previous promise to override the veto and the mayor's new position in support of Thompson's one-cent reduction. The veto override first went to the House, but even before members there voted, I reversed myself on the veto override and said I supported Mayor Byrne and Governor Thompson and that I would support the one-cent reduction in the sales tax. That was a difficult position to take after pushing for a total elimination of the sales tax all year long. I did it, though, because I wanted to support the mayor and the city of Chicago. Some of my own Democratic members were furious with me, and I had to deal with them. But it turns out I never had to take that position publicly, because the House failed to override Thompson's veto, the bill was dead, and it never got to the Senate for an override vote.

The drama wasn't over, though. Because of the veto, we had no tax relief at all, and that wasn't good, either. Thompson immediately called a special session to consider his one-cent reduction in the sales tax. They called it a "penny and a promise" because the governor also said he would consider additional sales tax cuts in the future if the state could afford them.[3] When the bill reached our chamber, Senator George Sangmeister immediately filed an amendment to eliminate the entire sales tax, which is what our bill earlier in the year would have done. I named myself as the temporary chair of the Senate Revenue Committee and tried to stop Sangmeister's amendment in committee, but I was unsuccessful and the amendment got to the Senate floor. It seemed like everybody wanted to talk about it, and the debate went on for about two hours. Downstate Democrats were behind Sangmeister in wanting to eliminate the entire sales tax on food and medicine. It became a Chicago versus downstate battle, except for Senator Daley and a few others who wanted to show their independence from the mayor. I worked the floor to help deliver votes for Mayor Byrne, so I had Savickas presiding because he was with us on this one. A defector from the downstate group was Sam Vadalabene of Edwardsville, whose vote I successfully secured. In the end there was a 27–27 tie, which was three votes short of the majority needed to pass Sangmeister's amendment. Then we passed Byrne's and Thompson's one-cent reduction, and "the promise" came through when we got another one-cent reduction the following year. It was really something.

Another big issue emerged when we learned in 1980 that Belvidere's Chrysler manufacturing plant could close because of the troubles the nation's number three automaker was facing. In those days, the industrial belt of Pennsylvania, Michigan, Ohio, Indiana, Illinois, and other states was losing manufacturing jobs. Illinois factories that we generally took for granted were shutting down in places like the Quad Cities and Galesburg. On the national stage, Chrysler CEO Lee Iacocca rose to fame and secured more than $1 billion in federal loan guarantees. The federal agreement included some provisions that unions and state and local governments also would pitch in to help.[4] The nation, frankly, was shocked that our auto manufacturing industry and steel industry were in a crisis. Just north of the Illinois border, a Wisconsin Steel plant shut down, wiping out four thousand jobs and causing a ripple effect of economic downturn in northern Illinois.

Some other states, along with Canada, were lining up to help Chrysler—Michigan, Delaware, Alabama, and New York—as was the city of Detroit.[5] I was among those who thought Illinois should step up to help Chrysler in Illinois. The idea was simple: the state would lend Chrysler $20 million. The bill, technically, was more complicated because we made it possible to give loans to other large companies that employed more than one thousand people, but everybody called it the "Chrysler bill" because that's what it was. We were concerned not only about the six thousand jobs that Chrysler provided in Illinois but also about places like Edwardsville, where my colleague, Sam Vadalabene, worried about the thousand employees of Cassens and Sons Transport Company, which had about seven hundred trucks that hauled Chrysler products.

The idea for the bill—to provide such enormous government loans to bail out a large private American industry—was experimental and very controversial. It's interesting to go back and read the remarks of my colleagues who voted against it.[6] "I think that as a matter of principle, this is probably a very bad idea, and we may rue the day we ever started down this path," Dawn Clark Netsch said from the Senate floor on June 25, 1980. A few minutes later, Senator Roger Keats, a Republican, poured more fuel on that argument: "You look at it the way you see an old friend who used to smoke four cigarette packs a day, and they're dying of cancer. You aren't happy to see them pass away, but God knows they did it to themselves; and I'm afraid Chrysler is in that boat. And anyone who knows economics understands that in order for growing industries to grow, the dying industries must die; and unfortunately, our auto industry, for reasons partially their fault and reasons that are partially the government's fault, is a dying industry."[7]

There were strong arguments on both sides. The Senate added an amendment so that Illinois would get the first lien on the mortgage of the Belvidere Chrysler plant if our $20 million loan was not repaid. That seemed a better solution than merely giving a direct, unsecured loan. We got thirty-two votes on the bill and passed it. I felt at the time, and still do, that if we could save six thousand jobs directly and thousands of others indirectly, it was worth a $20 million loan. Analysts still argue about whether Iacocca's bailout plan worked in the early 1980s. I think it did. Chrysler managed to bring itself back and continued building cars in America for three decades. Our loan was a good investment that helped a generation of workers. Not bad.

An unexpected pleasure occurred in October 1979 when President Carter invited Sheila and me to the White House during Pope John Paul II's visit to the United States. I got to meet the pope out on the South Lawn. Then the pope went from Washington to Chicago, where a ceremony and concert were held in Holy Name Cathedral on State Street. I ended up sitting pretty close to him. We attended with Congressman Dan Rostenkowski and his wife; Mayor Bilandic also was there. As a Catholic, I felt privileged to be in the presence of this leader, who really changed the papacy by traveling around the world instead of just staying at the Vatican all the time

Late in 1979, I filed my paperwork to run for reelection to the Illinois Senate in 1980. I had only token opposition. The Republicans ran a man named Robert Bova against me. The campaign had little of the contentiousness that Elmer Conti had presented eight years earlier or the meanness that Ronald Stolle had inflicted on me four years earlier. Bova was from the suburbs and tried to get votes by complaining that the Chicago machine was in Oak Park on my behalf. But he had no chance. I won handily with 70 percent of the vote. Frankly, I think the residents of Oak Park and my entire district appreciated what I did for them in the local community and in Springfield. So I won my fourth term, and I would win another four senatorial elections before retiring. None of these last five elections was a problem for me. This pattern often happens with local and state politicians. You have a tough time getting there, but once you establish yourself, the voters see what you're doing and reward you with reelection. You gain a lot with experience, and that's why I oppose term limits. The voters can still throw you out at any election. You can never take an election for granted, and I never did.

Overall, the Democrats did not fare very well in the 1980 elections. Ronald Reagan beat President Carter to take over the White House. Back in Illinois, the Republicans picked up three seats in the House of Representatives, just enough to give them majority control of that chamber. Soon enough they installed Representative George Ryan of Kankakee as Speaker of the House. He held that position for just one two-year term because the Democrats would regain control two years later and Michael Madigan would begin his first term as Speaker in 1983.

Democrats still controlled the Senate heading into the 1981 session, just barely. We lost two seats and had a hair-thin 30–29 majority. I assumed my Democratic colleagues would reelect me easily to a second term as Senate president. I had no idea what was coming.

Going into our session in 1981, the Senate Democrats were still feeling some unexpected effects of Mayor Byrne's victory two years earlier. Our caucus had a Jane Byrne faction and a Richard M. Daley faction. The black members were upset with both factions and hadn't coalesced around anyone except Harold Washington, who was being mentioned by a small South Side group as a possible candidate for mayor of Chicago, even though he had just been elected to the U.S. Congress in 1980.

Our caucus, as usual, had a dinner on the Tuesday night before we were scheduled to convene for the new General Assembly on the second Wednesday of January. By that Tuesday, it was clear that some Democrats were not yet ready to commit to me for my second term as Senate president. That was problematic for me because I needed every one of the thirty Democratic votes to get the constitutional majority. Some of the white ethnics were laying off, not prepared to vote for me, primarily because the black members were not prepared to vote. The black members suggested that I was responsible for, or approved of, Mayor Byrne's failure to appoint or reappoint two blacks to the Chicago Housing Authority Board. To this day, I don't understand why they blamed that on me. Netsch still wasn't happy that I had sided with Mayor Byrne and Governor Thompson the previous fall on the sales tax issue. She was telling all the reporters that I should not pay so much attention to the Chicago mayor.[8] To make it even worse, Senator Charlie Chew, who was ostensibly a friend of mine, was in a Chicago hospital, and Harold Washington was in Washington, D.C., after getting sworn in as a U.S. congressman on January 5. Washington had not resigned from his Illinois Senate seat, however, because he was fighting with Mayor Byrne over who his replacement would be. With Chew and Washington out of town, we were two short of thirty.

The next day, Governor Thompson did his constitutional duty in calling the Illinois Senate into session for the purpose of swearing in the newly elected senators and for the purpose of organization. It was obvious that we didn't have thirty Democratic bodies in the chamber. Besides Washington and Chew, four other senators were missing, although I cannot remember why: one Republican, Frank Ozinga, and Democrats Glenn Dawson, John D'Arco, and Jeremiah Joyce. Dawson and Joyce soon showed up and were formally recognized as present, but there were still only twenty-seven Democrats and twenty-eight Republicans in the chamber. Father John Smyth from Maryville City of Youth was there again to say the opening prayer, in anticipation of my reelection as Senate president. Thompson swore in all the new members, and then Republican senator David Shapiro of Amboy graciously stood up and said not enough members were present to elect a Senate president. He called for adjournment. I thought the governor and Shapiro, leader of the Senate Republicans, were doing me a favor by quickly adjourning until the next day, affording the opportunity for Chew to be discharged from the hospital and for Washington to come back from the nation's capital so that we could be a full complement. Then at ten o'clock the next morning, the governor took the roll call and announced that the next order of business was the election of a Senate president for the Eighty-Second General Assembly. Shapiro's name was placed into nomination, as was mine. This was standard procedure. Since the Democrats still did not have thirty bodies, one of my members moved that the Senate stand adjourned until February 10, but that motion was defeated. Thompson pressed to move on with electing a Senate president. Even worse, he ruled that the election of the Senate president would require the votes of a majority of members present, not a majority of all Illinois senators, as had been standard practice forever. Thompson himself repeatedly ruled four years earlier, when it took 186 ballots to elect Hynes as Senate president, that we needed thirty votes to elect a Senate president. This year, Thompson's surprise announcement meant that Shapiro possibly could steal the Senate presidency for the Republicans.

That riled the Democrats. Netsch appealed the ruling of the chair—Thompson—and I seconded that appeal. I also asked for an immediate caucus so that our members could keep their act together. We went into my office with the expectation of going back on the floor about forty-five minutes later, at about 11:30, if we could get this thing resolved. We devised a strategy about what to do if Thompson made up his mind to move ahead with the election of a Senate president even though he had only twenty-nine bodies, twenty-nine sitting Republicans—one less than a majority of the fifty-nine members of the Senate.

Thompson indeed called us back into session about 11:30, but the only Democrats on the floor were Netsch and me. That was our strategy. Netsch's motion challenging Thompson's ruling was to be debated, but first she moved to ascertain the presence of a quorum. I left the chamber. Netsch also left. The secretary started to call the roll. We figured that with only twenty-nine Republicans in the chamber, there was not a legal quorum of thirty, and no business could be conducted. Thompson did indeed stop the roll call when Netsch left the floor, because her motion was out of order without her in the chamber and without a quorum. We thought that would also stall a vote for Senate president, but much to our surprise, Thompson kept going with business of the day. Nominations were closed, and Thompson called for a vote on the Senate president.

Shapiro received all twenty-nine votes. I received none because no Democrats were present. Thompson declared Shapiro the president of the Senate for the Eighty-Second General Assembly. Shapiro gave a short rambling speech thanking everyone, and according to custom, a small group of senators escorted Thompson out of the chamber. Shapiro noted that there were no Democrats present, and the regular routine continued. The Senate—that is, only the Republicans—adopted a few housekeeping resolutions and formally introduced some bills. We always do that on the first day. Then they adjourned until February 3, the scheduled date of Thompson's State of the State message. Thompson and the Republicans left thinking they had a Senate president: David "Doc" Shapiro, a Republican. We certainly disagreed, and we were furious. We also were in limbo.

I didn't talk to Thompson before he left the Capitol, but I reached him by telephone while he was at the airport. He and Ty Fahner, the Illinois attorney general, and a number of others were heading out to Washington,

D.C., for the festivities surrounding Ronald Reagan's inauguration. I told Thompson that I was thoroughly disgusted and disappointed that he would run rampant over the Illinois Constitution and that I was going to file a lawsuit, so he ought not make any long-range plans for reapportionment until the lawsuit was over. I was referring to the fact that this was the year, according to the Illinois Constitution, that we would draw new maps for Illinois Senate and House districts as well as for Illinois congressional districts. I didn't want him rushing along with a Republican-led House and Senate to adopt new district maps that would be overwhelmingly favorable to the Republicans. I talked to Fahner, too, and I indicated that I would fax him a copy of the lawsuit, which I intended to file with the Illinois Supreme Court as quickly as possible. Two attorneys, Herman Bodewes and John Keith, and I began working on the lawsuit immediately and kept going until the wee hours of the morning. On Friday morning, we had it delivered by messenger to the home offices of each of the Illinois Supreme Court justices and faxed it to the governor in care of Attorney General Fahner at some hotel in Washington.

There was a lot of consternation among our membership about what ought to be done. Harold Washington was reluctant to come back from Washington. Actually, he was refusing to come back unless he had the opportunity to appoint his successor. He didn't like the fact that Mayor Byrne wanted her chief of staff, state representative James Taylor of Chicago, to get Washington's seat in the state Senate. So Washington refused to resign, just as he refused to come to Springfield to vote for Senate president even though he still considered himself a state senator and a U.S. congressman at the same time. I wound up talking with the Speaker of the House in Congress, Tip O'Neill of Massachusetts, and asked him to relate to Congressman Washington that he could not be on two public payrolls at once. I advised that if indeed he had been sworn in as a member of Congress and was getting paid, he ought to vacate his state seat and let nature take its course back in Chicago. It was literally a stalemate until the question of double dipping came up. Only then did Washington back off and agree to resign from his Illinois Senate seat. Jimmy Taylor was appointed to fill the Harold Washington vacancy. Meanwhile, Charlie Chew enjoyed a cure for whatever ailment he had, reportedly pneumonia, and got out of the hospital.

But the legal issues were not resolved. Our case reached the Illinois Supreme Court quickly. We asked the court to order Thompson to reconvene the Senate, to preside over another Senate president election, and to prohibit Shapiro from exercising any of the powers of a Senate president.

I told the Illinois Supreme Court that I was the "Senate president in exile." Springfield lawyer Herman Bodewes, who was making many of our arguments as the justices peppered each side with questions, told the court, "I suggest that if it takes less than thirty votes [to elect a Senate president] . . . there is absolutely chaos in that office."[9] The justices pelted Ty Fahner, who was representing Thompson, with questions about whether there had been a quorum when Shapiro was elected. Bodewes reminded the court that during the 186 ballots just four years earlier, Thompson himself kept ruling from the chair that thirty votes were needed to elect a Senate president. But Thompson changed his mind in 1981, saying he was "older and wiser" now.[10] We had other legal arguments, but Thompson's reversal was the main one. The court heard our arguments in late January but had not issued a ruling by the time the General Assembly reconvened February 3.

The drama continued on the day the House and Senate were supposed to hear Thompson's State of the State address. With Taylor officially taking over for Washington and Chew back in Springfield for our side, we finally had thirty Democrats and thirty bodies. First thing in the morning, we had a caucus and decided that we were not going to be walked upon like a doormat. An hour or two before the appointed time for starting the day's session, we went into the Senate chamber as a unified Democratic body and organized a new Senate ourselves. With no Republicans there, we went through the whole process again. I was elected Senate president with thirty votes, and we went through all the perfunctory organizing resolutions. So at that moment, there were in fact two organized Illinois Senates as a result of our action, although we considered the first one illegal. It is possible that ours was illegal, too, because Thompson was not there to preside, as required by the constitution.

Shortly after we organized with me as Senate president, the Republicans tried to start the day's business under the presidency of Shapiro. Taylor, who weighed about 250 pounds and was well over six feet tall, tried to block Shapiro from ascending to the podium, but it was more of a show than anything. "They restrained me, but it was good-natured banter between Senator Taylor and myself," Shapiro told the press later.[11] Shapiro called the Senate to order for the purpose of going over to the House for a joint session of the Illinois General Assembly to listen to Thompson's speech. We, the Senate Democrats, decided to boycott the governor's State of the State message because he had attempted to thwart the constitution. I had gone to the other side of the Capitol earlier and spoken with Mike Madigan, at this time House minority leader. I asked

Mike to pull his members off the floor so when Thompson was ready for his televised speech, there would be only Republicans in evidence on the floor of the House. That is in fact what happened. Madigan got up and questioned the quorum, and the Speaker of the House, George Ryan, was a little less than happy. It was Ryan's first opportunity as presiding officer with the governor standing there with him. There wasn't a Democrat on the floor except for Madigan, who was questioning a quorum. As soon as Ryan determined that he would not allow it, Madigan also walked off the floor. Thompson spoke for forty minutes to nobody except Republicans, and the press played that up.

The next week, the court issued a ruling in our favor. Illinois Supreme Court justices are elected in partisan elections, and there were four Democratic justices at the time. On a 4–3 vote, split along party lines, the court overturned what Thompson and Shapiro had done. The court also declared my February 3 election as Senate president to be null and void, but the main ruling gave us a victory. We prevailed on the most important questions: whether we needed thirty votes and whether there was a quorum on the floor at the time of Shapiro's election. The court instructed the governor to recall the Senate for the purposes of organizing and electing a Senate president and reminded him in no uncertain terms that it took a constitutional majority of thirty senators to elect a Senate president, not just a majority of those present. Thompson took the news well, saying of the supreme court, "They're the boss. It [the election] will be done over."[12] So Thompson called us back on February 17, and he had quite a bit of crow to eat on that day and subsequent days. In short order, the thirty Democratic senators voted me in to my second term as Senate president, and life went on. It was one of the most dramatic incidents in my fourteen years as Senate president. You might think that would have destroyed the political relationship between a Republican governor and a Democratic Senate president, between Thompson and me, but it didn't. It's fair to say I still don't like what Thompson did, but in our day-to-day operations for the next ten years, I don't think there were any lasting ill effects at all.

10. A Redistricting Fight

*Sam Vadalabene of Edwardsville became
the darling of the press corps that day.*

E VERY TEN YEARS WHEN WE DREW NEW LEGISLATIVE DISTRICT MAPS,
it was always a big issue, one of the biggest issues of the session. In
1981, the Republicans controlled the Illinois House, with George Ryan as
Speaker, and I finally settled into my second term as Senate president.
Both parties were working on maps favorable to their members. Then on
a Saturday morning late in the session, June 27, two Democratic Chicago
blacks broke loose from our fold—Richard Newhouse and Charlie Chew—
saying they would not go along with our Democratic map. Instead, they
were supporting a map put together by Senator Mark Rhoads, a Republican from Western Springs, who promised to make it more favorable to
blacks.[1] By peeling off Newhouse and Chew, Rhoads evidently thought his
map could get the thirty votes he needed to get it passed in our chamber,
which had that narrow 30–29 edge for the Democrats. That would upset
everything, because a chamber controlled by our party should be able to
draw and pass legislative districts that we ourselves put together.

With the Republicans controlling the House and the governor's office,
Rhoads might have been able to pull this off and get his map enacted
into law. He actually needed three Democratic defectors, because one of
the Republican senators was ill and not there.[2] Rhoads thought he had
Democrats Chew, Newhouse, and Tim Degnan, who had been appointed
to replace Richard M. Daley in the Senate when Daley became Cook
County state's attorney after the 1980 elections. Degnan was a Daley ally.
Meanwhile, unfortunately for Rhoads, Speaker George Ryan had his own
ideas about district boundaries. He was more concerned about House
districts, which were different from the ones being drafted in the Senate.
The truth is, in the big scheme of things, we weren't getting anywhere.

Rhoads was of the opinion that I had promised him a vote on his map, which was stuck over in the House. He said I promised him a vote sometime before five o'clock on that rare Saturday session, which was critical because every day is hectic in the last week of June. To put it mildly, Rhoads was not happy with me. I had a simple, direct response for him: "Your bill is in the House. There's no way I can direct the House to send it over here by five o'clock. That's just wishful thinking." He was getting more and more frustrated and was building up a full head of steam.

"Mark, the Speaker is of your party," I told him. "What the hell are you talking to me for? Go over and talk to him and tell him to get the bill over here. I'll let you call it. You'll get a shot at it, but I can't carry it over here." So Rhoads went across the building to the House. Soon enough, Speaker Ryan called me on the phone and asked me what was going on. I told him that Rhoads thought he had the map to end all maps because he had Newhouse and Chew on his side. I also let him know that Newhouse and Chew were boycotting a lot of Senate business and would continue doing so until they got Rhoads's map called. Then I asked George, "Are you going to send this baby over?" He said he didn't know, and I just said, "Let me know, will you?" I got the idea that Ryan was not going along with Rhoads's plan.

Rhoads came back and returned to his place in the Senate chamber. To say he was a little overheated would be an understatement. He rose and took the microphone, almost ripping it out of the stand. He called me a "son of a bitch" to start with, saying I failed to tell him the truth about getting a vote on his map. At that point, Chew was coming back onto the floor, and he asked Rhoads, "How we doing, Mark? We winning?" In fact, Rhoads was exploding. He had the microphone in his hand and was cursing at me, saying in impolite ways that I didn't do what I promised to do. I was not at the podium then but was directing my members from my seat on the floor. Rhoads was building up enough steam to come after me physically. He threw down his microphone and started in my direction across the aisle.

Senator Sam Vadalabene, meanwhile, small in stature but very loyal, was watching Rhoads closely. Mark wasn't paying any attention to Sam. It was Mark's moment of triumph, and he was coming after me, crossing into the aisle that separates Democrats from Republicans. But Sam stepped in and yelled at Rhoads, "Don't you talk to my leader that way." Then Sam hit him, grabbed him around the neck, and held him in a headlock.[3] Some of my friends, like Senator Ken Buzbee, will tell you that Sam actually punched Rhoads, and maybe he did.[4] I watched the swinging and the hitting, and I said, "Sam, don't kill the guy, just slow him down." After a little wrestling, other senators broke it up and things settled down.

Sam, who was sixty-six years old while Rhoads was only thirty-four, became the darling of the press corps that day, having mini-press conferences and talking about what happened. Sam did some of his press right at Rhoads's desk, remarking, "I saved your life, Mark. If you had gotten close to Rock, he would have killed you. I saved you, and don't forget it." Mike Royko, who was writing for the *Chicago Sun-Times* back then, had a great deal of fun with the incident. "You have to admire Vadalabene for punching a much younger man in the head," he wrote. "I found the whole thing entertaining."[5]

The Republicans' fury did not end with Rhoads that day. They were getting more and more irritated with Senator Terry Bruce, my assistant leader who was presiding over the chamber. They yelled that Bruce would not allow a fair debate on the maps. Deerfield Republican Karl Berning became so upset that he stormed the podium and kept screaming. Bruce just ignored him and carried on business, and Berning finally left the area.[6]

That shows you how heated the reapportionment discussions could be, and were. The way it works is that every ten years, the Democrats and the Republicans work on their own district maps, trying to gain an advantage by the way they assign various neighborhoods and blocks to certain districts. For us in the Senate that year, the groundwork was done in large part by someone known as "the mayor's guy." This person would come down from Chicago and help with the numbers. The mayor's office was mostly concerned about the aldermen and the ward committeemen and making sure they ended up in the right legislative districts. In 1981, Marty Murphy was the assistant city planner for the city of Chicago. He was sensational with numbers and understood demographics. He knew his business and worked closely with the Census Bureau staff to make sure the numbers were right. Big cities used to sue the Census Bureau after the official decennial census, saying its numbers were too low. Many grants and programs were formula-driven by population, and if you didn't get your numbers in the census, you spent ten years trying to get them back. Murphy was very good, and it just so happened he had lived across the street from me and was a close friend of mine. I don't think Mayor Byrne knew that I had that connection when she first appointed him. He was literally on his own to put the maps together for us in the Senate. Mike Madigan took a more hands-on approach in the House because he had many more people to deal with. In each Senate district, he had to put two representatives, and it grew messy for him.

I had Jim Donnewald draw the downstate map and Murphy work on the upstate map. Then I would call in each of my incumbent members and say: "Let's assume all of the other members are dead except you. Where do you want these lines drawn that would benefit you the most? If we can do it, we're going to do it, but remember we've got thirty other people with lines, too." We tried to get the districts as close as possible to what each member wanted. One member who gave me fits was William Marovitz, the Chicagoan who was always changing his mind about what buildings he wanted in his district. He had all those high-rises along the lake shore with a high percentage of Jewish residents, which was beneficial to him. About every twenty minutes Marovitz would change his mind, and he would want a different building, so we'd have to change the numbers.

But at some point, we literally lifted the matter out of the members' hands and gave it to the experts, one of whom was Murphy. He and a couple of other experts would go to Springfield. The state Democratic Party always had somebody there, too. It was a long process. Sometimes we would escape the Capitol and go to a hotel. We would talk about whether we were close to a finished map. Sometimes the reformers would weigh in, too, saying somebody like the League of Women Voters should draw the map. That's lovely. What I mean is that if your district is not involved, it's lovely. I don't know any public official who would want the League of Women Voters to draw these maps. But it always came up. Iowa and some other states eventually did something like that. Iowa put its map into the hands of an allegedly independent group. I don't think that process is any better than the way we do it. Everybody knows his or her own neighborhood better than anyone else. If you want proper representation for Latinos and blacks and everyone else, who are you going to give the responsibility to? Not the League of Women Voters.

There is a big political risk in the Illinois process because you take your chances every ten years. Whoever has the majority in each chamber passes its map out of the House or Senate, and then if there is a governor of a different party, as we had with Thompson, he would veto it. It's what happens. Then, according to the Illinois Constitution, the legislative leaders appoint an eight-person Legislative Redistricting Commission, half Democrats and half Republicans. If they can't agree on a map, which is usually what happens because they end up with a 4–4 tie vote, the next step is for the Illinois Supreme Court to give the secretary of state two names—one Democrat, one Republican. Then, not later than September 5, the secretary draws one of the two names, making it a nine-member commission and breaking the partisan deadlock. So the drawing of one name literally has a lot to do with how many Democrats and how many Republicans get elected in the next ten years. The writers of the Illinois Constitution thought that neither party would ever risk an all-or-nothing map victory based on a 50–50 chance, and they thought the eight-member

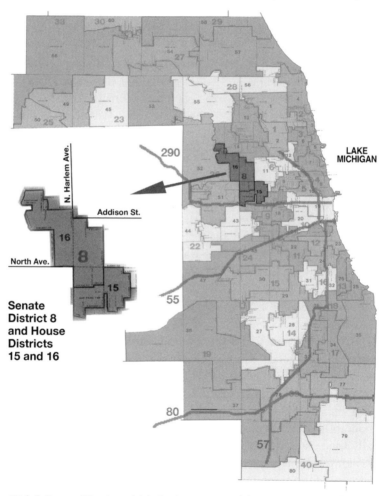

The Eighth Senate District, which Rock represented from 1983 to 1993. Illinois State Board of Elections; illustrated by Sherry Hutson.

commission would always agree on some compromise, but it didn't work out that way in 1981, 1991, or 2001. It turns out both the Republicans and the Democrats liked to take their chances, all or nothing, on that 50–50 possibility. The only times it didn't happen were 1971, when two Republicans inexplicably voted for Democratic maps, and in 2011, when the Democrats controlled everything and the process never went to a redistricting commission.

In 1981, the commission remained deadlocked. Secretary of State Jim Edgar had a little ceremony and placed two names in Abe Lincoln's top hat. He then drew the name of a Democrat, former governor Sam Shapiro. That gave the Democrats a 5–4 majority on the redistricting commission, which of course adopted a map favorable to the Democrats. So we won the "map fight" in 1981. Starting with the 1982 elections, we would control both the Illinois House and the Illinois Senate for the rest of the 1980s. I had been representing the Eighteenth District; under the new map, my territory became the Eighth District.

While reapportionment dominated the session, it was becoming clear that states were facing the "worst fiscal crisis they've seen since the Great Depression," and the problem would last for several years.[6] It's interesting to write these words ten years into the twenty-first century, because after the housing market collapse and stock market plunge in 2008 and 2009, the media were saying *those* were the worst years since the Great Depression, or if not that, the worst since 1983. The fact is, the economy was terrible in the early 1980s. It was always a part of our conversations, and it affected everything we did.

11. Going National and Beefing Up Our Party

The word of the hour in Washington was devolution,
and President Reagan wanted our help.

DURING MY FIRST DECADE IN THE ILLINOIS SENATE, there was no organized conversation between those in the Illinois legislature and Illinois members of the U.S. Congress except about what happened personally in one's district. You might get some information from your own congressman about the goings-on in Washington, D.C., but other than that, state legislators wouldn't hear much, if anything. Governor Jim Thompson had a state office in the nation's capital. I could argue about its effectiveness, but the fact is Illinois had an executive presence. Thompson's small Washington staff kept the governor and his people in the state Bureau of the Budget informed about what was happening in the capital. I visited that office a couple of times when I was on business for the National Conference of State Legislatures (NCSL). A polite way of putting it would be to say I did not receive a welcoming reception; Thompson's people in Washington didn't want to share any information with the legislature. They thought if Illinois was to get any news about Washington, it was going to come through the governor's office, period. Illinois legislators were thus increasingly unhappy with the flow of information about Washington to the legislative branch of government in Springfield.

So in 1980, after one of my trips to Washington, I talked to Bill Redmond, Speaker of the Illinois House of Representatives, about it. I said, "We're not getting the kind of information we should be getting from Washington, and the governor's people are playing it pretty close to the vest. I'm going down to talk to Thompson and either loosen them up enough to get what we want from them or perhaps do our own office." He asked what I thought. I said I preferred to have our own office. He replied, "Let's go get it." So Redmond and I walked downstairs and sprung the idea on the governor, and somewhat to my surprise, Thompson offered no resistance. He didn't have any problem with it. He just said, "You get it passed and get it on my desk and I'll sign it." I told him that was all I asked. Redmond and I engineered a larger appropriation for the Commission for Intergovernmental Cooperation to staff the office, and we opened our Illinois legislative office in September 1980. Five other state legislatures had an office in Washington: New York, Ohio, California, Michigan, and Pennsylvania.[1] Then we came along from Illinois, and we all ended up in the same building, in the Hall of the States at 444 N. Capitol Street in Washington, which is also where Thompson's office was located. We were within walking distance from the U.S. Capitol.

But we didn't get down to serious business for a few months, until February or so, after Reagan was sworn in. Frankly, we were preoccupied for a while; that was the year that Thompson tried to take over the Senate. President Reagan made it apparent during this time that he had a plan for the states in terms of the money they received from the federal government. He was going to take a whole host of programs, such as special education, mental health, and other social services, and lump them together in what he called "block grant" programs. Instead of having the money follow each of those individual programs, he would lump the funds all together and give them to the states. We could spread the money around however we wanted, within some broad guidelines. We couldn't take human service money and use it for roads, for instance.

At that time, I was also very active within the NCSL. I had been recruited based on a recommendation some years earlier from Senator Russell Arrington. The former Republican state senator from Illinois had been a big influence in the early years of the legislative leaders' conference. Before he died, he had talked to a number of those people, encouraging them to get me involved. He said that I was going to be in the Senate as long as I wanted, and he predicted that I would become one of the leaders. He thought it would be a good idea for Illinois to have somebody positioned at the national level. Those in the NCSL were very kind and would invite me to Washington for briefings. The biggest NCSL event was the national conference, but there were other meetings, too.

So, with our NCSL connections and our new legislative office, we had a good handle on what Reagan was going to do. I was appointed to an executive committee of the legislative leaders. Five or six of us had the opportunity to meet with the president himself and listen to his rationale for the existence of the block grants. He sprung it on us one day, before we had enough information to make an informed judgment about whether it was a good idea. But clearly it was going to happen.

Back home, the fiscal conservatives thought our Washington office was a waste of money because the Democrats obviously were going to run it. Illinois Republican lawmakers didn't like the idea of a separate Washington office for legislators because they felt secure that they would get all the information they needed from Thompson and his administration. But our legislative Washington office soon became one of the states' leaders in the nation's capital city. We launched some initiatives. For example, we began having regular meetings with the Illinois congressional delegation as a whole—Democrats and Republicans. There were some great people in Congress then from Illinois—among them Dan Rostenkowski, Sidney Yates, Bob Michel, Mel Price, and Ed Madigan, all of whom were legendary for bringing money back to Illinois. We made it very clear to them that ours was not a partisan office; it was a General Assembly office. So in my capacity as one of the NCSL leaders, I volunteered Illinois's participation in NCSL's activities and lobbying efforts, and our members would go to Washington on a regular basis to testify. Senator John Maitland, a Republican from Bloomington, was a terrific witness for state policies on education. Senator Ken Buzbee from downstate was an expert on budget issues. I testified a couple of times before the House Ways and Means Committee, because my friend Rostenkowski was chairman of that powerful committee. I thought it would be a good idea to put a friendly face in front of the chairman so that he would rule favorably on issues important to us. In any given week, if we were not in session in Springfield, we would have four or five people out there running all over Capitol Hill, getting briefed by cabinet staff, sharing information with the other states, and then bringing it back to Illinois and issuing memos or oral reports about the latest trends.

In 1981, the word of the hour out there was devolution. Much of the programmatic responsibility and money would be devolved back to the states, and we were all going to live happily ever after. It was a noble effort, and some of it worked. It was part of President Reagan's philosophy opposing big centralized government. Reagan had been the governor of California, and he understood what states needed. He thought it was expensive and wasteful for the federal government to send program after program to the states, along with administrative personnel. His idea, as I mentioned above, was to give the states big blocks of money and let them spend it. He wanted to meet with state leaders, and I was among those invited to go.

Reagan wanted our support, and he was very gracious. He did not appear to be very spontaneous, however. He had index cards in his pocket, and he would walk into a room and politely tell everybody to sit down. Then he would pull out the index cards, make a little speech, and put the cards away and, boom, he'd be gone. It was a one-way conversation. There was no discussion with him. One of us would just say, "Thanks; we'll do what we can to make it happen and give you all the credit you deserve." He did not waste a minute. When he left the room, his staff took over, and we would talk about the details. It was quite an adventure for a while, with Illinois in the forefront of NCSL activities. We had considerable input into the agenda, and it was fun for a long time.

When we opened the legislative office, our first executive director was William Holland. He had come to Illinois from Seattle University for an internship program and began working for the House Democrats in 1974.[2] By 1980, he was the director of the Illinois House Appropriations Committee staff for Speaker Redmond. Since he had been around the Illinois capital for about six years, I knew him slightly and was very comfortable with him. When I asked him if he wanted to take on the adventure of opening the Illinois legislative office in Washington, he said yes, moved to the nation's capital, and did a great job setting up the office. He had two small children at the time, and frankly, he thought it was the move of a lifetime.[3]

The Washington office was under the jurisdiction of the Illinois Commission for Intergovernmental Cooperation. I was the legislative chair of that commission, and our executive director in Springfield was John Lattimer. Holland reported to Lattimer, who helped us with national connections because he was also involved in the NCSL, even serving as the staff chair for a couple of years. Lattimer got me more involved in the NCSL, too. Once our office was up and running, Lattimer and Holland hired a couple of staff people and added some interns. They funneled a lot of information to Springfield for us, and they coordinated the many Illinois witnesses going to Washington to testify and meet with federal officials. I was in touch with Holland a lot, and sometimes I went out there. It was a great deal of fun to be involved in the mechanics and logistics of moving all these people back and forth, and it was rewarding for the people of Illinois because we knew what was going on.

By having such an active presence in Washington in the early Reagan years, we actually helped implement the block grant program. We worked with those on Reagan's staff who were designing the program, and we told them what would work and what wouldn't work, in our opinion, based on our experiences. Some of our advice they took, and some they didn't. Generally speaking, I think the program was implemented more gracefully and with less rancor than it otherwise would have been. We were part of a friendly collaboration to make sure that it worked, and the fact is that it did work.

Illinois legislators loved those community development block grants, and so did mayors around the state. We were getting additional money with fewer strings attached. Legislatures across the country could decide how the services and programs from these block grants could be delivered. We had something to say about every aspect of every program. Governor Thompson stepped up, too, creating two groups to look at how to spend the federal block grants. One was the eleven-member Local Government Advisory Committee chaired by Peoria mayor Richard Carver. The other was the nineteen-member Task Force on Human Services, which looked at social services, community services, mental health, alcohol and drug abuse, community development, and other issues.[4] It was a worthwhile exercise, certainly for us, and we made a lot of friends all across the country because our Washington office was so helpful. A number of states admitted that they could not afford a Washington office, so we let them work with us. We helped them as much as we could. We were well ahead of the game.

In 1981, there was a lot of speculation that I would run for governor the next year. I really thought I wanted to do that, and I spent the spring and summer of 1981 mulling it over. Two other prominent names in the field were former governor Dan Walker and Adlai Stevenson III, who had served as both U.S. senator and state treasurer. Stevenson had just finished his U.S. Senate career in January 1981. His name was fresh to Illinois voters, but I thought he would be a dud on the campaign trail. I was still ticked at Governor Thompson because he had tried that coup in the Senate earlier in the year. It was always on my mind that I should run and teach this guy a lesson in Politics 101—that the chief executive should not meddle in the business of the General Assembly. As I planned my campaign, I thought I could get the endorsement of Congressman Harold Washington, Mayor Jane Byrne, and Cook County state's attorney Richard M. Daley. That way, we could avoid any internecine warfare, and I told them that. "If we all get together and agree on a candidate, there needn't be any sniping or carping," I told them, and I thought I had them on my side.

If I were indeed going to run, I would have to start collecting signatures in the fall of 1981 and file the paperwork in December. Frankly, I was waiting to see who the state party might endorse. I certainly was in the running. I believed that the party's official backing was not to be taken lightly. Walker, Stevenson, and I were together in August at the Illinois State Fair in Springfield on Democrat Day. We took turns saying Thompson needed to be replaced, and some press reports indicated that Stevenson was drawing the most interest.[5]

Then Washington told me he had to back a black candidate. That's how Roland Burris, who was state comptroller then, got into the race. Mayor Byrne said she might support me, but she didn't want to continue to be at odds with Daley, who had just become the state's attorney. I used her argument to try to get some leverage. "I agree," I told her, "so let's get all three of you behind me." But Daley didn't go for that. He didn't like Jane Byrne; if she wanted something, he wanted something else. So that didn't work out. Jane then told me she was going to support Stevenson because all the reformers and so-called good government groups were going to back him. So there I was, trying to line up support, and all of my friends were going in a different direction. I stayed interested for another six weeks or so. A few people were telling me to stay in the state Senate, and a few others were saying I should run for attorney general. I was well aware that no sitting member of the General Assembly had been elected governor for sixty years, since Len Small of Kankakee did it in 1921.[6] I analyzed all the angles, and realizing my political support was nowhere to be found, I made up my mind by October 1981 just to run for reelection to the Illinois Senate in 1982.

Then another political opportunity arose, somewhat to my surprise. Jack Touhy, the former Speaker of the Illinois House, had been chairman of the state Democratic Party for nine years, after taking over for Mr. Ronan. Touhy let it be known that he was going to step down from the chairmanship. He didn't want any more statewide involvement; he had had enough. Frankly, the state party had changed for the worse when Touhy was state chairman, especially after Mayor Richard J. Daley died. All Touhy had to do in his first few years was follow whatever the mayor said. But Touhy had been on his own since Daley's death in 1976, and we had lost the visibility the mayor had given us statewide and nationally. For a few years, the Illinois Democrats were getting bad press for becoming almost nonexistent at the national level, and we deserved it. A party official told the *Chicago Tribune* in January 1982 that we had "the worst state party organization in the country, bar none."[7] The article went on to say, "Despite its size, Illinois has no representatives on the party's executive committee. The state's twelve members of the Democratic National Committee rarely attend committee meetings, and when they do, they are notable for their silence and lack of influence."

I was of two minds about our party. Early on, the operation under Mr. Ronan's leadership impressed me. We used to have a big Roosevelt Dinner every year in Springfield; the mayor came down from Chicago, and hundreds of other people attended, too. We would have a major fund-raiser at the St. Nicholas Hotel, which is near the Amtrak station. Chicago Democrats who used to serve in the General Assembly or work in Springfield thought it was fun to go down for a day, and they also knew they would get on a bus or plane immediately afterward and get out of town. I'm not sure if anyone knew how much money they raised. The state didn't require the kind of record-keeping that we have now, and the party leaders never released that information to peons like me. That was for the high-powered guys to know.

Democrats also had a presence at the Illinois State Fair back then, but it was on-again, off-again, as the years went on. The party would say it had two major downstate events—the Roosevelt Dinner and the state fair, but the part about the state fair was mostly bull. The Chicago party regulars didn't want to go to Springfield for the fair, and many didn't show up. Depending upon how hard the mayor pushed, each ward organization was responsible for getting a trainload or two busloads of the party faithful to the state fair. The message was: Get your fanny down to the fair.

I was in charge of our ward contingent—physically keeping people on the bus. Many from my ward would go regularly because Art McGloon had been the ward committeeman, and he would drag the party faithful to Springfield once in awhile. What would happen, though, is that guys would get off the bus and walk into the hotel and start rearranging tables so they could relax and play cards. We would get there about noon or a little after, and they wanted to go nowhere near the fairgrounds. I would stand there with my clipboard and bus arrangements and say, "Come on, guys, I've got to get somebody on this bus and go to the fair." I would wind up with only a half-dozen loyalists.

Once we got to the fairgrounds, on the north side of Springfield about three miles from downtown, I would shepherd them around so they knew where they were going. These city guys couldn't find their way around a small county fair, let alone the state fair, which was much bigger and covered a lot of acres, with all of the animal barns, food tents, carnival rides, grandstand, and the arena for animal judging. It would have been easy for them to get lost—on purpose. We would listen to a few speakers and do a one-mile march around the grounds. Then they would want to go back downtown to one of their favorite watering holes, or they would start a card game in "the office." We called it the office; it was actually

McGloon's suite at the Statehouse Inn a block north of the State Capitol. The Statehouse Inn is still there and has been remodeled and is doing very well. McGloon had extra tables and chairs brought in so they could all play cards. It was always a fun day. Then the trick was to round them all up and send them back to Chicago. The tendency was for one or more of them to stray and end up at some saloon so that nobody knew where they were. I was the cleanup hitter—the last one to leave Springfield, to make sure they all got out.

Touhy was one of the legislative alums who liked going back to Springfield once in a while. So when Touhy announced his plans to retire as state party chair, I knew he was serious, and it was an opportunity for the party to get more politically active. With the new congressional map in 1981, I wound up in a different district, a district with Touhy himself, just when he was stepping down. I could sense a dwindling of party loyalty. In an interview for a national magazine, I said: "I think the demise of party loyalty, as we have known it in the past, is a tragedy in our American system. . . . Party discipline is definitely lacking [in the states]."[8] From my seat in the Illinois Senate, I was aware of the disenchantment of some of the downstate Democrats. I thought I could help the state party, so I went to see Touhy and told him I wanted a shot at the party chairmanship.

First, I had to get on the state central committee, so I ran for Touhy's seat and won. Meanwhile, Mayor Byrne and others were making a big push to get Alderman Edward Vrdolyak to unseat George Dunne as chairman of the Cook County Democratic organization. That was a really big deal. Chicago and Cook County politics were still in disarray five years after Mayor Daley's death. Although I had been leaning toward supporting Dunne's reelection bid as Cook County chairman, I decided to join forces with Byrne in support of Vrdolyak. I had nothing against Dunne; I just felt that the Democratic Party of Cook County needed to be revitalized and thought Vrdolyak was the best person to help the party. Quite a few others felt the same way, including Aldermen Thomas Cullerton and Roman Pucinski.[9] Early in 1982, Vrdolyak won by a substantial margin and did indeed become the Cook County party chairman. That set the stage for me to get elected as the state party chair, which occurred in April 1982 with only token opposition from Waukegan mayor William Morris, a former member of the Crazy Eight. I still consider it one of the highlights of my political career. To follow Mr. Ronan and Speaker Touhy in the role of state chairman was a great honor for me.

I knew there was a lot of work to do. I wanted to get us involved in the national party, so I went to Washington, D.C., and beefed up our active membership and started putting Illinois members on committees. I persuaded the Democratic national chairman, Charles T. Manatt, to attend a Springfield fund-raiser. There were 1,200 people in the room, and almost nobody knew who he was. Certainly, they didn't know him personally. That's how out of touch the Illinois Democrats were.

One new idea I had for the state party was to have equal representation for men and women on the state central committee. It was a high priority for women, and for me, too. So I pushed legislation to double the number of state central committee members, from twenty-two to forty-four. (Illinois lost two congressional seats in 1981 due to national population shifts; we were down to twenty-two instead of twenty-four.) So we enacted a system in which one man and one woman were elected from every congressional district. It was one of my early initiatives to give women their rightful place on a level playing field. Previous to that, because of our good ol' boy system in Illinois, it wouldn't have happened that a woman would get elected to the state committee. Some thought women did not belong in politics at all, and they surely weren't going to put women onto the governing board of the state party. My response was to have two members from every district, one man and one woman. Privately, some of the men from Chicago didn't want it to happen, but they wouldn't say it publicly. The grumbling was all intramural, and I felt like the Lone Ranger. But we got it to happen, and it's been good for the party.

As the newly elected state chairman, I heard complaints from downstate county chairmen that they were ignored by Chicago. I vowed to make changes and made it a point to visit with the county chairmen personally. Before Democratic Day at the state fair, we hosted a reception for everybody in downtown Springfield the night before, and then we all went to the fair the next day. We truly beefed up our presence at the fair; that was important to the downstaters. In 1983 and 1984, I invited seven or eight of the Democratic presidential hopefuls to Illinois, and many showed up. Walter Mondale, who became the party's nominee for president in 1984, expressed his admiration for the state fair. He was sincere. I really liked Mondale. The former vice president was genuinely qualified for the presidency; he was probably overqualified. He was very smart—a midwestern guy from Minnesota with no pretense. What you saw is what you got. We traveled around Illinois together; I would get on the plane with him in Chicago and go to different places to help him campaign.

I was the state chairman for only about two years, and then I stepped down early in 1984 when I became a candidate for the U.S. Senate. I didn't think it was appropriate for the chairman to run at the top of the party's ticket, and so I resigned from the office of state chairman, having already received the endorsement of the state central committee for the U.S. Senate. Calvin Sutker from the suburbs took over for me, and a few years later state senator Vince Demuzio became the state chairman. That was a big deal because Vince had been one of the Crazy Eight; however, he proved to be a great assistant leader, loyal to me and to the party. He was from Carlinville in Macoupin County, a rural county south of Springfield. What I had been doing in the Senate and for the party gave some much-needed momentum and recognition to the downstaters.

My own staff was changing as well. Holland directed our Washington office for three years but never lost track of what was going on in Illinois. When my great friend Jim Donnewald was elected state treasurer in 1982, he asked my chief of staff in the Illinois Senate, Bob O'Keefe, to move to the treasurer's office. It was a great move for O'Keefe and created an important opening on my own staff. One day I was having breakfast in Chicago with John Lattimer, and the topic of who would be my next chief of staff came up.[10] Lattimer said he thought Bill Holland would be the best choice. Holland didn't like Washington, according to Lattimer. Frankly, I thought Bill liked Washington more than he apparently did. But Holland himself expressed an interest in being chief of staff. We had gotten to know each other because of the Washington experience, and I decided he was indeed the right guy to take over for O'Keefe. It all worked out because Holland decided he would indeed rather be in Springfield than in Washington at that point in his career. It was great timing for him. He had a period of transition from one job to the next but got to Springfield full-time early in 1983 for what would prove to be one of the busiest sessions of my legislative career.

12. Speaker Madigan

*It is fair to say that Mike and I had differences
in style and different views of government.*

WE STARTED 1983 BY MAKING HISTORY. Democrats regained control of the Illinois House because of the remap, and they installed Michael Madigan of Chicago as Speaker of the House for the first time. He would be the Speaker for most of the next three decades. Meanwhile, Democrats kept control of the Senate, and this year there were no shenanigans as I easily won my third term as Senate president. I became the first Democrat ever elected Senate president for three consecutive terms.[1] Amazingly enough, with Madigan and me, it was also the first time that the presiding officers of the Illinois House and the Illinois Senate were both from Cook County.[2] People probably remember Madigan as following George Ryan as Speaker. Ryan served only one term while the Republicans controlled the House, starting in January 1981, but he had to resign from the House after winning election as lieutenant governor in November 1982 and getting sworn in on January 10, 1983. George would spend the next twenty years in statewide office: eight as lieutenant governor, eight as secretary of state, and four as governor. But for two days at the end of the Eighty-Second General Assembly before the new representatives and senators were sworn in, the House needed a different Speaker, and the House Republicans chose Representative Art Telcser, a Chicago Republican and close pal of Ryan's. When the new Democratic majority was sworn in on January 12, 1983, they chose Madigan as Speaker for the first time. House Democrats had not been in strong hands under Bill Redmond's leadership, and they knew it. So the switch was a good move for them.

Madigan and I had entered the legislature the same year, 1971, when he was twenty-nine years old and I was thirty-four. He was from the Thirteenth Ward on the South Side, and I was from the Thirty-Seventh

Ward on Chicago's West Side. We had been in the legislature together for twelve years when he became the Speaker. I have heard some people suggest that Madigan and I didn't get along or that we didn't like each other. Those people don't know what they are talking about.

No question about it, Mike and I were, and are, friends. We didn't socialize together much, because Mike was pretty well convinced that it was in his best interest to have dinner virtually every night with his leadership team and maybe one or two others. But I didn't think that was necessary anyway. You could always find him in one of the better restaurants in Springfield with six or eight people—the same people from the House and once in a while with a visiting firefighter from Chicago or a visiting constituent.

We had a lot of access to each other. Over the years, I could pick up the phone and talk to his secretary and say, "I have to see him; I have to talk to him," and virtually always there was an immediate favorable response. I'm happy to say that the same was true on the other end. He would call my secretary, Betty Shipley, or one of the other close members of my staff, and say he wanted to talk to me. It was part of a good working relationship. If something got away from us—if there was a mini-revolt among our members, or if some piece of legislation happened to slip out of the Senate or out of the House and it was later thought not to be in the best interests of Chicago or of the Democratic Party—I could count on him to slow it down or kill it in the House. He could count on my same effort in my chamber. I would stop or postpone or shelve whatever the issue was whenever Mike and I reached an agreement.

We probably agreed on most of the substantive issues, as well as on some that were special to both of us. For instance, he and I put in the requirement that private schools be included in the state's capital program for schools. When Governor Thompson promoted a big capital program for higher education, Mike and I both insisted that private colleges and universities be included.

Also, Mike and I did our best for the city of Chicago, but we did it in different ways. He came up through the ranks as a ward committee-man, the Thirteenth Ward, and he considered it important to get jobs for people in his ward. I was not into that as vigorously as he was. Also, he never was hidebound as a real liberal or a real conservative, or even as a moderate. He would be very difficult to label, and that's been a part of the secret of his success. It would be impossible to identify him with one narrow political philosophy or ideology. Constituents don't know where he stands on a number of issues, even though he has some strong feelings. I think it's fair to say after almost forty years of dealing with him—twenty-two of those in the legislature and almost eighteen years since then—that he's generally not in favor of gambling as a legitimate revenue source. He didn't happen to believe in it, and I had to respect that. So when people would ask me, "Why can't you get a gambling bill out of the House?" I replied simply, "Because the Speaker's not in favor of it. You're going to have a tough time convincing him to do something that would further the expansion of gambling. It's not in the cards, no pun intended." Meanwhile, as he well knows, I actively helped the horse-racing industry over the years, and I pushed for off-track betting because I thought it was the right thing for the industry and for the state of Illinois. One big issue that we did not agree on was whether to go after a World's Fair for the city of Chicago in 1992. I was for it and he wasn't—something I'll explain in greater detail later.

It is fair to say that Mike and I had differences in style and different views of government. I think he would agree, though maybe not in the same words.[3] Madigan is an excellent legislative tactician, one of the shrewdest ever. He thinks through what he wants to do. He strategizes very well and is able to read and anticipate his members. He was very good in the caucus because he could literally predict where almost all of the members were coming from on every issue. I didn't seem to have that same facility, but I had a different caucus than he did. Mine was much more rambunctious, much more independent. I had only that slim majority in my chamber, so if one or two of them took a walk or threatened to go off the reservation, the whole building could crumble for me. Mike could afford to have four or five take a walk or be recalcitrant, and those members wouldn't have any impact because he literally could put something together without them. He didn't need their votes. He seemed to hold his caucus together very tightly, whereas I held mine together by handling very strong factions that were forever dividing my caucus.

Another difference was our approach to issues. I don't think he will be viewed historically as an ideologue. He did not pursue issues for their own sake but was more concerned in many instances with the politics of an issue than in the issue itself. He and I had some squabbles about that. I was notorious for focusing on issues instead of the politics, and he was equally notorious for giving such a high priority to the political consequences of everything.

When we dealt with the family medical leave issue in the late 1980s, for instance, we wanted to afford women the opportunity to take unpaid maternity leave with the guarantee that the job would still be hers eight or twelve weeks later. We worked at least two or three years on this issue and succeeded in passing it, only to have Governor Thompson veto it. Then we got it passed again, and Thompson vetoed it again. It was the number one effort for a while on the part of the organized labor movement. It was also the number one issue with the women's caucus in both the House and Senate.

In the Senate, Penny Severns, a Democrat from Decatur, was leading the way on this issue, and we were finally in a position to pass legislation. We had the votes. We had amended the bill to the point where the leave was unpaid and applied only to employers with fifty or more employees; there were also numerous contingencies. Different versions of the bill appeared in the House and Senate, so the issue was sent to a conference committee.

I thought Madigan was a little slow at first, a little dilatory, in appointing the conferees. Now, I understand that is a prerogative of the presiding officer. It's one of the hidden tools of the business. When you're supposed to put five members of each party on a conference committee to resolve the differences in a piece of legislation, you, as the presiding officer, should know what the position is of each of the five members you're appointing. You can appoint five who are opposed to something or five who are willing to fight for something or even some who don't care much and then leave it up to the wind. Or you can delay the appointments and nothing happens. Then it stays in political limbo, governmental limbo, because nobody's doing anything.

So I went over to visit with Mike, and I said I would like his help on this issue. "The sooner you can make these appointments," I said, "the sooner we can get this thing out of here. Because of the interest in it, and because organized labor is filling up the galleries every time we take a look at this thing, I'd like to get rid of it by passing it." He was not in such a hurry because politically, he thought we would be better off having it as an issue in the fall rather than as a fait accompli in the regular spring session. So we had a legitimate difference of opinion. We jousted back and forth, and one of the House members said to me, "You know, I'm getting a little tired of you trying to do what's right all the time. We've got a great political issue here." That helps explain the difference between Madigan and me.

In this case, the Speaker recognized that I was right, and we should have passed it. I knew he knew that. On the other hand, politically, he was correct. We could have stretched it out to our advantage. It was a great political issue, one that we intended to use, except I wanted it to be said, "Part of the success of the Democratic Party is that we were able to pass this as quickly as possible." I didn't mind sacrificing a little political benefit in order to try to get it done. Because of Thompson's vetoes of the family medical leave bills, as it turns out, this important policy did not become Illinois law until I was gone from the Senate, but it did finally pass and was enacted, and it's an example of sometimes having to stay with an issue for many years in order to see it through.

Sometimes, politically, Mike and I were on the same side. He was very supportive in response to some of my difficulties. In 1981, when Thompson and friends literally attempted to steal away the Senate from the Democratic Party, Mike stood with me, and we boycotted the governor's State of the State message. There were no Democrats on the floor of the House when the House supposedly was in joint session. Mike and I pulled off the protest, embarrassing Thompson. It was a show of force by us, the Democrats, that we didn't appreciate the governor getting involved in the leadership battles of the General Assembly. I think Thompson got the message. He didn't meddle again, certainly. Maybe he didn't have the chance, but he didn't do it again. For Mike, this was yet another opportunity to make the Republicans look bad. He thinks that's important.

Mike was very solicitous about his members and attempted to recognize what was important to them, and he tried to help them obtain what they wanted. In this way, I would say we were similar; each of us really tried to learn and understand what our members wanted.

It's probably fair to say that Mike had some concerns about my otherwise good working relationship with Thompson. He didn't think I should be so friendly with a Republican governor. Mike might say that Thompson picked me off politically, to the detriment of the Democrats, but I viewed my style as never losing sight of wanting to make government work for the people of Illinois. In any event, I would say that Mike and I had a civil and friendly rivalry. There is, frankly, always going to be some rivalry not only between Democrats and Republicans but also between House and Senate members, between House and Senate leaders, even when the same party controls both, as the Democrats did for most of the 1980s.

Wedding photo,
Sheila Graber and
Philip J. Rock, 1964.
Author's collection

Rock, running for the
Illinois Senate for the first
time, and his opponent,
Marie Pedersen, featured
on the cover of the weekly
paper the *Austinite*,
October 14, 1970,
published on the West
Side of Chicago.

From left, congressional candidate Mike Glasso, Illinois Attorney General William Clark, and Rock. Author's collection.

Rock enjoying a victory in his district office in Oak Park, along with Senator Jerome Joyce (*left*), Ed Arman (*behind Rock*), and Rock's brother, Mike. Author's collection.

Rock with young campaign workers in his Oak Park office. Author's collection.

Rock making a point in the Senate with Senator Vince Demuzio beside him.
Photo by Ken Burnette.

Leaders at the McCormick Place expansion ceremony, October 1984. *Left to right:* Governor James R. Thompson, Mayor Harold Washington, Cardinal Joseph Bernardin, and Rock. Photo by Kee Chang, Chicago Association of Commerce and Industry.

Rock attending a hearing in the suburbs at which people opposed the expansion of O'Hare Airport. *Left to right:* Rock, Representative Lee Daniels, Senator James "Pate" Philip, and Illinois congressman Henry Hyde. Author's collection.

Rock on the Senate floor with William Holland, his chief of staff. Author's collection.

Rock speaking from his seat in the Illinois Senate. Author's collection.

Rock making a point while holding up his scribbled notes on the back of an envelope, one of his trademark poses. Photo by Michael Fryer, *Chicago Tribune.*

Republican minority leader James "Pate" Philip (*left*) conferring with Rock.
Photo by Ken Burnette.

Rock and Illinois senator Jerome Joyce (*center*), a great friend of Rock's from Kankakee County, visiting with presidential candidate Michael Dukakis, 1988. Author's collection.

House Speaker Michael Madigan and Rock meeting the press. Photo by Michael Fryer, *Chicago Tribune*.

Governor James R. Thompson and Rock singing "Danny Boy" at a fund-raiser for Maryville Academy. Chicago alderman Ed Burke is at the piano. Author's collection.

Mayor Richard M. Daley (*left*) with Rock and Dan Fusco, Rock's law partner. Author's collection.

Rock in the Old State Capitol with leaders of the Illinois Women in Government program in the 1990s. *Left to right:* Maralee Lindley, Margery Benson, Alice Phillips, Linda Kingman, Rock, Betsy Tracy, and Bonnie Ettinger. Photo courtesy of Bonnie Ettinger.

Rock at his Oak Park office after leaving the Senate, 1996. He was still the Oak Park Township committeeman.
Wednesday Journal of Oak Park and River Forest.

13. Getting Behind the Tax Increase of 1983

*Harold Washington made history when he beat incumbent
mayor Jane Byrne and Richard M. Daley in the primary and
then topped Republican Bernard Epton in the general election.*

JIM THOMPSON WAS ELECTED IN 1982 TO A THIRD TERM as Illinois governor. (There are no term limits for governor in Illinois.) He squeaked out a win over the Democratic candidate, Adlai E. Stevenson III, by 5,074 votes. For a few weeks, nobody knew for sure who won. Stevenson went to court to fight for a recount, but after weeks of legal wrangling, the Illinois Supreme Court rejected Stevenson's challenge.

By the time Thompson's third term began on the second Monday in January 1983, Springfield already was buzzing about whether Illinois might increase the state income tax. It had become clear to everyone only after Thompson won reelection in 1982 that the state was in deep financial trouble. He took a lot of heat when he started talking about the state's budgetary issues because he had given no indication of major problems during his campaign. I guess he knew there was going to be trouble, though, because he put together a blue-ribbon tax reform commission, chaired by James Furman, executive vice president of the Chicago-based MacArthur Foundation. The commission released a report in December 1982 advising an income tax increase from 2.5 percent to 3 percent on individuals and a 50 percent decrease in local property taxes allocated for elementary and secondary education.[1] Those on the commission called this a "tax swap." They had eighteen additional recommendations, such as broadening the sales tax to include professional and trade services, not just sales taxes on material goods. Their idea would cause consumers to pay sales tax on services from attorneys, plumbers, barbers, artists, doctors, and many others.

Within days after all the swearing-in festivities, I became the first legislative leader to call for passage of a state income tax increase. In doing so, I was ahead of the governor. I taped programs for WBBM and WMAQ radio in Chicago, which played on the third Sunday of January, and called for an increase in the income tax from 2.5 percent to 3 or 4 percent. I also said we needed to pump up the gasoline tax from 7.5 cents to 9.5 cents a gallon. The state had a structural deficit of about half a billion dollars in fiscal year 1984, which was already half over, and we were going deeper into the red. To generate a large amount of new revenue, we always looked for a variety of revenue streams, not just one. Thompson initially called for an increase in liquor, cigarette, and gasoline taxes, but he hadn't said anything about income taxes. I said it would be too minor to increase only the sin taxes and the gasoline tax.[2] I told the governor to do everybody a favor and tell it like it is. Many of my friends, political and otherwise, thought I was suffering from "politically terminal lunacy" by going public with the idea of an income tax increase before anyone else did.[3] I did not know what the political repercussions might be for getting out first with the proposal.

Illinois had not increased the income tax since its inception in 1969, fourteen years earlier. I told the radio audiences and reporters that twenty-eight states had increased some taxes in 1981, and thirty states did so in 1982. So we weren't the first state needing more revenue during that difficult recession. Some people say the worst time to raise taxes is during a recession because citizens already are hurting. But the truth is, some people *always* say it's the "worst time" to raise taxes. The economy was indeed terrible in 1983. The numbers seem staggering even now: Illinois lost 350,000 manufacturing jobs between 1971 and 1982, and the percentage of Illinoisans working in manufacturing deteriorated rapidly from 31 percent to 22 percent during those years. We also gained 134,000 trade jobs and 288,000 service jobs during that time, but overall, those service sector jobs paid a lot less than the lost manufacturing jobs.[4]

Since Thompson didn't mention the income tax increase in his inaugural address, we waited to see what he would say in his State of the State address, which ordinarily is part of a festive day. We members of the Senate would go across the third floor of the Capitol to the House chamber, where we would all listen to the governor talk about his proposals for the year. Speaker Mike Madigan and I took our places behind the governor—like you see on television when the president of the United States speaks to a joint session of Congress. Thompson took what one reporter called "the gamble of his career" when he did indeed propose to raise $1.87 billion in new revenue primarily by raising the state income tax from 2.5 percent on personal income to 4 percent.[5] But that's not all. Thompson proposed other tax and fee increases to generate all the revenue he thought we needed:

- corporate income tax, from 4 to 5.6 percent (the Illinois Constitution requires a ratio of 5 to 8 between the individual and corporate income taxes, so if we raised the individual tax rate, we'd have to increase the corporate rate, too)
- liquor tax increases (various rates) of 67 percent on wine, beer, and spirits
- gasoline tax, from 7.5 cents to 11 cents a gallon
- license plate fees for pickup trucks and large automobiles, from $30 to $48 annually, plus a 20 percent increase in other truck registration fees.
- license plate fees for small automobiles (defined as 35 horsepower or less), from $18 to $36 in 1984 and then to $48 in 1985[6]

The atmosphere in the General Assembly was more somber than usual for a State of the State address. We didn't do all the normal cheering and applause for the governor, but he poured it on, quite eloquently. He announced in his speech, "It is my duty to tell you, my fellow citizens, that I believe that we can no longer save and cut, stretch and borrow, nor put off until tomorrow the pressing human needs of today. For fourteen years this state has gotten by, sometimes well and sometimes not so well, without any increase in the income tax. . . . But the same cruel recession which has been punishing so many citizens has taken its toll on the ability of your state government to maintain a standard of decency in the delivery of some human services, a standard of excellence in education, and a new standard of achievement in economic development."[7]

My initial reaction was that Thompson might be asking for too much, but sometimes that's what you do because you figure the request will be whittled down along the way. I also thought that some kind of "tax swap" was the only way we could get an income tax increase passed. The Furman commission had recommended one on a large scale; I believed if we couldn't get that, we had to provide some kind of property tax relief. We did not have the political ability to pass a lone, naked income tax without affording some relief to the beleaguered conservative Republican taxpayers in the suburbs. Even if it would be only $50 or so per homeowner, I thought it would be good to send a message that we knew citizens were paying their taxes, and we wanted to give them a little rebate. So I supported adding a property tax relief provision into the bill. Conceptually,

I supported the much larger kind of tax swap proposals that by now have been around for decades—from the Furman commission in the 1980s to the Ikenberry commission in the 1990s to Chicago senator James Meeks's bill during the Rod Blagojevich and Pat Quinn years at the turn of the twenty-first century. All of these proposals would provide truly significant property tax relief and increase the income tax so that the income tax becomes a much greater provider of revenue for education and other state services. I think that's the right way to go. Realistically and politically, though, such an increase is virtually impossible to pass because it is too big a hit on the income tax. When the increase is too much, perhaps double the current rate, people won't go for it. Everyone would love to get rid of the property tax or reduce it considerably, but statewide, local taxing bodies raise billions of dollars from it. How could we possibly replace it? I didn't think it could happen.

Madigan, meanwhile, argued we might not need a permanent tax increase; a temporary increase might be adequate until the economy recovered. "If the problem is short term," the Speaker said, "there's merit in considering a short-term solution rather than something Illinois will live with forever."[8] We were already beginning to see the kind of leader that Madigan would become. He was different from the previous Democratic speaker, Bill Redmond: more hands-on than anybody in terms of dealing with his members, very meticulous and methodical, kind of laid-back. Madigan strived to anticipate and have a remedy for virtually anything that came up. He was not a rabble-rouser and certainly didn't get up and yell every day—that was not his style—but you had the feeling that he understood what was going on and what he wanted to do. He was not as strongly supportive of the tax increase as Thompson and I were, but he wasn't totally against it, either.

Thompson and legislators who supported the tax increase had a tough sell. Members of Thompson's own party from both the House and Senate immediately told him in a private meeting they were not too crazy about the tax increase.[9] Some of my members, among them Dawn Clark Netsch, thought that the governor was engaging in trickery because his campaign comments had contained no hint of any dire financial condition. The Illinois State Chamber of Commerce and Illinois Manufacturers Association led the interest groups in lambasting the governor's proposal for a tax increase. The chamber's president, Lester Brann, said, "This is the worst possible time in our state's economic history to be proposing massive tax increases."[10] About the only encouraging sign was the silence or neutrality of many associations and newspapers. At least they weren't against us. Most education groups and the American Federation of State, County, and Municipal Employees supported the tax increase, undoubtedly because they saw it as the only way to fund increases in pay for teachers and many government workers.

We had three major strategies to build support for the tax increase in the next three or four months. First of all, Thompson would spend a lot of time personally selling the need for more revenue. He assigned Greg Baise, his patronage chief and later the head of the Illinois Manufacturers Association, a leading role in selling the tax increase. Thompson and Baise appealed to education groups, social service providers, public employee unions, the Illinois Municipal League, and many others. He went to the Municipal League because it was a big deal for local governments to keep a one-twelfth share of the income tax for local governments. Thompson also dispatched cabinet members around the state to sell the plan, and he himself tried to visit one major media market a week in Illinois, visit with community leaders, and make at least one speech that would be covered by the media.[11] Thompson was a gifted speaker and campaigner, always able to work a room and charm a crowd. He loved mixing with people and was very good at it. Thompson did something else, too, to get people's attention: he presented a "doomsday budget" early in the session to make everyone see how drastic the cuts in human services and schools might be if the state had no new revenue. There was something in it to make everyone nervous: cutting $200 million from local school aid, including at least $60 million from Chicago public schools; cutting $100 million from higher education, allegedly forcing 1,000 faculty layoffs; eliminating the General Assistance Welfare program and state-paid medical care for the working poor; releasing prison inmates before their sentences had ended; and—something that would prove to be a major issue in this session—forgetting a much-needed operating subsidy for the Regional Transportation Authority, which was so important to me and many other Democrats.[12]

While Thompson was doing all of that, I was not having an easy time trying to get individual legislators on board. After no bill emerged for six or eight weeks, I formed the Select Committee on Budget and Finance to make some noise. I named Netsch, already chair of the Senate Revenue Committee, as chair of this special committee, with two appropriations chairmen—downstater Ken Buzbee and Chicagoan Howard Carroll—as cochairs. I also lined up chairs of Senate committees related to issues most negatively affected by Thompson's proposed cuts. Then my counterpart on the Republican side, James "Pate" Philip of DuPage County, appointed Republican spokespersons from those same Senate committees to the select committee. I don't think Pate was too crazy about the tax increase, but he knew Thompson really wanted it, and so he reluctantly provided some help from the Senate Republicans.

One problem that many legislators had with Thompson's proposal was that he didn't provide many details on how he wanted to spend the new money from the tax increases. So Netsch's committee called Thompson's budget person, Robert Mandeville, whom we all respected, to appear at a hearing. He tried to make it clear that $1.6 billion would not generate a lot of new money for the legislature to spend as it wished. He used charts and visuals to show that even with the tax increase, the state—which had so many debts and owed so many bills—would still spend less on programs in 1984 than in 1983.[13] That was not welcome news, because if we were going to vote for a tax increase, we would have much preferred to create some new programs or have all members go back to their districts and say how the increase would help their local community.

On February 22, we received some other startling news. I was watching television that evening and learned that Congressman Harold Washington had defeated incumbent mayor Jane Byrne and Cook County state's attorney Richard M. Daley in the three-way Democratic primary for mayor of Chicago. Jesse Jackson was standing at the podium, waiting for Washington to come give his victory speech. Jackson must have had that podium for thirty minutes. He always loved the limelight, although one commentator wrote that Jackson's "identification with Washington may have turned off many potential voters" in the general election a few weeks later.[14] Analysts agreed that having two high-profile white candidates made it possible for Washington to win the primary, especially because Daley and Byrne were beating each other up. Noted columnist and professor Paul Green called it the "ultimate battle royale." He also wrote, "Few local campaigns in this country, indeed, in the world, have ever generated such sustained intensity as Chicago's 1983 mayoral primary."[15] Byrne started out with a 20-point lead in the polls, and she had raised millions of dollars to run for reelection. But in a very close race in which both the *Tribune* and the *Sun-Times* endorsed Daley, Washington got 37 percent of the vote; the incumbent Byrne, 33 percent; and Daley, 30 percent. I had supported Byrne for reelection; I had been at her inauguration four years earlier with a front-row seat in Grant Park and had been interacting with her on friendly terms in one way or another since our consumer protection days in the late 1960s.

Mainly because Washington was black and because the primary was so ugly, the Democrats had a major battle on their hands in the general election in April. Washington's opponent was Bernard Epton, a reform-minded Republican from the near southeast side. No one had paid attention to the Republican primary, which Epton won easily. But in the general election campaign, he went after the "white ethnic" Democrats who had voted overwhelmingly for Byrne or Daley in the primary and were seemingly unlikely to vote for a black person for mayor. I realize it is not politically correct to describe a campaign so bluntly in racial terms, but it happened to be true. A biography of Washington reported samples of really terrible, racially charged literature. "Your vote for Mr. Epton," said one piece, "will stop contamination and occupation of the City Hall by a Mr. Baboon, elected racialy [sic] with the votes of thousands of baboons."[16] If Washington were elected, another flyer asked, "will they put basketball hoops on the Picasso [sculpture downtown]? Will Water Tower Place be renamed Watermelon Place? Will the CTA be renamed Soul Train?"[17] It was awful. Epton himself used racial code words in his television commercials, including the notorious phrase "Vote for Mayor: Before It's Too Late."[18] It was quite a campaign. I agree with Paul Green's analysis that the general election campaign "deteriorated to the gutter and below in the closing weeks. Neither man exhibited much wit, charm, or polish as they tore into each other, leaving no aspect of the other's character or record untarnished. . . . Washington questioned Epton's mental health, [and those on Epton's team] intensified their charges that 'Washington was unfit to be mayor because of his historic disregard for the law.'"[19] In both the primary and general elections, Washington's opponents kept reminding voters that Washington had been convicted a decade earlier for failure to file his income taxes. It all became a national spectacle, and former president Jimmy Carter sent people from other states, such as Georgia and Alabama, to help Washington. I advised these visitors to be careful about what they said to whom: "It's a little nasty out there, so make sure you know exactly who you're talking to before saying anything."

On election day, Washington won, but barely. He got 51.8 percent of the vote and a margin of 48,250 out of 1.3 million votes cast. He received more than 98 percent of the vote in sixteen of the fifty wards but less than 20 percent of the vote in fourteen wards. Some of those wards were still plenty unhappy that Byrne had upset the Democratic organization's candidate, Michael Bilandic, four years earlier and that Washington had defeated the organization's pick, Richard M. Daley, this time around. There's no question that race as well as party organizational concerns had a lot to do with the outcome and the huge discrepancies in many of the wards.

Washington became the city's first black mayor, and as the state Democratic chairman, I supported him and his victory in the general election. I remember being with him just before election day, and we were all courteous, as we should have been. It didn't take very long, though, for new kinds of power struggles to go front and center in city politics. Commonly called the "council wars," the battles pitted organizational Democrats against reformers who considered themselves anti-machine. I was close to, and identified with, people like Aldermen Ed Vrdolyak, Edward Burke, and William Banks—those who were really at war with the Washington faction. I had friends on both sides, and I thought the best thing was to keep them neutralized insofar as legislative action in Springfield was concerned. When I returned to Chicago during this time, I would certainly hear about the fights. They were calling Chicago "Beirut on the lake," and I just reminded everyone that the General Assembly had a different mandate than the city council. I asked of all them—Burke, Vrdolyak, Washington, everybody—not to bring their fight to Springfield. I told them the fighting on the city council floor was their business, I was not going to get involved, and I would appreciate it if they would not involve the legislators in Springfield in their fights. "I'll stay out of your business, and you stay out of mine," was my message to the Chicago factions. I think my Senate members, particularly those from Chicago, came to the realization that they didn't want to fight a long-distance war.

Nonetheless, it's fair to say that after Washington was sworn in, his first year was not his finest hour. He was besieged on all sides. He had to deal not only with the white ethnic committeemen and all their employees but also with the blacks who said in no uncertain terms, "It's our turn. We are going to run this place," meaning city hall. They were pushing him to fire and replace everybody. The new mayor was having a tough time in Chicago and not getting help from Springfield, nor was he getting much help from the party. What I tried to do with Speaker Madigan was keep the council wars away from Springfield. If we had kicked each other around in Springfield based on the alliances in the Chicago battles, the only winners would have been the downstaters. Madigan and I were successful at this, I think. We literally sat both sides down and said, "It's not going to happen down here," and for the most part it didn't.

In any event, Washington's victory in 1983 changed the general climate for the remainder of the spring session, when the income tax issue dominated everything. Thompson decided that he wanted Philip to carry the income tax bill, and Pate agreed, somewhat reluctantly. So the three leading proponents of the income tax increase were a Republican governor and the Democratic and Republican leaders of the Senate. It was a bipartisan effort. Speaker Madigan—remember, it was his first year as Speaker—had said very little about the tax increase, and Representative Lee Daniels, the Republican House minority leader, seemed opposed to it. We still had a long way to go. In early April, the *Sun-Times* reported that only twelve senators favored an income tax increase, seven opposed it, and the other thirty had various positions in the middle.[20] Mindful that Madigan had said something about a temporary income tax increase, Thompson decided after his statewide travels that a permanent income tax increase had no chance of passing. So he and Philip put in a bill, SB 1297, that would increase the income tax for four years from 2.5 percent to 4 percent for individuals and from 4 percent to 5.6 percent for businesses. Saying it would be for four years rather than forever was an early compromise based on Madigan's thinking. Meanwhile, Thompson's doomsday budget was still out there. But it was only April, still very early to negotiate something of this magnitude by the end of June, which was at that time the date when we concluded a spring session.

I started the month of May by calling an unusual Committee of the Whole in order to have a full Senate hearing on the merits of Philip's bill. Thompson showed up and spoke directly and in great detail about the need to increase revenue for human services and education. He said that people had asked him why he didn't first cut state spending before requesting a tax increase. "We have," he pointed out. "Together we have cut back hundreds of millions of dollars in the last three years. We have cut."

He used the same rhetoric with the issue of layoffs. "When business people say to me, 'I've had to lay [people] off; why don't you lay [people] off?' And the answer is, we have. We have, and in some places it's really hurting." Thompson was really good: "My friends, I have gone nearly everywhere in the state of Illinois[;] I've spoken to chambers of commerce, to organized societies; I've visited schools, mental health institutions, correctional facilities[;] I've met with your constituents. Yes, I've heard opposition [to the tax increase,] but I've also heard support; I hope you will hear some support today. I've gone to the public. I've made myself available in town meetings. I intend for the balance of this legislative session to work unceasingly for an appropriate tax increase for the State of Illinois to keep us number one. That is my obligation and I will not retreat from it. I will work publicly, I will work legislatively, and I will not turn my back on the needs of the people of the State of Illinois who you represent, but I need your help."[21]

Then there was a parade of witnesses, and we tried to drive home the point that the state needed the extra revenue for education, human services, municipalities, and other necessities. The committee meeting began in the morning and went into the early afternoon. Unfortunately, even with the promise not to make the tax increase permanent and with a hint that we would entertain some property tax relief—something requested by Republicans such as Aldo DeAngelis and Adeline Geo-Karis—we did not get enough movement in our favor by the time a critical deadline for bill passage came, on May 27. The day before, Thompson, Philip, and I met privately to see if we could launch a compromise acceptable to our caucuses. We agreed to cut the increase back to 3.5 percent and add a small homeowner property tax deduction, and then Thompson spent a day talking to individual senators, trying to get them on board. I counted votes. We needed thirty, and I don't think we ever got more than twenty-five or twenty-six, including Democrats and Republicans. So I didn't call Philip's bill for a final vote, and the bill died because we missed the deadline for passing it out of the Senate, according to our rules. We entered the month of June needing another strategy.

Incredibly, Thompson had been working hard on Lee Daniels, the House minority leader from DuPage County. The governor believed all along that if he could get the support of Daniels and some House Republicans, he could get his income tax increase. Thompson thought it would be more difficult to get support in the House than in the Senate, on the theory that House members have to run for reelection every two years and so are reluctant to vote for a tax increase when they will be filing petitions for reelection just a few months after a vote. Thompson loves to tell the story about using his morning jog in Springfield to convince Daniels to support the tax increase. As Thompson put it, "I would knock on his kitchen door at six o'clock in the morning and ask for a cup of coffee. [I would go] into his kitchen and sit myself down and start talking about the tax increase. The next day I brought him a pound of coffee, and the next day I brought him a coffee maker. He finally surrendered. He didn't want me knocking on his door at six o'clock in the morning."[22]

Maybe it worked. During the first two weeks of June, a lot of people were taking different positions, and Thompson was getting testy. A few aldermen even came to Springfield, including the anti–Harold Washington Ed Vrdolyak, who said he supported an increase but stipulated that there needed to be more for Chicago. Vrdolyak was still positioning himself as Chicago's leader, even though Washington was mayor. Because Washington was so new, it was unclear how he or the black legislators would line up, but the mayor eventually said the Chicago Democrats supported a tax increase. On the morning of June 16, Daniels emerged in support of a temporary increase in the income tax. He distributed what they called the House Republican Policy Committee Report.[23] The major pieces were an income tax increase to 3.5 percent for only eighteen months and an income tax deduction for homeowners equal to their total property tax bill.

That was a major breakthrough, but there were still many ideas out there. I frankly thought I had already compromised considerably in the past five months in order to get the revenue the state needed and to get to where we were. I believed from the beginning that we needed a permanent income tax increase. But I had already agreed to back off to a four-year proposal, and then the Daniels plan got it down to the temporary time frame of eighteen months. Philip and I had been out there consistently trying to drum up support while the House was lying low. That wasn't the most pleasant position politically, but it was necessary. Most of my priorities, such as the schools, the disadvantaged, and Chicago mass transit, needed more revenue.

Thompson called for a summit meeting of the legislative leaders at the Governor's Mansion four days later, on Monday, June 20. So I went down there that morning with my chief of staff, Bill Holland, and press secretary, Judy Erwin. We met with Thompson and the other leaders—Madigan, Philip, and Daniels—and some of their staff people. With the Daniels plan, we had something new to work with, but there were no guarantees.

We staked out our positions and agreed to keep talking. After that first summit meeting in the mansion, we began meeting every day in the governor's office in the Capitol. It was more convenient for us and our members, with my office on the third floor of the Capitol and the governor's office on the second floor, than going a few blocks away to the mansion. Members of the press would hang around all the time, waiting for one of us or all of us to emerge, and each day they would want to know if we had an agreement.

Initially, everyone was pretty contentious. It was not a happy time. A couple of them did not want any tax increase at all, namely Philip and Daniels. Madigan just said, vaguely, "Let's see what we've got here," and I was the only one who said, "Let's get the income tax increase." I had my caucus pretty well talked into it, or at least enough of them. Philip was just going along with the show, with some reluctance. He didn't like it, but he recognized that for Thompson to get what he wanted, and for Philip to get what he wanted from Thompson, he was stuck; he had to support it. Despite Daniels's public pronouncements, he was not giving the governor any solace or comfort at all. Whatever Thompson would say, Daniels would say the opposite. Without property tax relief and a temporary time frame for the income tax increase, Daniels said, we could count him out. Thompson led the meetings and talked more than anybody, trying to keep things moving. Madigan volunteered almost nothing in the meetings; he kept his ideas to himself. Based on my public statements for six months, everybody knew where I was: I was in favor of it. I was also suggesting very strongly that absent a tax increase, we would have a horrendous time with the budget as we knew it. There would be significant cuts. I wasn't kidding. I wasn't bluffing. That was the reality.

It might be that the press made too much, and still makes too much, of those summit meetings. Frankly, there was a lot of sitting around. After a lot of light patter at first, we got into the substantive issues, and somebody picked up or refined where he had left off. We would talk for a while, and then the standard mantra was: "I'll have to check with my caucus. I can't make any decision without my caucus." So then the meeting would break up and all of us would call a caucus or set a caucus for the next morning, depending on the time of day. It became tedious, and the longer it went, the worse it got, because we were not eating right or sleeping right, tempers got short, and we had to listen to a lot of sentiments and opinions that didn't advance the cause.

We had twelve summit meetings between June 20 and June 30.[24] One thing I can say for certain: all four of us leaders, plus Thompson, genuinely wanted the end result to be something that was in the best interests of the people of Illinois. We did not agree on what that was, but we did agree not to go out after the meetings and bash one another, and we didn't. I would also meet regularly with members of my caucus to inform them about which issues had come up.

After a few days, it finally became known that we were also talking about a permanent increase in the sales tax from four cents to five cents for every dollar spent. The permanence of the sales tax increase would help offset the temporary nature of the income tax increase. I frankly cannot remember whose idea it was; it came up in the caucuses and some of our conversations, and it was just talked about and eventually became a part of our proposal. We were getting closer to a final plan. Along with adding one cent to the state sales tax, we also decided to remove the final two-cent sales tax on food and medicine. Daniels credits Philip with bringing these ideas to the summit, while Daniels and Madigan held firm on having a temporary income tax increase.[25] I opposed an increase in the liquor tax that had been in the original plan, and, indeed, it disappeared entirely during the summit discussions.

I was aware that some people believe I gave away some political edge by being the first one to support a tax increase. But without the strong public support of Thompson and me, I think we would have been deadlocked and gone into special session. I helped to create an atmosphere in which we could at least talk about instigating a tax increase. There was a certain level of trust between Philip and me, even though his more conservative Republican ideology made him far less assured of the necessity of the tax increases.

As always happens in a legislative session, we were down to one or two days before the scheduled adjournment day, and we emerged with a final plan. Thompson told the press, "It's a question of this or nothing." I presented the plan to my members the night of June 28 and told them the only alternative was terrible budget cuts on a lot of issues we really cared about. Predictably enough, my members had mixed feelings, and I knew some of them would not support the plan. Philip and I had to count votes for the next day. It didn't help that Mayor Washington's contingent called the compromise plan a total disaster the next morning, but we had to keep pushing.

The Associated Press noted that our final plan, which was actually two bills, was "Illinois' largest tax boost in history."[26] The highlights presented to the House and Senate included these increases:

- the state income tax, from 2.5 to 3 percent for individuals and from 4 to 4.8 percent for businesses, retroactive to January 1, 1983, and expiring on June 30, 1984 (many did not believe the tax would be "temporary," but it was, and it did expire)
- the state sales tax, from 4 cents to 5 cents per dollar, effective January 1, 1984
- the gasoline tax, from 7.5 cents a gallon to 11 cents a gallon, starting in 1983, then to 12 cents a gallon on July 1, 1984, and to 13 cents a gallon on July 1, 1985
- license plate fees, from $18 to $36 for small cars and to $48 for pickup trucks and large automobiles; the small-car fee also would go up to $48 on July 1, 1984

The package also permanently eliminated the remaining two-cent sales tax on food and drugs, effective July 1, 1984; exempted manufacturing equipment replacement parts from the sales tax, effective July 1, 1984; allowed counties and municipalities to share in the new temporary income tax net revenue through a revenue-sharing formula; and allowed homeowners to take a property tax deduction from their income tax, beginning with the filing of their 1983 tax returns.

There was more, all spelled out in the conference committee's 102-page report. All four caucuses met for a final look. I talked to my members about it, and Philip and I and some of our staff started counting votes.

On the last scheduled night of session, June 30, the House took up the main income tax bill first. With twenty-three Republicans and forty Democrats voting aye, the bill carried by a 63–55 vote on HB 1470, which was amended to include the conference committee report. Then it came over to the Senate. I knew it would be close. I asked Terry Bruce, the assistant majority leader, to preside so I could be on the floor. Our galleries were packed; they told me it had been the same way in the House minutes earlier. Some House members came over to our chamber and stood around the back to see what we would do. Speaker Madigan also came in and sat next to me.[27] He had delivered over in the House; he had done his part.

A Republican senator, John Davidson of Springfield, became the lead Senate sponsor of the new bill. Philip and I worked it out that way. So according to our rules, Davidson rose to speak first. More than a dozen senators followed to speak for or against the bill, and some asked questions of Davidson. He guided the debate very well, explaining various aspects of the conference report, which included the signatures of all four legislative leaders. Senator Richard Newhouse, like many Chicago Democratic senators, did not like the increase in the sales tax at all, but he said he had the support of the people in his district for an income tax increase to keep services going. The sales tax is part of the package, he said, "and if that is what is required to keep our communities afloat, then I am prepared to vote for this measure."[28]

It was during my turn to speak that I said my friends "thought that I was suffering from politically terminal lunacy" when I had proposed a tax increase back in January. However, it was now or never. It was this bill or nothing, and I pointed out to "those of us who represent in whole or in part the city of Chicago" that in this bill, "the people we represent across all those lines, education, public aid, mental health, children and family services, will receive $600 million more in services than they would receive under the alternative. $600 million!"[29] I also used my time to highlight that we were dealing with one of the most important reasons that government exists—to help people:

> What happens in a bad economy? Where do people turn? You and I know that. That's why we're here. They turn to the government. . . .

Nobody here, either house, either side of the aisle denies the needs, the needs of the unemployed, the needs of the school kids, the needs of the medically indigent, the needs of our wards, the people with whom we have been entrusted, the wards of the state that are cared for by the Department of Mental Health and by the Department of Children and Family Services, our wards. Nobody denies the needs of the poor, the elderly, the handicapped, and the list goes on. . . .

[C]ompromise was and is and will always be in this body [the Senate] inevitable. And so we compromised to what I think is a halfway reasonable level of allocations; not what everybody wants; certainly it's not what everybody wants, and it's probably more than some people want, but I ask you to seriously consider the alternative. . . . The present and future needs of this state are undeniable; and I suggest to you, so is our responsibility. I urge an aye vote.[30]

Then Senator Bruce called for the vote. We needed thirty, and I thought we had them. The voting began. It happens quickly, electronically. My own light on the tally board, next to "Mr. President," was green, along with twenty-eight other green lights. For a short amount of time, there were twenty-nine red lights as well, making it 29–29, with one vote still out. Then Senator William Mahar, a Republican from Homewood, voted. It was green, giving us the narrow 30–29 margin we needed to pass the increase in the state income tax and the sales tax. Of our thirty votes, nineteen came from Democrats and eleven from Republicans. It was a genuine bipartisan effort on the part of Pate Philip and me, and we prevailed.

Immediately after that, we took up the other bill, HB 1305, to increase the gasoline tax and license plate fees. We passed this one by a 33–26 margin. Again, we were counting carefully, and we did a little switching. My good friend Jerome Joyce from Kankakee County voted against the income tax increase but in favor of the gasoline tax increase. Philip and I both voted in favor of both bills, but I told downstater Vince Demuzio, a member of the Crazy Eight for whom my respect was growing, that I didn't need his vote on the gas tax increase. So I pulled him off that vote, and it probably looked good to his Macoupin County constituents that he voted against these taxes. But I needed Vince's vote on the income tax increase, and I got it. It turns out we were the fourteenth state to increase taxes that year, and I suppose more followed.[31]

Some people say the tax increase of 1983 was the issue that formalized the practice of the governor having late-session summits with the legislative leaders. That is true to a certain extent, although it obviously wasn't the first time a governor had met privately with legislative leaders. I had done some of that myself with Governor Walker a decade earlier. Maybe it's because we met for ten days in 1983 over a highly contentious issue that this practice came to be expected in later years. Our meetings with Governor Thompson ultimately produced a final compromise. While we all may have held a little bit back, we also shared a lot of candor around the table. The idea was to get something done. For the remainder of my years as Senate president, we continued to have summit meetings with the governor and legislative leaders. But as time went on, I think it evolved into something more: more control by the leaders over legislative action and over their members. Early on, we tended to have those summit meetings only on big issues, but I also allowed Republicans to have their say on the floor of the Senate and to have their bills heard. Rank-and-file members, in my view, now have less of an opportunity to have their bills heard if the presiding officer doesn't want to call them or bottles them up in some committee. The process shuts out some of the members. To the extent that it does, it's unfortunate, because they deserve to have a say in what happens on issues big and small.

14. Boosting Regional Transportation

*The RTA provides a classic study into the kind
of hostility that can and does arise among
Chicago, suburban, and downstate citizens.*

ONE THING WE DIDN'T GET DONE IN THE 1983 SPRING SESSION was
the resurrection of a much-needed subsidy for the Regional Transportation Authority (RTA). For some reason, Governor Jim Thompson
and Mayor Jane Byrne had negotiated a deal in 1979 to eliminate any state
subsidy to the RTA. That proved to be ill advised because the RTA was
running $100 million in the red, and there seemed to be no way to get
it back on track financially. So during the income tax debate, some of us
talked about a new formula that would generate an additional $75 mil-
lion for the RTA. I strongly supported it, although the arguments against
a larger state subsidy had been mostly winning for more than ten years.

The RTA provides a classic study into the kind of hostility that can
and does arise among Chicago, suburban, and downstate citizens and
their representatives. When the RTA first came into existence in 1973,
suburban residents were angry about spending money on the city of Chicago's transportation system. Such ranting has continued off and on,
really, for almost forty years. In 1973, in my second term as senator, the
Illinois Department of Transportation was barely a year old. Republicans
controlled both chambers of the General Assembly, but only by a slim
one-vote majority in each chamber. Both of its leaders—Senate president
William Harris of Pontiac and Speaker W. Robert Blair of Park Forest—
were the main RTA advocates. Both Governor Dan Walker and Mayor
Richard J. Daley also wanted a regional transit authority, but each had
different plans on how to make it happen. All the public transportation
services were on their own and threatening to increase fares significantly or stop running. Joseph A. Tecson, an early regional transportation

advocate and expert, summarized the problem succinctly: "In 1973, public transportation provided a crisis atmosphere in Springfield. . . . The CTA [Chicago Transit Authority] was issuing statements that it would be forced to either raise fares or cut services. Suburban bus companies were threatening to go out of business, because they were running out of money to meet payrolls and pay for fuel. The commuter railroads, except for one, were operating in the red and were filing petitions with the Illinois Commerce Commission asking for substantial rate increases."[1]

That is why it made sense to a lot of legislators, including me, to establish a regional transit authority for Chicago and for the counties of Cook, DuPage, Kane, Lake, McHenry, and Will. Public transportation couldn't pay its own way around the region, so I thought the state had to do something. There were many studies, including those from a task force put together by Governor Richard Ogilvie and from the Illinois Transportation Study Commission, which held a series of public hearings chaired by Speaker Blair. Thirty-one Chicago business and labor leaders organized a coalition urging us to create a regional authority to provide for coordinated public transportation services, facilities, and funding. It's interesting to look back and read in the *Chicago Tribune* that the coalition sent a telegram to "four top political leaders," meaning, at that time, the governor, the House Speaker, the Senate president, and the mayor of Chicago.[2] Today, the "four leaders" would mean the majority and minority leaders of the four caucuses in the Illinois General Assembly and not the Chicago mayor, so times have changed in that regard.

At any rate, the idea of a regional transit authority had bipartisan support but became controversial. In the fall of 1973, we had five "special sessions" going in addition to the regular session of the General Assembly. A special session typically is called to address a specific topic. The RTA was the topic of the third special session, but nobody could agree on what to do. The most divisive issue centered on imposing a half-cent sales tax increase in the RTA region to subsidize public transportation and, of course, on how to spread out the money for bus and train services. It was becoming clear we weren't going to pass any RTA bill by the scheduled adjournment on Saturday, November 17. Members said the issue was dead; so did the front pages of all the newspapers.[3] Thanksgiving was less than a week away. A few of us stayed around the next week and almost missed our Thanksgiving dinner to hash out all of the details about the RTA. Then we were back in Springfield on the Saturday after Thanksgiving to continue negotiating so we would be ready when everyone else returned to Springfield on Monday.

We were ready. We presented a package of sixteen bills to the third special session of the General Assembly just after Thanksgiving weekend and had a contentious debate on the Senate floor. The downstaters contrasted the proposed sales tax increase on everybody in the RTA region to the statewide gasoline tax, which, they argued, was appropriate for downstate roads because it was a users' fee. That is, drivers who use the roads pay for the tax on gasoline, which in turn directly provides money to build and maintain roads. Those lawmakers objected to increasing a general sales tax on everybody because that went beyond being a users' tax. Everyone who paid that sales tax would not be using the trains and buses.

"I have to tell you that one of our colleagues [from Chicago] refers to us downstaters as manure kickers," said Senator Harber Hall, a Republican from Bloomington who opposed the RTA bills. "It doesn't offend us when he does call us manure kickers. But when he says, 'I voted for your manure kickers' roads so you [should] vote for the CTA,' he and Dawn Clark Netsch leave out one thing. Those roads are paid for by user funds . . . not the general taxpayer. Why don't they say that?"[4]

I believed then, and I said on the floor, that public transportation was an issue for the whole state and not just for the users. One of the big compromises we made was to call for a binding referendum on the establishment of the RTA in those six northern counties. That referendum was not in the earlier bills. Our Thanksgiving weekend summit got everything sorted out. Needing thirty-six votes to get the bill passed, we prevailed by getting thirty-eight votes. Republicans controlled the Senate at that time, and it was a major bipartisan effort in our chamber, led by Harris and our Democratic leader, Cecil Partee.

There was one more hurdle before the RTA could get up and running: passing the referendum in the spring of 1974. The question, which was included in the RTA bill, was clear: "Shall a Regional Transportation Authority be created for Cook, DuPage, Kane, Lake, McHenry and Will counties, Illinois?" There was a lot of opposition in the suburbs from those who I thought, frankly, would benefit from the RTA. Supporters formed a group called the RTA Citizens Committee, led by George Ranney Jr., who had served under Governor Ogilvie and was one of those who put together the RTA bills.[5] As with everything connected to the RTA, the referendum on March 19, 1974, was hotly contested. In the five counties outside of Cook, DuPage delivered the most votes—27,224—but 75 percent of the voters in DuPage County voted against it. In fact, if it were up to the citizens in those five counties, the RTA would have died and been buried in a locked vault. Only because of the Chicago voters, where 71 percent voted in favor—delivering 456,475 votes—did the RTA become a reality. Thank goodness our bill didn't say it had to pass in each of the six counties. The final vote overall was 684,266 to 671,287, a slim 50.5 percent approval.

Table 2
RTA referendum approval, percentage by county, March 19, 1974

Cook (inside Chicago)	71
Cook (outside Chicago)	41
DuPage	25
Kane	11
Lake	25
McHenry	9
Will	11
Overall vote	50.5

That's how we got the RTA—a divisive issue then and a controversial issue for almost four decades. Speaker Blair later lost an election and his seat in the House of Representatives because of his support for the RTA. His suburban constituents punished him for it.

It's hard to remember any legislative session in the subsequent twenty years when an RTA subsidy was not on the horizon. Every time we would go into session, we would have half a dozen members putting in bills trying to dismantle the RTA, change its direction, get their money back, or get additional money. They never stopped complaining. The people in the collar counties would say, "This isn't doing us any good. We need to get out of the RTA. We want the buses, but you can keep the trains, the Metra. They cost too much." Even sensible lawmakers like Senator Jerome Joyce of Kankakee County wanted to get rid of the RTA. I said to him, "The people in the region are moving west. In the near future, you're going to see more people in Kankakee, Kendall, and Will Counties, and they will have to have a way to get around." But he and others would insist that they didn't want it. That was the echo throughout the whole RTA district.

I always believed the RTA had to be state-supported for the benefit of everyone who needs public transportation. There is no way that public transportation could make it independently. Anyone who would suggest that we either don't need to subsidize public transportation or it should somehow be self-supporting doesn't know how it works or why it is critical to the state of Illinois and the people who depend on it. We need the RTA.

In the middle of the RTA, of course, sits the Chicago Transportation Authority, which has never operated very well. It wastes money and is not frugal, but its leaders come hat in hand to the state, saying they represent public transportation in the big city and deserve to get the lion's share of the funding. Then you look at a small transportation district like Jim Donnewald's in southern Illinois, and it might get one taxi and one bus. That's it. But in Chicago, they still say there is too much for downstate. That's why the tension will be with us forever. Some people believe they are getting taxed without receiving anything in exchange.

Something I used to do with new members, especially downstaters, was invite them to the suburbs to see the RTA system. I would start by asking them to my house, which had a train stop not too many blocks away, at Austin Boulevard. I would put them up at my house overnight and then say, "We've got to get up early to go see the commuters." I would walk them over to the Lake Street "L" at Lake and Austin and watch the commuters get on board about 7:15 or 7:30. Around eight thousand of them would get on the train for the fifteen-minute trip to downtown Chicago. I will never forget standing there one day with Senator Ken Buzbee, who was born in the little southern Illinois town of Anna, and I said to him, "There are more people on this train at this moment than you have in your whole county." Then I said, "All we're asking for is a little money." I know these members had to be impressed.

The system moves thousands of people, and it costs money. However, I do not believe the RTA has been well managed. That is our fault, not having more oversight of some kind. I think some of us were much too defensive about how things were going. We were so supportive of the regional transportation concept that perhaps we ignored the fact that the RTA management ignored some basic management principles and didn't plan well enough or manage the fares carefully enough. It's also fair to say that experts in the field of mass transit were telling us that some of the RTA leaders didn't know what they were doing.

That history about the RTA provides the context in which the major RTA subsidy controversy arose during the 1983 session, when we were also considering the income tax increase. We had been living for four years without the state subsidy, and we had to get it back. We tried to pass the $75 million subsidy right after passing the income tax increase, but there was enough lingering unhappiness with the RTA operations, the so-called Chicago control, and the structural deficit that a lot of members got together, including quite a few from the suburbs, to propose significant RTA reforms as well as a restoration of the subsidy. Governor Thompson supported the reforms, Speaker Madigan supported them, Mayor Washington supported them, and I supported them. The Chicago supporters would endorse the reforms if they could get the millions.

A couple of studies had been done in 1981 and 1982, with Glencoe mayor Florence Boone taking a leading role, that frankly had a number of good ideas.[6] For example, to help control costs, they suggested a provision prohibiting the linkage of wage increases to changes in the Consumer Price Index. Inflation had been at record levels in the late 1970s, and so unions liked to negotiate cost-of-living adjustments connected to the inflation rate. Reformers wanted concessions from the unions—principally, for the unions to forgive a $33 million loan to the CTA from its pension fund.[7] The main opponents of RTA reforms were Alderman Ed Vrdolyak and some of the Chicago unions.

We actually proposed eliminating the existing RTA board—the structure and all of its members, including chairman Lewis Hill—and replacing it with a new thirteen-member board and three service boards: the existing CTA plus the Commuter Rail Board and the Suburban Bus Board. So that, naturally, generated opposition from Hill and his allies. But that way, the operation would become more decentralized and the suburbs would have a little more power. The main reason that Mayor Washington supported the whole package was that he needed the state subsidy for the city. He was the new mayor and took a lot of heat from the unions and black constituents who were members of those unions.

The House did indeed pass the new RTA subsidy and the reforms right after it passed the income tax increase at the end of the June session. All eyes were on us in the Senate. Then Washington stepped up and made a few additional demands. For some reason, he wasn't satisfied with the proposed subsidy, and he let everybody know it. But I said publicly that I thought we could pass it the way it was; it was the bill that Thompson wanted, too.

Union members who felt they were giving up too much were in the gallery, cheering for various senators as they rose to speak in opposition to the bill. Senator John D'Arco of Chicago, among others, said we would betray the labor unions if we voted for the bill, despite the fact that pro-labor representatives such as Speaker Madigan and John Cullerton, both of Chicago, and Jim McPike of Alton had voted for the bill in the House. I was also pro-labor and in support of the bill. To endorse Washington's new opposition to the bill, Senators Charlie Chew and Emil Jones spoke up forcefully against it. Opponents worried about some shift of control to suburban Republicans on the new RTA board.

Senator Roger Keats, a Republican from suburban Kenilworth, was the bill's main sponsor in our chamber. I felt especially passionate on July 2, 1984, as I rose to speak near the end of a long and contentious floor debate.[8] My concern was for the 1 million people who depended on public transportation. I insisted that we should be mostly concerned about those beleaguered riders, and that's why we had to give up a little something, such as the city's control of the board, to restore the state subsidy. Despite my pleadings, we mustered only twenty-five votes, and so we lost that day in the Senate. But I knew we would have another chance during the veto session in November.

In the meantime, Governor Thompson met with Mayor Washington to see if they could work out a compromise. I joined those conversations. Washington finally backed off on his demand to get more than the $75 million. To satisfy the thirteen downstate mass transit districts, we also had to adjust the formula for distributing the money. It was reported to be the first major deal that Washington and Thompson made since Washington had become mayor a few months earlier.[9]

The unions were livid, thinking Washington had sold them out. They came down en masse for the Senate vote during the veto session and packed the place. This time, they had a friend in Alderman Vrdolyak, who was happy to be there in opposition to the mayor. It was quite a sight to see Washington working with Thompson and some suburban Republicans for votes on this bill. Unusual allies, indeed. I again spoke as strongly as I could, saying it was now or never for a subsidy to Chicago for the RTA. This time we won, with thirty-seven votes, one more than we needed, with five of the six black senators voting with us—showing some courage, in my opinion. With our vote and the governor's signature, the old RTA board and its chairman, Lewis Hill, were going out of business, to be replaced by something better.

So you can see why I say that 1983—with the tax increase and Washington's election and the restoration of the RTA subsidy—was one of my busiest and most productive legislative sessions.

There's much more, actually.

For one thing, I thought we finally had to respond more forcefully to the horrific crimes of John Wayne Gacy, a Chicago native who had a house in the suburb of Norwood Park. He was well liked in his community and threw big barbecues and block parties. I'm embarrassed to say he also started to become active in local Democratic politics, doing things like dressing up as Pogo the Clown to entertain children, sometimes in hospitals.[10] He had his own decorating business, PDM Construction;

unfortunately, some of his young employees became his victims. It was later discovered that he would lure young men and boys to his home, where he would show them magic tricks and eventually handcuff them, have sex with them, and then kill them.[11] He built a trap door in a bedroom closet floor that led to a large crawl space under his house, where he buried twenty-seven or twenty-eight victims; he disposed of five or six others in the Des Plaines River southwest of Chicago.[12] He was arrested just before Christmas in 1978 and was convicted in 1980 of murdering thirty-three boys and young men between 1972 and 1978, making him one of the worst serial killers in American history. (After continuing to grab a lot of publicity from his southern Illinois prison cell for fourteen years by selling his paintings and maintaining a 900-number for people to call to listen to him declare his innocence, he was executed by the state of Illinois on May 10, 1994.)[13] His treatment of boys and young men sickened everyone.

That kind of a news story and publicity often leads to legislation. It turns out that while Gacy was awaiting trial and not long after he was convicted, the national media gave considerable attention to several other cases involving missing children. In the Atlanta area over the course of three years, "the bodies of [at least twenty-nine] young boys and girls were discovered in lakes, marshes and ponds along a roadside trail."[14] Then on July 27, 1981, Adam Walsh was lost at a Florida shopping mall. His parents, John and Reve Walsh, turned to police and were furious about the absence of a coordinated effort locally and nationally to search for their six-year-old son. John Walsh has since become famous for dedicating his life to the cause of finding missing people, especially children, and for his many appearances on the television program *America's Most Wanted*. All of those stories raised awareness about issues related to missing children. It was in 1983 that President Reagan declared that every May 25 would be National Missing Children's Day to bring national attention to this cause.

Sam Amirante, who had been one of Gacy's lawyers and is now a retired judge, actually came up with the idea of doing something in Illinois to go along with the national movement. He told me that he was hearing from the families of missing young men. I found out later that the state's Department of Law Enforcement had 13,000 reports of missing children in 1983.[15] I was joined by a few other senators in sponsoring the Intergovernmental Missing Child Recovery Act, which Amirante also worked on. We wanted to give funding to law enforcement agencies under the Illinois State Enforcement Agencies to Recover Children program (commonly called I-SEARCH) to help them work together to find lost, missing, and runaway children. The bill also charged I-SEARCH units with developing plans that incorporate the most efficient ways to maintain a computerized network. We wanted Illinois to connect into the FBI's national monitoring program and to develop regional alerts when children are reported missing. That is the kind of issue that no lawmakers oppose, and they shouldn't. Our bill passed unanimously, and Thompson readily signed it.

My hometown of Oak Park joined with neighboring River Forest to establish its own I-SEARCH board. A social worker by the name of Diane Eckert developed some really great local programs. The board consisted of a police youth officer from each town, a preschool development expert, local citizens, and my district office manager, Pat Arman.[16] They developed age-appropriate programs on child safety, "stranger danger," runaways, and date rape for all of the public and parochial schools in our communities. A police officer and Diane Eckert did the classroom presentations. The program developed a good relationship between students and police as "helpers," and school administrators were very impressed. One year, at my annual picnic in the local forest preserve with about a thousand people, we had a youth officer from each town there to fingerprint and show children their police cars and explain items they wore on their uniforms. A local printer gave us thousands of I-SEARCH packets, and the Boy Scouts came to help.

The fact is, sexual abuse is a major social problem. We became attuned to it because of the publicity about certain cases, and we continued to learn more about it over the years. Pat Arman tells a few stories that are very disturbing—but are the very reason that we follow up by sponsoring legislation and initiating programs.[17] One time we had an early-morning meeting in our district office for all elected officials in Oak Park and River Forest. They learned that statistics would suggest that even among that relatively small group, at least two of them probably had been sexually abused in some manner during their lifetime, and they were told what to do if anyone ever confided in them. About an hour after our meeting ended, someone who was there told the social worker about a sibling who had abused that person and possibly another of their siblings when they were young. We contacted the social services office in town and explained to the director that we were sending someone over and what the issue was. The victim later told us that they (I don't want to say "he" or "she" in order to help protect this person's identity) attended counseling and then spoke to the other sibling about possible abuse. Both had indeed been abused. The story is sad, but it's important that we put these programs together to allow people to get help for themselves.

Just one more story about this: A kindergarten child who went to our local I-SEARCH program spent a summer at her grandmother's house. When she returned home, she immediately told her mom that she needed to talk to the police lady from school. The officer elicited from the child that an uncle had been touching her "private parts" when she was at her grandma's house; the girl had been taught that that was wrong. She described what had happened, and the uncle was investigated and arrested.

Another major initiative of mine during this session was a program to pump up the economy. After the 1982 elections, I called staffer Peter Creticos into my office and said, "We all ran on the economic development issue; we better have something to show that we are really serious about it." In fact, all of us were talking about it. Madigan had some ideas, Thompson had some ideas, and then the legislature created its own special Commission for Economic Development. We basically were all critical of Thompson for not doing enough to spur economic development in the previous six years. Even Republican senator Stan Weaver of Urbana joined us in this criticism of Thompson.[18]

I put Creticos to work on it. He wanted to try something different. I have to say that Creticos was not a big fan of the Department of Commerce and Community Affairs, which ordinarily would take a leading role on a major initiative like this.[19] Creticos did a lot of work in just a few weeks and eventually determined that we would have a bill for every member of our caucus. That's how we would get it done. Thirty-one members, thirty-one bills, and that's just the framework. I remember House members and even some Senate members barking at us in the Senate as "prairie dogs" because our projects seemed to multiply like prairie dogs. It wasn't that big a deal, but as the package was coming together, a few members would come up to me and others and say, "Woof, woof," just kidding around, really, about our Prairie State 2000 initiative.

Creticos had the job of pulling together all kinds of ideas and then putting them into a package. He looked carefully at the work of a man named Pat Choate from Oklahoma, who much later became Ross Perot's vice presidential running mate in 1996. Choate back then was with a group called the Northeast-Midwest Coalition, and he had the innovative idea of creating something like individual, personal accounts to be used for people to get retraining for jobs.[20] We began to focus on the idea of providing incentives for retraining and setting up a fund that people could tap into if they needed to retrain for a different career. Illinois manufacturing jobs were on the decline. We knew we were headed toward something much different in the economy—we now know it was the transition from a manufacturing to a service and knowledge economy—and so we settled on providing retraining for workers. The workers could get vouchers for job training at community colleges, universities, or vocational schools. I called this the "G.I. bill for Illinois" because, while the economy was putting people out of work, we needed to prepare an entire generation of workers to be ready for a new economy. We called our plan Prairie State 2000 to signal that we were looking ahead almost two decades to the turn of the century. It was innovative in the early 1980s to embark on this kind of policy change. By the time we finished, we had thirty-eight or thirty-nine bills with six major components:

1. Job training and education assistance
2. Business and tourism development
3. Investment incentives
4. State government reorganization as it pertains to the Department of Commerce and Community Affairs
5. Assistance for local government
6. Agriculture and natural resource development

There was a little something for everybody, and we persuaded twenty-three Republicans to cosponsor the bill, too.[21] In the end, the major bills were not controversial, but there was some grumbling about the individual bills—nothing too serious, though, because we managed to pass the whole package. It was difficult for members to keep track of exactly what we were doing because we were considering almost forty bills, one after the other. But I was on the floor, and Terry Bruce did a great job of keeping things moving from the podium. I knew what was in the bills, and I think the members trusted me.

15. A U.S. Senate Race against Paul Simon

I had passed up opportunities to run statewide for comptroller
in 1978, for governor in 1982, and for attorney general in 1982.

IT'S NO SECRET THAT I WANTED TO BE THE DEMOCRATIC NOMINEE for the U.S. Senate in 1984. I planned to challenge incumbent Republican Charles Percy, who almost lost his reelection bid in 1978 to an upstart Chicago attorney named Alex Seith. I had a lot more political experience than Seith, and I was often mentioned as a possible statewide candidate. I had passed up opportunities to run statewide for comptroller in 1978, for governor in 1982, and then for attorney general in 1982.

When you want to run for higher office, you start mentioning your interest to people and then see what happens. Reporters and politicians and insiders pick up on it, and names start floating. So certainly in the early going, a year before the March 1984 primary, my name was out there. So was Paul Simon's. Simon had been lieutenant governor from 1969 to 1973, during that historically unique time when we had a Democratic lieutenant governor and a Republican governor, Richard Ogilvie. (That Republican-Democratic alignment in the top two positions would be impossible now because of changes in the 1970 Illinois Constitution.) Simon ran for governor in 1972 but lost to Dan Walker in the Democratic primary. Then Simon briefly joined the faculty at Sangamon State University in Springfield (which later became the University of Illinois Springfield), where he started the still-flourishing Public Affairs Reporting program and was one of three cofounders of *Illinois Issues* magazine, along with Sam Gove and Samuel Witwer. Then Simon moved to Carbondale to run for a congressional seat being vacated by Congressman Kenneth Gray, and Simon won that seat in 1974.

In 1983, Paul was in his fifth term in Congress and had a reputation as a reformer and a man of great integrity. I had known Paul since my first years in the state senate, when he was lieutenant governor. I approached him privately early in 1983 and told him that I intended to run for the U.S. Senate and that I would be seeking the endorsement of the Democratic State Central Committee. For me, getting the party's official slating was critical to my candidacy. Without it, I would not run. I was the state chairman at the time, but I never assumed the party would automatically slate me for any office. I asked Paul if he planned to enter the race. He assured me that he would not, and he expressed no ambivalence. I took him at his word. He acknowledges in his own autobiography that he did not intend to run. "I had no plans to run," he wrote, "not eager to take on a statewide race and all the fundraising that goes with that."[1] The press also reported that Simon was "leaning against it," and it's interesting now to remember that David Axelrod was the reporter for the *Chicago Tribune* covering this run-up to the primary.[2] Simon's nonparticipation was good news for me, because the potential field was getting crowded with Alex Seith and Roland Burris, who had become the first black person elected to statewide office when he first won the comptroller's position in 1978. I can't say there was a front-runner in the early going, but I was pleased that Simon was staying out.

I recruited former House Speaker Bill Redmond to head my exploratory committee. Percy seemed vulnerable. The Republicans helped our cause even more in 1983 when a Republican congressman, Tom Corcoran of downstate Ottawa, declared he would formally challenge Percy in the Republican primary. Corcoran considered himself the conservative alternative in a party that is often divided by its conservative and moderate groups. None of the Democrats had made formal declarations yet, but soon enough, I learned that Simon wasn't exactly staying out. He was exploring his chances. He hired a campaign manager and a powerful pollster, Peter Hart of Washington, D.C. In June, Hart released a poll showing Simon as the first choice of more voters than any other possible candidate. Burris was second, and I was last.[3] It's an understatement to say I wasn't too happy with Simon, because we both learned early in our political careers that your word means everything. You can agree to disagree and argue about issues and everything else, but you don't go back on your word. He broke his promise to me, and he was in the race to stay. His reasoning was that a lot of influential Democrats urged him to run because they thought he would have the best chance of beating Percy.[4]

The primary was still eight or nine months away, too early to get overly concerned about anyone's polls. He and I didn't talk about it. He didn't call me, and I certainly didn't call him to ask why the change. There was talk that he was concerned about being challenged for his own congressional

seat in conservative downstate Illinois. That possibility and what he perceived as his growing popularity must have caused him to change his
mind and run for the U.S. Senate.

Then in the summer of 1983, one by one, we all formally got in: Burris
and Seith, then Simon. I got a strong boost from Mayor Washington,
who came to the Oak Park Democratic Party picnic in late July on my
behalf. That caused a stir because it signaled that Washington might not
endorse the black candidate, Roland Burris. While the mayor fell short of
endorsing me that day, he told the crowd of a thousand people at Thatcher
Woods Forest Preserve in River Forest, "If there's anyone in public life
that deserves it, it's him."[5] I thought that with the mayor's tacit support
and the formal backing of the state party, I could take away some of Burris's support and prevail over both Simon and Seith. I also assumed that
I could get Alderman Ed Vrdolyak's support in the city, even though that
would mean bitter rivals, Vrdolyak and Washington, might be backing
the same person. I was the last one to hire a campaign manager: William San Hamel, who had run Mike Bakalis's race for governor in 1978
and Tom Tully's successful Cook County assessor campaign in 1974. I
felt ready. I was forty-six years old when I went to the Bismarck Hotel in
downtown Chicago with Sheila and all four kids, and I proudly made my
formal announcement at the end of August:

> I welcome the challenge of this race because of my commitment to
> do all that I can to help Illinois realize its full potential as a state and
> as a people.
>
> Mr. Percy's 16-year record in the United States Senate must be ques-
> tioned. I believe he has short-changed the people of Illinois. Despite his
> top position in the U.S. Senate, Mr. Percy has a record which reflects
> a serious lack of concern for the primary issues affecting the lives of
> the 11 million people of Illinois. The 700,000 working men and women
> who today stand in an unemployment line instead of the production
> line are a painful reminder of misguided federal policies.
>
> Fairness must be the overriding principle in all economic programs,
> and by almost any calculation, Illinois has not been fairly treated. . . .
> There is no excuse for Illinois to rank 47th among the 50 states in return
> on our federal tax dollar. We cannot afford to pay out $1.21 for only a
> dollar's worth of federal services.[6]

Simon pushed hard to get the state party's endorsement. He thought
he was going to walk in and walk out with the party's blessing after he
got all kinds of encouragement to run, despite his pledge not to do so. But

much to his chagrin, I won the endorsement, and I was proud to carry the party's banner. It gave me the boost I really wanted.

I was off and running and thought I had a great shot in the primary. By this time, there were four main contenders: Simon, Burris, Seith, and me. One Saturday in the fall of 1983, the four of us gathered at Sangamon State University in Springfield, and I laid out a principle that I stuck to for the rest of my campaign. I said I would not bash other Democrats; I would not go negative. "I will not indulge here today in criticism of a fellow Democrat," I said. "That simply will not happen." I meant it, and I didn't do it. I don't think that's the right way to behave in a primary. Simon, meanwhile, was being touted as the front-runner because of the polling, and he had this to say about me: "He's been so outstanding [in the Illinois Senate that] I want to keep him as the senate leader a few more years."[7]

Mayor Washington stayed neutral. He was supposed to come to one of my January fund-raisers, but he didn't show up. His official excuse was that he was attending a funeral or some other function, but the truth is that my support of Vrdolyak for another term as Cook County party chairman and Vrdolyak's support of me in my campaign irritated the mayor quite a bit. Then Washington skipped somebody else's fund-raiser a week or two later. I guess he just didn't know what to do. His support of me could have helped me a lot with the city's black voters. He knew that I had successfully represented African American neighborhoods my entire career on the West Side of Chicago, but apparently it wasn't enough to get his endorsement. He never did endorse anyone. He finally told me a month before the election that he would stay neutral to the end, and that disappointed me.

I traveled a great deal during the seven- or eight-month campaign. I went through most, if not all, of Illinois's 102 counties. Once I got to a place, I was fine, but getting there, I have to admit, I dragged my heels. I'm not as outgoing as somebody like Jim Thompson. But something else was going on. Despite the press attention, I never did think there was much general public interest or groundswell of support for this four-man primary. I didn't understand it then, and I don't now. I do know that Thompson tells people to this day that he advised me in a friendly way not to run, not because he supported Percy so much, which he probably did, but because he knew I would not enjoy all the glad-handing you have to do when running for an office like U.S. senator.[8] I remember telling *Tribune* reporter David Axelrod: "I like people, but I'm just not that comfortable with [campaigning]. Maybe it comes from spending time in a seminary, where we were told to speak only at the proper time, or maybe I'm like my father. I'm by nature a quiet, reserved person."[9]

I did appreciate the *Tribune*'s endorsement a month before the primary:

[Rock has] developed into one of the most knowledgeable people in Illinois government, instrumental in much of the legislation that has made the state work better in recent years.

Like Paul Simon, Phil Rock has a reputation for decency. But, unlike Mr. Simon, he's willing to submerge his traditionally liberal views when the money isn't there. . . .

Gov. Thompson often acknowledges how much he depends on Phil Rock to get his programs through the General Assembly; Mr. Rock does deliver—usually in exchange for support of his own legislation, such as reforms in child-support collections and a set of economic incentives [Prairie State 2000] approved last summer. Depending on your mindset, you can call that old-fashioned wheeling-dealing or you can call it smart, pragmatic politics; in any case, Gov. Thompson and Sen. Rock have made it work well for the people of Illinois.[10]

I trailed in the polls during the whole campaign. A couple of weeks before the election, I had only 6 percent of the voters behind me. Getting name recognition was a problem for me, because I didn't have enough money for advertising, and I was the only one of the major candidates who had never run statewide. I hoped that the party endorsement and the support of the Cook County Democratic organization would render the polls meaningless and carry me to victory. I spent most of the final stretch in the Chicago area, and some of the party leaders worked hard for me. Party regulars showed up for me big-time at rallies in the final week. More than a thousand people came to Queen of Angels Hall in Ed Kelly's Forty-Seventh Ward, for example, for an old-style rally with bands and beer. That was a great deal of fun. A few other aldermen, such as Vrdolyak, Roman Pucinski, and Ed Burke, also sponsored big rallies for me. I asked their precinct troops to get the voters out because the reputation of the regular Democratic organization was on the line.

But, frankly, I was concerned because I wasn't sure the endorsements meant a great deal. I was firmly disappointed in the state central committee, for instance. Don't ask me what a lot of those people or the captains in the wards did, because in many instances, they didn't do anything. Part of the reason was that in those days, the U.S senator couldn't do a thing for you—couldn't get you a garbage can, couldn't speed up your social security check. At the precinct level, the U.S. senator was viewed as a political eunuch who couldn't do anything directly for people. He was not part of the party apparatus, so many of the state central committeemen just lacked interest. It was discouraging to go around and try to generate some enthusiasm. I tried to explain the issues, but the audiences didn't seem to pay any attention. It was an eye opener for me. These were the ruling members of the party, the committeemen of the party, and the possibility of having a U.S. senator like me didn't make a whit of difference to them.

A moment of levity, I guess you could say, occurred just before St. Patrick's Day. I was at the WBBM studios on the near North Side along with the other candidates. When I left, my driver, Jerome Williams, and I discovered that my car was missing. It had been stolen from its parking spot at 400 East Erie. I quickly acquired another vehicle to go to other functions, and the police found the car somewhere on the South Side shortly before midnight.[11] Missing were the four wheels and a few other parts, but the thieves left my campaign literature and buttons in the vehicle. I don't suppose they cared who their U.S. senator would be, either.

I was labeled the "conservative" candidate in this race, primarily because of my pro-life position and my endorsement of government support for parochial schools. I said consistently during the whole campaign that I was pro-life and would support a constitutional amendment to ban abortion. That was the major reason the Chicago contingent of the National Organization for Women supported Simon and not me, despite all the work I had done in the legislature for abused and neglected children, to assist victims of domestic violence, who are almost all women, and to add an equal number of women to the Democratic State Central Committee.

I rolled into the primary election day short of money and down in the polls, with my hopes pinned on a very strong Chicago turnout. Indeed, I did do well in both Cook County and the city of Chicago, but in the rest of the state I got very few votes. As the numbers came in, it sunk in that not only would I not win but I would come in fourth. The final tally was disappointing:

Simon	556,757
Burris	360,182
Seith	327,125
Rock	303,397

The only thing left for me to do was go out and thank my supporters, which I did. I felt terrible, getting only 19 percent of 1.57 million votes statewide, while Simon got 35 percent.[12] I told Bruce Dold of the *Chicago Tribune* the next day, "I'll have to sit down and re-evaluate my position. Maybe I'll just go back to being a lawyer on LaSalle Street," referring to my private law practice with Dan Fusco and others.[13] I was $200,000 in debt, in part because I had taken out a second mortgage on my Oak Park house to finance the campaign. It's impossible to describe, especially for a private person like me, precisely how it feels to lose an election like this. It's not a good feeling, to say the least.

I took some solace in the fact that I was still the Senate president. I had a very supportive family and great law partners, and I did indeed have some friends in politics in both parties. Mike Lawrence, a syndicated columnist for Lee Newspapers, wrote what I considered a very thoughtful column about me a couple of weeks after the election:

> Relatively few people . . . have grasped the essence of the gentleman from Oak Park. . . . What most Illinoisans do not know is he is far from a mindless partisan—that this intelligent, thoughtful legislative leader has been, in fact, a valuable ally to the Republican governor [Thompson] when it has come to problem-solving, that he has been such an ally despite entreatments from fellow Democrats to let James Thompson suffocate in turbulent waters.
>
> Even in the Capitol, he is largely misunderstood. His frequently gruff persona belies an essential decency and sensitivity. It is, ironically, in part a byproduct of his intensity in trying to make government work for those who need help.[14]

It helped a little bit to read such kind words, but some bitterness and a lot of disappointment lingered. The young *Tribune* reporter, David Axelrod, left the news business not long after the primary and began a new career as a political and media advisor based in Chicago. He went to work for Simon's general election campaign in 1984 as communications director and then was promoted to campaign manager. Much later, Axelrod was a senior strategist on Barack Obama's successful campaigns for the U.S. Senate and the presidency. During his own tough U.S. Senate primary in 2004, Obama won Simon's endorsement, which was crucial because it wasn't at all clear that Obama was going to win that race. The Axelrod-Simon-Obama connection is yet another example of how relationships and contacts make a difference in politicians' lives for a long, long time.

Meanwhile, Simon, then fifty-five years old while I was forty-six, went on to beat incumbent Charles Percy in the November general election and became Illinois's new U.S. senator in 1985. He won reelection in 1990 but decided not to run in 1996. Instead, he went back to Carbondale to launch a public policy institute at Southern Illinois University. He passed the baton to another downstater, Richard Durbin of Springfield, who won in 1996 and has been reelected twice, in 2002 and 2008. Durbin was my parliamentarian for a while in the state senate, and I think he, too, had gone to work for Simon's senatorial campaign in 1984. Meanwhile, another former staffer of mine in the state senate, Bill Houlihan, became one of Senator Durbin's top staff people in the last fifteen years or so, serving as his downstate administrator in the Springfield district office. Sometimes I reflect on those relationships that began in the 1980s: there is a bond, an almost sacred bond, that ties people together in the political arena, despite all our mischief and fighting and disagreements.

I still appreciate the kinds of political relationships that were possible at the time I lost my U.S. Senate campaign. Loyal Cook County Democrats remained truly loyal. Speaker Madigan supported me. Great friends like Illinois state treasurer Jim Donnewald were with me all the way. After the election, it was two Republicans, Thompson and Pate Philip, who sponsored a fund-raiser to help erase my debt. They held it at an upscale Frank Lloyd Wright–designed private home in Oak Park. That would not happen today among leaders of the two parties, I don't think.

Given all that happened and how it turned out, I think that my desire to run for the U.S. Senate was a bit ill-conceived. My timing was off, and in retrospect, so was my campaign. What I told Bruce Dold about not being a gregarious campaigner hurt me politically more than I had anticipated. I would have preferred, obviously, to have won.

After the primary, I never really talked to Simon again, except for maybe once, when I called to tell him good-bye. I would see him from time to time, because we would be at the same functions or in the same room. Paul and I were always civil to each other, but that's about it. At Paul's request, I did try to assist his wife to get some rides on the state airplane at times, and I think that helped a little. Some people with whom I had worked in the Illinois Senate became big Simon boosters over the years, and that's fine, but it's fair to say that I was not among them.

16. Year of Major Education Reform

The state seems to pass one of these major
capital plans every ten or fifteen years.

GOING BACK TO THE ILLINOIS SENATE HELPED TO HEAL THE WOUND. For a few months, the press continued to mention my "disappointing fourth-place finish" in the primary, but I was moving on. When we convened for the Eighty-Fourth General Assembly in January 1985, my members were bickering about who should be on the leadership team. There were a couple of openings because Gene Johns of downstate Mt. Vernon had died the previous August and Terry Bruce, also from downstate, got himself elected to Congress. The downstate people wanted to keep their influence, and the black caucus was no longer settled on Kenny Hall from East St. Louis as its nominee to the leadership team. Plus, with Harold Washington in as mayor of Chicago, some wanted to get Frank Savickas out of his Senate leadership spot because the white ethnics were not perceived as being sensitive to the concerns of the African Americans. As I've said before, I try to let these groups decide these things for themselves, but this year was a little tougher.

Dawn Clark Netsch had wanted to be on the leadership team since arriving in the Senate in 1973, but there was never a place for her. She thought this might be her year, so she put some pressure on me and had some of her supporters do so as well. Among those adding pressure on Dawn's behalf were the two state representatives in her Chicago Senate district: John Cullerton and Jesse White, the future secretary of state. But I sat down with her and explained that I couldn't put her in leadership. She was a little too liberal, too reformist, to be a member of my team. Richard Luft was a better choice due to geography as much as to anything else, since he was from Pekin in central Illinois. Pekin and its neighboring city, Peoria, were decent Democratic strongholds. The people from central Illinois had a legitimate gripe that they weren't getting the attention that they should, so Luft became the Terry Bruce fill-in on my team. Luft was fairly acceptable to most of the downstate members. He wasn't a serious ideologue; he didn't have any serious animosities. He liked to play golf, and he got along with everybody.

Filling out the rest of the group in 1985 was a challenge. I had had some issues with Gene Johns, the caucus chairman, in the previous session. He was from southern Illinois and felt that he was being ignored, which was also affecting the other downstate Democrats. I tried as politely as I could to tell him the downstate senators didn't want any part of him as a spokesperson. But he didn't want to hear that, and so in order to assuage a little subgroup that supported him, I appointed him as the caucus chairman in 1983. That's almost equivalent to an assistant leadership position, but certainly not as important as the floor leader. That role had gone to Vince Demuzio, who was assuming what I considered the "Donnewald role" as a downstate leader.

Demuzio and I were becoming close friends, and his stock in our caucus was rising. He had become my floor leader, and I was happy with that arrangement. He was the guy standing there with the files, trying to make sense out of everything, and handled all of the day-to-day stuff while trying to keep the downstaters on the reservation. That was rarely easy in my caucus. It took a lot of time. Demuzio spent many hours "hearing confessions" in his office for all these members who wanted to realign the stars and the moon so that they could get what they wanted. It was quite an adventure for him, and I thought he did a great job.

Table 3
Democratic Senate leadership teams, 1979–93 (Rock as president)

1979–81 Terry Bruce, James Donnewald, Kenneth Hall, Frank Savickas
1981–83 Bruce, Donnewald, Hall, Savickas
1983–85 Bruce, Vince Demuzio,* Hall, Gene Johns,* Savickas
1985–87 Charles Chew,* John D'Arco,* Demuzio, Richard Luft,* Savickas, Sam Vadalabene*
1987–89 D'Arco, Demuzio, Luft, Richard Newhouse,* Savickas, Vadalabene
1989–91 Earleen Collins,* D'Arco, Demuzio, Ted Lechowicz,* Luft, Vadalabene
1991–93 Collins, D'Arco, Demuzio, Jerome Joyce,* Lechowicz, Savickas, Vadalabene

Note: An asterisk following a name denotes that the person was on the leadership team for the first time.

Johns, meanwhile, got in a huff and said he would not accept the position of caucus chairman again, telling me it was beneath him. I responded, "Well, if you're looking around, this is like musical chairs: there aren't any chairs left. If you don't want that one, I'll make arrangements to get somebody else." I think Johns's illness was slowly encroaching. He was not a healthy man. He had been missing some floor time and was spending a great deal more time in his office. Johns passed away in 1984.

To replace Johns directly as the caucus chairman, I had to consider that I had factions all over the place. I thought there was one guy who could at least get them all together in a room: Sam Vadalabene of Madison County. Everybody liked Sam, who would tell jokes and take some of the tension out of the air. He was a great human being. I asked him to be the caucus chairman, and he was delighted.

There was a secret to Sam's success in the caucus, and a lot of people didn't understand how he did it. Besides his great personality, he made it his business to get along with many interest groups and many House members because he wanted to get his own bills passed. Sam's strategy was to handle between fifty and seventy-five bills, one each for many different groups every session. The veteran lobbyists and other players always went to him; downstate and union leaders went to him. Then he gave every House member one of his own bills to handle or sponsor, and he in turn would agree to handle one of theirs. If he handled a House bill for a member of the other chamber, he would expect that member to honor his bill when it got over to the House. It was a way of scratching each other's back. Sam gave almost every Democrat one of his bills—House and Senate Democrats, all of them. The presumption was that when one of his bills was called, every Democrat would support it because every one of them had one of Sam's bills, and he would support their bills. He was a master.

It helped that Sam was well liked, too. He brought a lot of projects and concrete back to Madison County in his career. That county is probably six inches lower than the rest of the state because of the concrete and asphalt he brought in. Sam was legendary. In 1983, Governor Thompson came to testify in the Senate, appealing for the income tax increase. We were about an hour and a half into the hearing, and all we wanted was for Thompson and budget director Bob Mandeville to say this was a grand idea so we could wrap things up for the day. Before Thompson got off the stand, I asked, "Has anybody got any questions for the governor?" Up jumped Sam. He said, "Governor, is it true that you're more inclined to help those who help you?" Thompson, of course, picked right up on it and said, "Senator, if you can stand any more concrete or asphalt in your district, you've got it!" So from then on, Sam made no bones about the fact that he was going to support the tax increase that Thompson wanted, and he expected to reap the benefit. And he did.

Frank Savickas is another story. He hung around on the leadership team only because the white ethnics kept putting him there. He and I didn't get along very well, but he was the hero of the white ethnics. I had to keep him. As for the black caucus, I was sorry to see the Chicago members remove Kenny Hall of East St. Louis as the black representative on the leadership team. I gave them the right to self-deliberate, which may have been my mistake in this case, but it's the way I ran things. I didn't think Hall would have any problem getting himself selected by the black caucus. But Charlie Chew and Richard Newhouse roughed him up politically and managed to get the other blacks behind Chew, who really wanted to be in leadership. So Chew got onto the leadership team and Hall was out. But then, unfortunately, Chew got throat cancer, was gone from Springfield most of 1986, and died during the year. So he didn't get a chance to do much in his leadership role.

To fill out the team, I also wanted my friend John D'Arco of Chicago. I thought he could help watch my back and let me know if one of the factions was plotting to go off the reservation.

As we moved into the session, we had thirty-one members. For some silly reason, Newhouse voted "present" on the day of organization when I won my fourth term as Senate president. I don't know why he did that, but I still had the thirty votes to keep the presidency for another term.

While it's fair to say that education is a big agenda item every year, things were lining up for 1985 to become the year of education reform. It had been brewing. A well-publicized study emerged in 1983 that was aptly called *A Nation at Risk: The Imperative for Educational Reform*. "Our nation is at risk," the report began. "The educational foundations of our society are presently being eroded by a rising tide of mediocrity that threatens our very future as a nation and a people. What was unimaginable a generation ago has begun to occur—others are matching and surpassing our educational attainments."[1] It sparked a dialogue in the nation and in Illinois about what we needed to do to reform our educational system. The teachers always said we needed to pump more money into the system, but others were saying we had to do a lot more than that.

Reform and frustration were in the air, so by a joint resolution of the House and Senate in 1983, we created the Commission on the Improvement of Elementary and Secondary Education. Senator Art Berman of

Chicago, who had some expertise in education, and Representative Richard Mulcahey from the northwest part of the state cochaired the twenty-person commission and did a tremendous amount of study. I gave Berman a free hand, and he ran with it. They conducted fourteen public hearings all over the state for citizen input. Two of their major thematic questions were, "How adequate are the state's expectations for instructional standards and pupil performance across all ages?" and "How can we assure that our schools are adequately preparing youth for higher education and/or public/private employment?"[2] That was more than twenty-five years ago, and those questions are still being asked today.

In every era, some people think they are discovering or expressing new problems for the first time. Schools and teachers in the 1980s faced great pressure that went way beyond instruction and learning. The superintendent of the Chicago schools, Ruth Love, said at a conference on education reform in 1984, "We are now asked in the public schools to provide parenting, socialization, assimilation, manners, morals, immunization, sex education, and it could go on and on. I think it's about time that the schools determine what they are willing to be held accountable for."[3] The Chicago Public Schools CEO would probably say the same thing today, as would superintendents and teachers around the state.

The Berman-Mulcahey commission highlighted three great concerns when it delivered its final report to the legislature in January 1985: concern about lack of clarity regarding the purpose of elementary and secondary education in Illinois, concern about a decline in student achievement, and concern about the quality of teaching and leadership from principals.[4] These issues were consistent with the national attitudes expressed in *A Nation at Risk*. "It was the first time in 30 years that the gap between public expectations and school performance had become so great as to cause wide and serious concern," said Ted Sanders, who took Donald Gill's place as the state superintendent of education in January 1985. "The time was ripe for change, and the changes likely would come from a conviction that our schools over the years had somehow become less than accountable, our teachers less than competent, our curricula less than rigorous, and that an unacceptable process of decay had set in."[5]

Sentiments about education reform were approaching an all-time high in 1985. Other forces were in play: Thompson had ideas, Speaker Madigan had his approach, and the Illinois Project for School Reform, headed by Mike Bakalis, was looking at virtually all the same issues that the commission addressed. What we had, literally, were hundreds of ideas that needed to be sorted out. The Berman-Mulcahey commission, as it turned out, paid a lot of attention to ideas pushed by the Illinois State Board of Education and presented the legislature with fifty-seven recommendations.[6] We had a couple of caucus meetings, and I outlined my plan of attack. I said I didn't want to end the session with something called "school reform" that all the reformers and education leaders would criticize as the wrong solution. That wouldn't solve anyone's problem. So this commission was not a group that sat there and just listened. Berman did a masterful job. During the spring, he kept a lot of senators, House members, superintendents, principals, teachers, and other educators down in Committee Room 212, a large, ornate, comfortable hearing room on the second floor of the Capitol. Berman practically locked them up until they agreed, or came close to agreement, on how we were going to respond to the recommendations. Although the discussions got hot and heavy, Berman put a comprehensive package together. Two Republican senators, Bob Kustra from the suburbs and John Maitland from Bloomington, also immersed themselves in this issue. It also helped that I got along well with Ted Sanders, who had some really smart people on his staff who knew how to get things done. Everything was falling into place for major education reform, or so it seemed.

During the hearings, the head of the Chicago teachers' union always made sure there was a full complement of teachers in the room. The unions had a lot to say, and they had confidence in Berman. They knew Berman was on their side. In my view, nobody else could have dealt with those folks as effectively as Berman did. They didn't trust Maitland. Maitland was always very interested in the formula used to distribute money to school districts—I called him a "formula guy"—and he wanted to skew the formula away from Chicago. The unions didn't trust Kustra, either. He was a voice from the suburbs saying, "We don't get enough."

Every once in a while, Berman would come to a bend in the road or find something that people couldn't agree on, and then they would send it up to the third floor to us—to Pate Philip and me. For example, there were provisions on special education and bilingual education. My feeling was that special education was being short-suited, that it was not receiving its just due. So Berman and I decided that special education had to be a part of the package. Maitland and Kustra didn't want it, but I said it was essential that it be in there. "Let's deal with it head-on," I told them, and we did.

The scope of the reforms was so massive that we had to pull out all the stops to keep things going. In May, I called for a summit meeting of legislative leaders and school officials to sort out hundreds of ideas and dozens of proposals. Philip and House minority leader Lee Daniels liked the idea, but Speaker Madigan initially said he wasn't sure whether he would participate.[7] That was just typical Madigan. Thompson was calling for a tax increase of eight cents a pack on cigarettes and a 5 percent tax on out-of-state telephone calls to pay for the education reforms. So, as is generally the case on major initiatives, we had to deal with the revenue generation and the substance of the reforms at the same time. We had to answer how we were going to pay for what we wanted to do. Thompson told us in his State of the State speech to send him a serious reform package only if we had a way to pay for it. One thing that helped us increase the cigarette tax that year was that soon, the federal tax on cigarettes would be reduced. So we raised the state tax on cigarettes and included technical language saying that as of a certain date, the combined federal and state sales tax on a pack of cigarettes would be twenty-eight cents. It was complicated, but so was the entire bill.

Around mid-June, Thompson and about a dozen people, including some senators, flew to several cities in one day to continue to drum up support for the legislative package.[8] Then we ran into overtime that summer, as we always did. This year, we were in overtime to make sure we got everything right, not because we couldn't agree on the major issue of education reform. Madigan and I, along with the Republican leaders, had put together a conference committee to hash out all the details. The conferees really went to work: they met with everybody, they listened to everybody, and they put together a report that became the substance of SB 730. The governor's office was deeply involved in this, too. There were disagreements and compromises and some unusual alliances. The Illinois Education Association, the powerful teachers' union then led by Ken Bruce (brother of Terry Bruce), found itself in support of Superintendent Sanders on some major issues.[9] The teachers were really pleased to be a part of the reform process. That was a bit unusual because the powerful IEA doesn't mind butting heads with the superintendents. What finally came to the Senate chamber on July 2 were forty-seven provisions for major education reform. The following is a partial list of those provisions:

mandatory testing of students at various grade levels

"report cards" on the performance of school districts

a requirement for the State Board of Education to identify
state goals for learning in six areas: language arts, math,
social science, biological and physical sciences, the
fine arts, and physical development and health

new emphasis on improving the training of teachers and
the relationships between teachers and principals

a basic skills test for teachers and what was called a kind of
"bar exam" for new teachers in an attempt to make sure
teachers were qualified to be in the classroom[10]

new mandatory teacher evaluation requirements

early childhood education

optional full-day kindergarten

some consolidation of districts

gifted student and talented teacher programs

bilingual education requirements

startup grants for dropout prevention

a major reading improvement program

expanded school food programs

establishment of the Illinois Mathematics and Science Academy

Just before the vote, I rose and thanked the four senators who had put
so much effort into the reform package: Berman, Maitland, Demuzio, and
Joyce Holmberg. I was proud of the way the legislative process worked. We
had seriously grappled with the issue for a couple of years. "This is one of
the finest hours a leader can have to see a work product like this," I told
my colleagues. "For those who attended the summit meetings, and they
were many, when you get that [spirited] a group together, all concerned
about education and children, and come out with a work product like this,
we can all be proud."[11] The bill passed our chamber by an overwhelming
56–2 margin, and the reforms became law.

Nobody liked everything—which happens with this kind of legislation. As Berman observed, "School boards aren't excited about the school
report card, unions weren't excited about the learning outcomes, small
districts had trouble with the consolidation studies, the business community and politicians weren't happy with the new taxes."[12] But as Thompson
put it when he signed the legislation: "This is an extraordinary day for
the people of Illinois. [The General Assembly] passed the most important
education program in the history of Illinois. It was a vote for the future
of every child and grandchild in this state."[13]

The 1985 legislation has had a remarkable and lasting effect on Illinois. The Illinois Mathematics and Science Academy, for example, was built in Aurora with the help of Build Illinois funds, a capital development program that Thompson also pushed during the 1985 session. Still trying to help the economy and address the state's infrastructure needs, Thompson designed the Build Illinois program to provide $2.3 billion in bonding authority for buildings, roads, housing, colleges and universities, and other projects in the next eight years. He mentioned Build Illinois early in the year in his State of the State address. He also talked to Madigan and me about it, and we got on board. It was said to be the state's largest building program in fifteen years.[14]

The state seems to pass one of these major capital plans every ten to fifteen years. After Build Illinois came Governor George Ryan's $12 billion program called Illinois FIRST (an acronym for Fund for Infrastructure, Roads, Schools and Transit) in 1999, and then the next one didn't pass until Governor Pat Quinn's first year in office, a $26 to $31 billion program in 2009. There are two aspects to every major program like this: the projects and the financing. It's easy to draw up lists of projects because every member has them, but it's not easy to settle on a final list. For Build Illinois, there was a lot of jockeying about how to pay for all of these projects. My Chicago colleague senator Howard Carroll and I thought we could raise most of what we needed by putting a sales tax on the private sales of cars. We all considered this a good source of revenue, and it wouldn't offend businesses because it was on private sales of cars, owner to owner. Nonetheless, it became complicated and tense as the final deal was worked out by Thompson and the leaders, particularly Madigan, who came up with $500 million in projects for Chicago. Carroll and I also discovered that 80 percent of Thompson's projects would go to Republican districts, and that didn't sit well with us.[15] Ultimately, Build Illinois was successful. It funded not only the Illinois Mathematics and Science Academy but also projects like the State of Illinois Center in Chicago, McCormick Place North (partially, anyway), the elegant new Illinois State Library building in Springfield across the street from the Capitol, a major bridge renovation over the Mississippi River connecting St. Louis and East St. Louis, and on and on. Thompson loved going around the state, breaking ground and cutting ribbons with legislators and local officials.

The year 1985 was a year of big ideas, in fact. But not every important piece of legislation that year grew from a big idea. One issue I dealt with was quite personal to me: Alzheimer's disease. Alzheimer's results from a destruction of brain tissue and subsequent loss of brain function, causing a steady loss of memory that makes it much harder for people to speak, think, and carry on daily activities.[16] My dad was diagnosed with this tragic disease at the relatively young age of fifty-five and subsequently died. It wasn't easy to watch, and it made a big impact on me. I took an interest in learning more about it and conferred with a doctor at Rush Presbyterian–St. Luke's Hospital,[17] Dr. Jacob Fox, a neurologist who was a world-renowned expert on what was then a rather new medical subject. Many doctors didn't know how to diagnose the condition and didn't know what to call it when they came across it.

At that time, we learned that an estimated 50 percent of all nursing home admissions in Illinois could be attributed to Alzheimer's and related disorders. We also got clear evidence that the disease had been causing "serious financial, social and emotional hardships on the victims and their families."[18] So, working with some House members, we drafted and passed a series of twelve bills that called for education and dissemination of information about Alzheimer's. I asked Dr. Fox and some of his colleagues to go to the other hospitals and tell other health care professionals about the disease. It didn't make a headlines splash, but it was there, and people could take advantage of it. In our legislation, we established a program for Alzheimer's research in Illinois and created a statewide system of regional and community-based services for Alzheimer's victims. We also mandated the creation of an Alzheimer's task force within the Illinois Department of Public Health, with members appointed by the governor and the legislative leaders, and required that an Alzheimer's state plan be submitted every three years to the governor and the General Assembly. It was all to make sure that we got on top of this issue.

History shows that our bills had plenty of foresight. In 2007, the General Assembly adopted another resolution requiring an updated comprehensive state plan. Subsequently, the 2009 report from the Alzheimer's Disease Advisory Committee referenced our series of bills of twenty-four years earlier. It found that by 2010, there would be about half a million new cases of Alzheimer's in the United States every year, taking a huge toll on the victims and their families. "In Illinois, more than 347,000 caregivers provided nearly 300 million hours of unpaid care to persons with Alzheimer's [in 2007]," the report said.[19] Those are staggering numbers and don't begin to describe the actual suffering that families endure. The 2009 report then made a series of short-term and long-term recommendations for combating this terrible disease, one that, in my opinion, the government must continue to address.

17. The Debacle of the 1986 Elections

Madigan called a news conference one morning, and that afternoon, the organizers of the world's fair gave up.

The idea for a world's fair in Chicago had been bouncing around for seven years, at least since architect Harry Weese proposed it to celebrate the one hundredth anniversary of the successful 1893 Columbian Exposition.[1] The idea was to have an authorized world's fair in 1992. Maybe Weese, who had other big plans to revitalize the South Loop and Navy Pier, wasn't the first to talk about a fair, but he got credit for it. Frankly, I liked the idea and was in favor of it, as was Governor Thompson. The Chicago business community also supported it, especially the Civic Committee of the Commercial Club. Jane Byrne had supported it when she was mayor, and when Harold Washington took over that position, we thought he would be in favor of it, too, but he was a little uncertain. At any rate, we started to make a big push in the early 1980s to get support for a fair. Then we tried to get some funding in 1983. All we could muster then was $8.8 million for a feasibility study and a small staff. Thompson put his Department of Transportation director, John Kramer, in charge of the new World's Fair Authority. Peter Creticos left my staff to work on the fair, and Washington added Jim Compton of the Chicago Urban League to the team.

Despite the push from Thompson, the world's fair had opponents from the beginning. Their big questions: What would it cost and who's going to pay for it? Those are great questions; those are the questions about everything. In this case, I thought we could work it out. But as time went on, opposition mounted. We were waiting for a feasibility study, which finally came out late in June 1985. It said we could pay for the fair with $511 million from private investors, $277 million from the state in general revenue, and another $220 million backed by bond sales.[2] Speaker Madigan was rather cool to the idea all along, and he enlisted the help of Adlai Stevenson III to oppose it. It was one of the few major issues about which Madigan and I disagreed so publicly in the ten years that we simultaneously ran our respective chambers. I wanted the world's fair and he was against it. Stevenson was preparing to run for governor again the next year. Any time you get Stevenson on your side, you also get the reformers and the Lake Shore people backing your cause; so support for the fair was not as strong as I would have liked. The opponents zeroed in on the expense and the resulting political questions: What do we get? What's in it for us? That's the standard conversation in Cook County.

Sensing additional concern from the suburbs and downstate, Kramer and his team tried and failed to design a world's fair that would extend into the neighborhoods and suburbs. The idea was to have international events everywhere, even around the state, but, frankly, skepticism ruled the day.[3]

Madigan had his own advisory committee on the world's fair. After years of discussion, he abruptly announced the morning of June 19, 1985, that he would not support state funding for the fair, saying it was not financially sound. Thompson's support, meanwhile, was quietly wavering. Following Madigan's announcement, Kramer soon declared that he was shutting down the fair's planning office. It was over. As the *Chicago Tribune* put it a few months later: "One morning last June he [Madigan] called a news conference to announce his opposition to the proposed 1992 Chicago World's Fair. That afternoon the fair's organizers gave up."[4] I don't think too many leaders were particularly saddened by the fact that the fair wasn't going to happen. It was well meaning and was going to be a showcase for the city, but we in Chicago weren't ready for a world's fair. Mayor Washington never fully embraced it; that wasn't his style. He didn't like that big stuff, and he wasn't enthused. So when you get the mayor and a few well-known politicians opposed to it, you're not going very far. The fair was finished long before it ever got started.

Another issue on which I f aced a lot of opposition was off-track betting. I had pushed for it and couldn't get it through the General Assembly. We wanted to allow racetracks to have two off-site locations around the state where people could gather, have a beer or two, enjoy the races, and do a little betting. Predictably, the gambling opponents always showed up. The opposition included a church coalition that didn't want any betting or gambling of any kind, and certainly not the expansion of gambling. Opponents would come to see me, and I would listen to them. I told them that among my other faults, I go to the horse races. Sometimes I win and sometimes I don't, but it's something I enjoy. I always thought the opponents were better organized than we were. They had mailing lists ready to go, and all they had to do was publish the trouble of the day—like our push for OTB—and they could get their supporters to wind themselves up and respond. I think it's fair to say they still are better organized than gambling proponents, even with all the lobbyists and the money floating around from the casinos.

Opponents of gambling think it jeopardizes discretionary income that people could use for better purposes. They take the position that the state should not encourage or otherwise make gambling available in Illinois. I think we're going to have gambling whether it's legal or not, so you can argue whether you're better off with gambling that is regulated or gambling that is unregulated. I believe if you're going to have gambling, you should have regulation.

In 1985, when I made a new push for OTB, two other senators joined me in sponsoring a bill to establish the Off-Track Wagering Association and to set the rules for OTB: Stan Weaver, a downstate Republican, and Sam Vadalabene, who had horse racing in his district across the river from St. Louis. We had strong leadership in the Senate, but in the House, Madigan was a bit reluctant and formed one of his ad hoc groups to consider the issue. This time, he put one of his rising stars, Representative John Cullerton of Chicago, on the issue. Cullerton, who was chairing the House Horse Racing Committee, was an astute politician who, like me, had gone to Loyola law school. His father's first cousin was Parky Cullerton from the Thirty-Eighth Ward.[5] Parky had been an alderman and then the Cook County assessor. At any rate, we barely passed the bill in the Senate as the 1985 session rolled along, and then it lost in the House the last week of the session despite Cullerton's support. But we weren't finished with the issue in this session.

Cullerton kept doing his homework. He wanted to know how much money OTB would raise, how much the state would realize in revenue, how much the local governments would realize, and what it would all cost. With those facts and figures, we could negotiate the ratios and the distribution of the revenue. Although our bill failed, the House had another, more comprehensive bill. It included OTB at two locations per racetrack, as well as affirmative action plans for minority and female employment at the tracks, background checks of racetrack employees, and provisions to help the DuQuoin State Fair in southern Illinois.[6] The bill started to pick up steam in 1986. By that time, the bill did not contain the phrase "off-track betting," but it did include "intertrack wagering," which everyone understood was the same thing. The House and the Senate passed different versions of the bill, so we had a conference committee; the future of the bill was in doubt as the veto session was coming to an end in December 1986. There was a lot of confusion, because by then we were dealing with the "Second Corrected Conference Committee Report on House Bill 2486."

I called a meeting on the last day of the session, December 5, 1986. By that time, Richard Duchossois, whose Arlington Race Track had had a bad fire the year before, was mad at us because he wasn't getting everything he wanted in tax breaks to rebuild the track. For Cullerton, who had stayed with the issue for two years, that meeting was his first time in the Senate president's office, even though he had been in the legislature since 1979.[7] That's worth noting because Cullerton would become the occupant of that office when he became Senate president twenty-three years later, in 2009. Thompson was also pushing for an agreement, calling it an economic development issue. Duchossois was in Springfield as we negotiated the details. We agreed to reduce the state's share of the revenue and give 2 percent of the revenue to local governments. Local governments typically want some percentage of new revenue streams like this, and giving it to them makes it easier for every legislator to support. They can say to all the mayors in their districts, "We made sure we got some additional money for you." We also required the tracks to pay $500,000 to charities and $250,000 to Gambler's Anonymous every year. We took the bill to the Senate, where we got plenty of votes to pass it. Then we watched as the House put sixty votes on the bill, the minimum it needed to pass. Cullerton, I am told, still has a copy of this roll call framed and hanging on his office wall.[8]

That's how we got OTB parlors in Illinois. At the time, there were seven tracks, which were allotted two OTB sites each, for a total of fourteen. Those tracks were Arlington, Sportsman's, Maywood, Hawthorne, and Balmoral in the Chicago area, Fairmount Park in Madison County, and the Quad City Downs in the western part of the state. The total number of OTB sites has by now increased considerably beyond the original fourteen. I was pleased that Springfield got an OTB site in a shopping center on Wabash Avenue, just a few miles from the Capitol. Since I do enjoy the races, I would go there to have a little fun at night or make a few bets during the day, if there was a break.

A month before we passed that legislation, the state and nation had the quadrennial November general elections in 1986. For the Democrats, however, the primaries in March had been much more interesting. There was still a lot of ill will under the surface, with Washington as the Chicago mayor, the council wars between the organizational Democrats and the "would-be reformers" still going on, and Cook County state's attorney Richard M. Daley positioning himself to be the mayor someday. I had a personal interest in the state treasurer race because Jerry Cosentino, who had served a term as state treasurer from 1979 to 1983 but left to go back to his trucking business, challenged my friend Jim Donnewald, the incumbent, in the primary. I thought the Democrats were double-crossing Donnewald, and so did the others who had served with him in the General Assembly. Cook County Democrats didn't consider it a double cross. After all, most Democrats, especially those from Cook, didn't know who Donnewald was. Cosentino went around from person to person to build his case. The reaction that Cosentino received in Cook County was, "It's only the state treasurer; who really cares? We'll support you." Another Democrat who challenged Donnewald in that primary was Pat Quinn, who had made a name for himself in the late 1970s as a populist and received a lot of publicity for the group he founded, the Coalition for Political Honesty. In the three-way race featuring Donnewald, Quinn, and Cosentino, I was sorry to see Cosentino emerge as the winner, making Donnewald a one-term state treasurer. Quinn, meanwhile, took his defeat in stride and ended up running for treasurer again in 1990, when he won and served one term. (He then ran for secretary of state in 1994 against George Ryan and lost.)

I also had a primary opponent in 1986: Nicholas LaPonte, who had a very high opinion of himself. He was an assistant attorney general working in Chicago and called himself an independent, which he considered a badge of honor. I was surprised by the primary challenge. I was the Senate president at that time and was always visible back home in the district. Everybody who knew state government knew I had some power at my disposal. LaPonte tried to say that I didn't care about my constituents, something that challengers usually say about incumbents. The local weekly paper, the *Oak Leaves*, criticized LaPonte's "negative campaign" and endorsed me, saying, "As president of the Senate, Rock has considerable clout in Springfield. Municipalities and school districts in his district use that clout, as do social service agencies seeking grants. His position is a major benefit to the district."[9]

LaPonte tried to run a professional campaign by canvassing the neighborhood, putting up signs, and taking down my signs. But he never made a dent, and I easily defeated him. It ended up being embarrassing for Cosentino that he hooked up with LaPonte. There were "LaPonte-Cosentino" signs around Oak Park, for which Cosentino called me later and apologized.

The biggest news in the state was how the Democrats bumbled the primaries. They didn't work hard enough in the precincts. Adlai Stevenson didn't have serious competition for the Democratic nomination for governor, but after that, things fell apart. Illinoisans learned what the word "LaRouchie" meant. Lyndon LaRouche Jr. was a political gadfly, the kind of extremist nobody pays attention to. He ran for president about five times and was the presidential candidate of the U.S. Labor Party, whatever that is, in 1976. He called himself an economist, but really, nobody cared what he said about anything.

For reasons unknown to any serious Illinois politician, some followers of LaRouche ran a group of candidates in the Democratic primaries for all Illinois statewide offices in 1986. How embarrassing it was to wake up the day after the March primary and learn that Democratic regulars George Sangmeister and Aurelia Pucinski had lost to "LaRouchie" candidates Mark Fairchild and Janice Hart in the races for lieutenant governor and secretary of state, respectively. So the Democrats had these two fringe candidates as their nominees. As a party, we had dropped the ball. Part of this was attributable to all the fighting going on in Cook County. Harold Washington and archrival Ed Vrdolyak had focused on local races, and so did many of their precinct captains. They had neglected to include Sangmeister and Pucinski in their preelection messages to their troops.[10] The media ignored the LaRouchies altogether, as we all did. When we lost the two races, we tried to fight it in court; I helped to write a brief, but legally, we didn't have a leg to stand on. So 1986 forever will be remembered as the year the Democrats had two off-the-wall LaRouchies as their candidates for statewide office.

Stevenson didn't want to run with Fairchild as his running mate, so he withdrew as the Democratic candidate and ran instead with the real Democrats and a slate of candidates under a new Illinois Solidarity Party. It was a mess, frankly, because the Solidarity Party had to satisfy the legal requirement of having a full slate of statewide nominees or it couldn't get on the ballot. Stevenson took Michael Howlett Jr., the son of our Democratic nominee for governor in 1976 and a sitting Cook County judge, as his running mate for lieutenant governor, and they added a woman named Jane Spirgel to run for secretary of state against Jim Edgar. Edgar was a very popular Republican incumbent, and we didn't have much of a chance, if any, of unseating him anyway. All of the other Solidarity

Party candidates besides Stevenson and Howlett said, literally, "I'm on the Solidarity Party ballot but don't vote for me. Vote for the Democrat." They were talking about our two Democratic incumbents, Attorney General Neil Hartigan and Comptroller Roland Burris, who were running for reelection. They stayed on the Democratic ballot with some of the LaRouchies because they had won their primaries.

The LaRouchies caused us even more trouble because Calvin Sutker, the chairman of the state Democratic Party and a state representative from Skokie, lost his primary race to return to the state central committee in another LaRouchie upset. So we had to choose a new state chairman. Sutker had just replaced me four years earlier, so we were looking a little foolish, like the Democrats were losing stability. With Sutker out, former senator and current Chicago city treasurer Cecil Partee became the favored candidate, getting the backing, surprisingly, of both Vrdolyak and Washington. Vrdolyak wanted a Cook County guy, and Washington wanted a black, so Partee was okay with both of them. Meanwhile, a few of us wanted to separate the council wars from the state party. We also needed to get away from the LaRouchie debacle that had just occurred in Cook County. We looked downstate.

I was among those who thought my assistant leader, Senator Vince Demuzio of Carlinville, could get enough support to become the state chairman. Residents of Demuzio's county—Macoupin County, southeast of Springfield—call it "central Illinois," but in Chicago we considered it southern Illinois. No doubt it was downstate, though. I supported Vince for chairman. There was some talk that Speaker Madigan wanted to be state chairman, but I know for certain that he didn't want it then, because I was involved in the decision making. In another surprise endorsement, State's Attorney Richard M. Daley swung to Demuzio. It was a way for the mayoral hopeful to oppose Vrdolyak and Washington at the same time; plus, Demuzio had supported Daley in his run for mayor against Washington three years earlier. In Cook County at that time, it seemed that nobody trusted anybody. Think of the unusual alliances that developed: Washington and his rival Vrdolyak supporting one candidate (Partee), and Daley and me supporting another (Demuzio). What a crazy year. I told Vince he was a logical choice. He had some troops loyal to him, especially some of the younger guys and for sure the downstate guys. So he ran and he won, and we moved into the general elections with a downstate state chairman for the first time in almost forty years.

After all that, the outcomes did not favor the Democrats in November. Stevenson lost to Thompson again. Edgar easily won reelection as secretary of state. However, Democrats Hartigan and Burris won reelection as attorney general and comptroller, respectively, while Cosentino beat his Republican opponent, Springfield mayor Mike Houston, by a 56–44 margin. So the statewide constitutional offices remained evenly split between Democrats and Republicans, but it could have been worse.

During the campaign, Republicans tried to capitalize on the Democrats' turmoil by making it known they would try to take over control of the Illinois Senate by winning a few seats. They did knock out LeRoy Lemke of Chicago, but we held onto the other targeted seats. Meanwhile, it was a very sweet victory in the Decatur area, where a city councilwoman named Penny Severns upset the ten-year Republican incumbent, James Rupp, the former Decatur mayor. *Illinois Issues* called this our "sweetest victory," and that's accurate.[11] Penny was a brilliant, energetic thirty-four-year-old with unlimited potential. She became a great senator and our party's nominee for lieutenant governor in 1994, but sadly, she died of breast cancer in 1998 at the age of forty-six. From a numbers standpoint, her victory in 1986 offset Lemke's loss. So we maintained our slim 31–28 margin in the Illinois Senate heading into 1987, while Madigan and his troops also maintained Democratic control of the House.

Almost lost in the LaRouchie craziness and the ongoing council wars was a historic victory for Hispanics and the diminishment of the longtime stranglehold by white ethnics on certain Chicago districts. A community organizer by the name of Miguel del Valle challenged incumbent Edward Nedza in the state senate primary in the Fifth Senate District on the near northwest side. That area's demographics were changing, and the district had a significant majority of Hispanics.

Del Valle canvassed the whole ward, promising a different kind of leadership. Nedza relied on his precinct captains, who ultimately could no longer deliver for him. Del Valle beat Nedza to become the state's first Hispanic senator. Then Nedza was convicted in 1987 of racketeering, extortion, and tax fraud for using his political muscle to obtain an illegal interest in the sale of vendor licenses for a flea market in his neighborhood. He was sentenced to eight years in prison.[12]

Del Valle, meanwhile, was an up-and-comer. He was the premier community organizer for Hispanics. Born in Puerto Rico, he earned both bachelor's and master's degrees from Northeastern Illinois University. He was intense. At first he seemed a little overwhelmed. I talked to him a few times and pointed out to him that he was the first Hispanic senator and could make a run with it—pass some bills and get lots of support because he would find his colleagues standing up for the Hispanics. The fact is, though, del Valle was very quiet, very low key, almost never heard from, in his early years. In my opinion, he let some opportunities go by. Later on, he did get more vocal and active and became a leader in the caucus. In retrospect, I would say he did it the right way. He didn't make any waves. At first he found himself in the black caucus, which didn't help. I guess he joined that group because he was a minority.

Times have clearly changed for the better in that regard, with growing respect for Latinos and their political muscle. Del Valle remained a state senator for twenty years before becoming the Chicago city clerk under Mayor Richard M. Daley. Over the years, his stature in the Senate rose. As more Latinos were elected to the General Assembly, del Valle cofounded and cochaired the Illinois Legislative Latino Caucus and founded the Illinois Association of Hispanic State Employees.[13] Del Valle was a pioneer and represented something significant in state government—the emergence of Latinos as a force to be reckoned with.

18. Illinois Women in Government

It was amazing how candid the women were. The
conferences attracted some big-time national
speakers, such as Helen Thomas and Molly Ivins.

IN THE 1970S, IT WAS CLEAR THAT WOMEN were becoming more active
in government and running for public office more frequently. Alan
Rosenthal, the distinguished director of the Eagleton Institute of Politics
at Rutgers University from 1974 to 1994, had noted the trend. He studied
how more women were winning elections to state legislatures around the
country. It used to be a good ol' boy prerogative to be a member of a state's
general assembly, but that was breaking down. Rosenthal put together a
conference concerning the subject of women in government. He invited
political and legislative leaders from around the country to participate,
including Willie Brown, the Speaker of the House in California, and me,
because he believed it would be more successful with representation from
the big states. The Center for American Women and Politics, the premier
center for the study of women in politics, is operated within the Eagleton
Institute at Rutgers and was hosting the conference along with Rosenthal.

Linda Hawker was a member of the Illinois Senate staff and attended
Rosenthal's first major conference in San Diego in the early 1980s. The
conference was designed to prepare women who were already politically
active to run for Congress. Linda did not attend to prepare to be a candidate but to learn all that she could. It's fair to say that Rosenthal helped
women understand that they could bring a different point of view to government. Hawker was very impressed with the conference and came back
with the idea of adapting that experience to create an Illinois conference
for women. She talked to me and some others on the staff about it. I told
her to go for it, and we agreed that the Office of the Senate President would
help. Hawker soon got others involved, including Judy Erwin, Loretta
Durbin, and Linda Kingman. With the help of Rosenthal's center and staff,

they organized a three-day weekend conference called Illinois Women in Government (IWIG). They invited women from around the state who were county board or village board members or otherwise involved in public life—the ones who ran for public office and prevailed. They also looked to their Springfield contacts and included women in state government and women legislators. More than a hundred women attended that conference at Sangamon State University (which in 1995 became the University of Illinois Springfield). It was important to us that it was bipartisan, even though my office had a big role in organizing it. Among the Republicans attending were Maralee Lindley, the Sangamon County recorder; state senator Adeline Geo-Karis; and state representatives Josephine Oblinger and Kathleen Wojcik. Members of the press gave presentations, too, and I was honored to give the luncheon keynote speech on Saturday. The conference was a great opportunity for women who were in the distinct minority in a man's world, such as Rock Island county board member Margery Benson. She came to the conference and loved it, and she ultimately was one of the apostles who spread the word about IWIG.

Many topics were covered at that first conference. Practitioners and university professors gave presentations, as did at least two Democratic senators, Dawn Clark Netsch and Joyce Holmberg. Workshop topics included property tax reform, time management, pay equity, women and children in poverty, and infrastructure. After the conference, several participants said that they definitely were going to run for a higher office. I kidded some of them that we had started something very powerful, but they shouldn't tell anybody what was coming.

It was a roaring success, so IWIG did not stop with just one conference. Quite a few Illinois women attended additional Eagleton Institute conferences over the years, and in Illinois, IWIG developed a board that was very active. IWIG began to have annual conferences, which became more sophisticated over time. We secured the involvement of the state's Intergovernmental Cooperation Commission, because we meant for IWIG to include government at several levels and wanted to make sure people knew it was bipartisan.

Many state legislators came to these conferences, especially the women. Over time, the annual conferences attracted between 200 and 250 women, and it wasn't just the women who noticed how successful all of this was. Over the years, we started to attract a significant number of corporate sponsors—and men. Secretary of State George Ryan hosted the opening reception in 1994 at the Illinois State Library, for example. That was the same year that Governor Jim Edgar, Lieutenant Governor Bob

Kustra, Comptroller Dawn Clark Netsch, and Attorney General Roland Burris either took part in or hosted different parts of the conference. Alice Phillips, a prominent Republican lobbyist, also became very active, as did Naomi Lynn, the Sangamon State University president. It was really something. While I helped to get it started and my staff was very involved, I had little to do with the actual planning or running of the conferences. As time went on, the Illinois Senate became the sole sponsor, and the conference moved to a downtown Springfield hotel, with some of the workshops or receptions in the Capitol itself or in the Old State Capitol, which is where Abraham Lincoln served in the Illinois legislature. It was all very impressive. There were all kinds of great seminars and sessions on everything from what you should wear in a media interview, to how to present yourself in campaigns, to various policy issues. Most women members of the Senate and the House were involved at one time or another.[1]

One year, Maralee Lindley, Sue Suter—who had progressed in her career to be a state agency director at the Department of Rehabilitation Services—and others talked about power and how they were able to rise to their positions. It was amazing how candid they were. The speakers advised conferees to stop thinking about power as a dirty word. How else were they going to change anything in government if they didn't ascend to some of the powerful positions? That session on power really energized women, because they still had too few role models in politics and government. The conferences also attracted some big-time national speakers, such as Helen Thomas, the renowned United Press International writer, and Molly Ivins, the popular columnist and humorist from Texas.

These conferences flourished for about fifteen years. IWIG no longer exists, but a couple of other programs emerged to support women who want further engagement in public life. One is the Illinois Women's Institute for Leadership (IWIL), which was founded in 1999 for Democratic women. The other is the Illinois Lincoln Series for Excellence in Public Service, which started in 1994 for Republican women.[2] The Lincoln Series gives fellowships to women who wish to be in a public policy–making role within five years. Some of the women who are active in either IWIL or the Lincoln Series were leaders in our IWIG program, so the movement has carried on.

It's fair to look back and say that Rosenthal, Rutgers, and the Center for American Women and Politics were really on to something when they started having those national conferences. The Center for American Women and Politics has been tracking the number of women in Congress, state legislatures, governor's offices, and other positions since the mid-1970s.[3] The Illinois Senate had two women members in 1975, and that number grew to twelve by the time I left the Senate.[4] The House, meanwhile, increased from fourteen women in 1975 to thirty-three women in 1992. The overall percentage of women in the Illinois state legislature increased from 5.9 percent in 1975 to 18.6 percent in 1992, and the percentage climbed to 27.7 percent in 2009, with most of the latter increase occurring in the House. That made Illinois fifteenth among the states in the percentage of women in state legislatures in 2009, when 49 of the 177 legislators were women.[5] Depending on your perspective, 28 percent of the total might not be enough progress, because it doesn't come close to the percentage of women in the Illinois population. What I can say is that I am very proud of the women on my staff who took a leadership role in the 1980s and 1990s to educate and train other women for higher levels of public service. They would say, I'm certain, that their conferences were terrific networking and bonding experiences. They thought it was important that IWIG was bipartisan because it was not about advancing either party but about the cause of women in government. The success of IWIG can be found not only in the training and education but in the lifelong relationships that developed or were enhanced as a result of networking that occurred in the planning and implementation of IWIG conferences.

The Senate Democratic staff had a high-level opening before the 1987 session because Kenneth Wright was leaving the important position of secretary of the Senate. The title "secretary" might be misleading, because the secretary of the Senate is an administrator who handles the business side of the Senate operation and provides an enormous amount of support to the senators. When we're in session, the secretary is positioned in front of the presider's podium in the Senate chamber, keeping track of bills and votes and the day's activities. The secretary also understands all the procedures and sometimes helps the presider make sure that the business of the Senate is being conducted properly.

Linda Hawker, then a special assistant to chief of staff Bill Holland, approached me at some point about the upcoming vacancy, and at first I had no response. I wasn't sure. I knew Hawker well from her involvement in IWIG and her work on the staff. After she asked me about the job, she went to Decatur, forty-five miles east of Springfield, and ran Penny Severns's successful campaign for the Illinois Senate. I was very impressed when I went over there and saw what Linda and Penny were doing. Penny was an impressive candidate, but she may not have won without Linda's campaign savvy. So after the elections, I had to make a decision about the new secretary of the Senate. Linda was well-regarded by my entire caucus, and she had the support of the downstaters. I weighed my options and decided to give Linda the job she had requested. During the veto session after the elections, when she was back in Springfield, I called her in and told her she had the job. It wasn't a long conversation at that point; maybe I surprised her with the abrupt news. I'm glad she accepted. We both knew she was making history, because Hawker in 1987 became the first woman secretary of the Senate, and she stayed in that role for twenty years, although she was the "assistant secretary" when the Republicans controlled the Illinois Senate from 1993 to 2003. Behind the scenes, she was just remarkable, serving as a mentor to many senators and helping in so many ways with the overall operation of the Senate. She provided the kind of service that often goes unrecognized in public service, but I know for a fact that members of my caucus knew how outstanding was her work on behalf of the Illinois Senate.

The 1987 session started as several others did, with three senators holding up my election as Senate president. My wife, Sheila, and my mom were in the elegant Senate chamber on the second Wednesday of January to observe my being elected to a fifth term. But Netsch still wanted an assistant leader's position and didn't get it. Some of my members backed her very strongly, but they knew I wasn't going to do that, and I didn't free a position for Netsch, which created some angst among her supporters. Plus, I tried to replace Frank Savickas on my leadership team, which led to Senators Jeremiah Joyce and Tim Degnan coming to his rescue. On the first vote for Senate president, Netsch, Joyce, and Degnan voted present as a small protest. That gave me only twenty-eight votes in a Senate with thirty-one Democrats. Here we go again, I told my family and friends, although those probably were not my exact words.

I listened to my members' demands once again, and I agreed to put a woman into the next available leadership position and on the powerful Senate Rules Committee. There were six Democratic women senators at the time. Netsch chaired the Revenue Committee, a very important committee, and two years later, I made my first appointment of a woman to my leadership team by adding Earleen Collins of Chicago. Because of the compromises we reached, Netsch told the *Chicago Tribune* it was the first time the role of women was being addressed in the Senate and in the Democratic Party.[6] I think, obviously, that she was overstating things.

19. The Cubs and the Sox

I told Pate that the Cubs were staying in
the city in that beautiful park we have.

SOME OF THE MAJOR ISSUES WE PLANNED TO DEAL WITH IN 1987 were carryovers from previous sessions. Political pundits and the press sometimes complain when Congress or the General Assembly doesn't accomplish something one year, as if it's the end of the world. But it usually isn't, because we could, and often did, pick up an issue the next year or the year after. For instance, in the late 1980s, the General Assembly became really interested in the Cubs and the White Sox baseball teams and the Bears football franchise, all based in Chicago.

The Cubs still played all of their games in the daytime in the early 1980s, and there was a movement to legalize night games at Wrigley Field. But the Wrigley neighbors objected and initially enjoyed political support. In 1982, the state actually passed a law banning night games at Wrigley, with Governor Thompson citing an "undue hardship" on residents of the neighborhood.[1] A year later, the Chicago city council stepped in and prohibited lights at Wrigley Field. When the Cubs made the playoffs in 1984, Major League Baseball announced that the team would lose home-field advantage in the World Series if they got that far because they didn't have lights, but the Cubs didn't make it to the World Series anyway.

The lack of lights also led to conversations and threats that the Cubs might abandon the North Side of Chicago and move to DuPage County, which was then ruled by Senator Pate Philip, the Republican minority leader and DuPage County Republican chairman. "Uncle" Pate was in the forefront of this one, and he had a little fun with it. I was totally opposed to the DuPage County move, and I told Pate, "You can't do that. Are you going to build a new stadium? What are you going to do with Wrigley Field? You can't move the Cubs to DuPage County." He ran with it anyway for a while. I think a couple of people in the Cubs front office would have quickly gone through with such a move. They had visions of selling almost twice as many tickets as they sold at Wrigley, where the capacity seating was just more than 39,000 at the time. Residents of Wrigleyville were intransigent about amenities such as lights, more seats, and better parking. So Pate told the Cubs they could do it all in DuPage County, and he received a favorable response from some in the Cubs organization. In my judgment, it always sounded like a conversation in a bar: one of the Cubs' owners said, "Wouldn't it be great if . . ." and Pate said, "Hey, hey, terrific idea! I'll get ahold of this guy and this guy and we'll move it along." But Pate did not get the kind of local response he thought he would get, so then he wanted to have a local referendum on whether DuPage should open its arms to the Cubs. I advised him, "You've got a mailing list for your county; send everybody a letter and ask people what they want." He did send something out, and the results were not in his favor. I told Pate, "I want you to know you're not getting my help on this one. The Cubs are staying in the city. They're staying in that beautiful park we have. Yes, it needs to be fixed up, but they're staying." Pate's overture to grab the Cubs didn't last very long, but it surely stirred things up.

Also at that point, there was a lot of talk about moving the Bears to a new stadium in the suburbs. The Bears weren't happy with Soldier Field in downtown Chicago and were floating ideas to get help for a new stadium, a domed stadium, a combination convention center–stadium, or maybe someplace in the suburbs, whatever deal they could get. The Bears had lobbyists in Springfield and Chicago, just trying to get the best deal possible. According to Pate, everybody wanted to move to DuPage County, so the Bears should move there, too. There was just so much talk.

Meanwhile, in 1985, as the Cubs were trying to figure out how to have a few night games, a Cook County circuit court judge ruled in favor of the Wrigley Field neighborhood residents and against the team. The judge said there was something wrong with ending a seventy-year tradition of daytime baseball. Negotiations and court battles went back and forth for a couple of years. I was involved in some of the discussions because it was clear that if the Cubs were ever to play at night, the neighborhood would get some concessions, including some changes in state law. Supporters of night games came to me and said they would go along with legislation to keep the noise down later at night. They called it an anti-noise pollution law. In other words, we could enact restrictions on transportation and noise if the Cubs did install lights. Negotiations continued and, finally, after the 1987 season, there was an agreement in which the Cubs could play up to eighteen night games every season through 2002. I agreed with the reasonable contingent who said there were already eighteen games that started at three o'clock in the afternoon. The idea was to allow for those eighteen games to start at night. The city council adopted an ordinance to that effect early in 1988, along with other provisions such as prohibiting the sale of beer after 9:20 P.M. and having no organ music after 9:30 P.M. It was quite a compromise. I have to chuckle that as the lights went up in the next few months, down went all of Pate's notions about the Cubs moving to the suburbs.

The first night game at Wrigley was scheduled for August 8, 1988, against the Philadelphia Phillies. A ninety-one-year-old man named Harry Grossman flipped a ceremonial switch to turn on the lights at 6:06 P.M. The game started at 7:01 P.M. but then was rained out in the fourth inning. So the first official game was completed the next night, with the Cubs beating the New York Mets, 6–4. As a season ticket holder, I was able to buy more tickets for that game, and I had more than any lobbyist. I gave tickets to some members of the Senate and to lobbyists, too. I invited them all to Bernie's Saloon before the game, and when we were all there, I kidded them, saying, "Where's the press now, taking pictures of me giving you tickets to this game?" It was really fun.

While that hubbub was going on, the White Sox were busy with threats of their own—the biggest of which was a possible move to St. Petersburg, Florida. That city was building a domed stadium, initially called the Florida Suncoast Dome but now called Tropicana Field, to lure a baseball team—maybe the San Francisco Giants, maybe the White Sox. The White Sox were indeed considering a move if they didn't get a new publicly financed stadium to replace rundown Comiskey Park on the South Side of Chicago. Looking back, it's interesting that the Cubs controversy overlapped with that of the White Sox, but the issues were different. For the Cubs, it was night games; for the White Sox, it was a new stadium. Everybody admitted that the old Comiskey Park, which looked dilapidated, was structurally dangerous.

With the Florida threat looming in 1986, the Sox gave us in the General Assembly until the end of the 1986 legislative session to get something done. The idea for an Illinois Sports Facility Authority sprung up in the space of a week to ten days in Springfield to assure we would have a new ballpark and some financial breaks for the team's owners. It was a new legal "authority" that could help with the financing of the stadium. But the complicated deal had serious opposition. We wanted to create a 2 percent hotel and motel room tax in Chicago and use that money and also up to $5 million from the state and city to retire $120 million in bonds, which would pay for a new 45,000-seat stadium.[2] Thompson was behind it, Washington was behind it, and I, of course, supported it. We got the thirty votes we needed in the Senate, but over in the House, it initially fell short by six votes. Thompson then squeezed out six more votes, achieving the bare minimum in the House to create the sports facilities authority and keep the White Sox happy for the time being.

But more trouble bubbled up, primarily because Washington and Thompson couldn't agree on who would control the sports authority. Despite passage of the law, nothing happened to implement the sports authority in 1987, and there was no progress toward the construction of a new stadium. Then Washington died of a sudden heart attack on November 25, 1987, just a few months into his second term. It is unfortunate he did not get to be mayor longer. He was really starting to establish himself and was beginning to make progress, but he didn't have enough time to see a lot of his plans come to fruition.

The city council selected Eugene Sawyer as the new mayor, and the Illinois Sports Facility Authority finally hired an executive director, Peter C. B. Bynoe, in the spring of 1988. By then, the Sox again were talking very seriously to the Florida boosters. The new Florida Suncoast Dome would be ready to open in 1989, and there were obvious political problems in Chicago and Illinois. The principal owners of the Sox, Jerry Reinsdorf and Eddie Einhorn, let it be known that they had a renewed interest in St. Petersburg, and the deal from Florida seemed more lucrative to the team than the package we had put together a year and a half earlier. The public statements from the Sox and from those coming out of Florida made everyone nervous. We were in serious danger of losing the Sox, and frankly—although the team was a big deal to Democrats on the South Side and to avid fans such as Dawn Clark Netsch and the late mayor Washington—not everybody cared.

It was up to the General Assembly. Chicago could keep the White Sox if we could finance the new, more appealing leasing plan developed in the spring of 1988 by the Thompson administration and the baseball team. That's what the Sox owners said, even as they kept the Florida connection very much alive. There was skepticism, to say the least, about involving state money in that kind of project. It was easy for critics to say the money could be better spent on education. When the new plan came to the legislature, Republican senator Aldo DeAngelis from the south suburbs declared that approval in favor of the Sox seemed virtually impossible. There was also a report that only five of sixty-seven Democrats in the House supported the plan.[3] Thompson stepped up his efforts. "This is our baseball stadium," he said. "It will belong to the people of Illinois, not the White Sox; they're simply the tenants."[4] At that point, Speaker Mike Madigan told Thompson that the governor had to find twenty-four Republican votes in the House and that he, the Speaker, would get commitments from thirty-six Democrats, getting to the sixty for passage. That is called a "structured roll call," a plan in which each party caucus commits to a particular number of votes in a bipartisan effort.

The issue came down to the last couple of days of the session, as big issues often do. Reinsdorf and Einhorn came to Springfield, and we had a big public ceremony where they signed the lease. For the owners, signing the lease was a show of faith that they expected the General Assembly to approve the financial package for the stadium. The Republican minority leaders, Pate Philip in the Senate and Lee Daniels in the House, were on board. All four legislative leaders—Philip, Daniels, Madigan, and me—plus Thompson and someone from the mayor's office, were there to exhibit a united display of support for the "Chicago" White Sox. We wanted the citizens of Illinois and the Florida baseball backers to see how united the Illinois leadership was. It was the kind of great theater that Thompson could pull off.

Then another day passed, and we were into the final night of the session. That was critical, because after midnight we would need thirty-six votes, not thirty, to pass the bill, and the House would need seventy-one votes, not sixty. We were literally racing the clock. Florida officials reported that their agreement with the White Sox would become official the next day if Illinois failed to act, which, frankly, seemed very possible to me. Already it was past 11:00 P.M. I had counted votes and believed we had enough, so we had a brief debate. Senator Tim Degnan stood up to say that twenty-two of twenty-six major league stadiums then in existence had state or municipal support. That was his way of saying a publicly financed stadium was not so novel any more. I don't know if he was right about either number, but it sounded good. I didn't have to speak; we needed to get the vote finished and send the bill to the House. Degnan reminded us that time was winding down, and he called for the vote. Sure enough, we had thirty votes, the bare minimum. Then we adjourned and went to the House chamber to see what would happen. It was tense.

Numerous reporters and lobbyists from Florida were in Springfield that entire week. We had Florida television cameras in the building, and Thompson was enjoying his TV time. Everybody was scurrying around, watching Florida TV news reports. The Florida people thought they were getting the Sox; the only things that might derail their plan were the new leasing deal and the coalition we had put together in the last few days. When the House took its vote, only fifty-four members voted for it, and midnight was minutes away, literally. It's really interesting, and legendary in Illinois legislative history, what happened next. Representative Jim McPike, House majority leader, was presiding, and he did not formally close the vote. Normally, within thirty seconds after the presider calls for a vote, which happens electronically, he or she then asks the clerk to make it official. Not this time. Madigan was working the floor for six more votes.

McPike stood at the podium and said: "Have all voted? Have all voted? Have all voted who wish?"[5] The presider does that in the House and the Senate on nearly every roll call. Then McPike asked the clerk to tally the final vote. But instead of announcing the vote at that point, as he routinely would, he did something different with only fifty-four green votes on the House tally board. McPike recognized Representative Terry Parke, who had asked to speak, and McPike said, "Representative Parke would like to change his vote from no to aye." And Parke said, "That is correct." Then McPike said, "Representative [Lou] Lang changes his vote from no to aye." McPike made that declaration without formally asking Lang or recognizing Lang, a Chicago Democrat.[6] Maybe there was a nod from Lang, maybe not. It was Madigan rounding up votes, and Lang was okay with that.

"Representative Rea. Representative Rea"—McPike was trying to get Rea's attention—"Representative Rea changes his vote from no to aye."[7]

McPike continued that kind of formality with four more representatives, because one whom he "selected" did not actually want to change his vote. McPike just moved on to the next one. As soon as he or Madigan got three more members to change from no to aye, a change in a total of six votes, McPike immediately declared that the bill to save the White Sox for Chicago had passed with sixty votes. McPike also declared that the time was 11:59 P.M. on June 30, and he quickly adjourned the session for the night. That was critical because two minutes later, the session would have been in overtime, and the House would need seventy-one affirmative votes for the bill to pass. News accounts reported that the House vote actually was completed at 12:03 A.M. the morning of July 1, not four minutes earlier. The time on the printed roll call vote was indeed 12:03 A.M.[8] It very well may have been after midnight when Madigan and McPike were rounding up those final votes, but McPike's ruling prevailed, and the White Sox got their new stadium and stayed in Chicago.

A few nights later, Thompson and quite a few Sox supporters gathered to celebrate this victory in McCuddy's saloon, across Thirty-Fifth Street from the old Comiskey Park. The governor was still trying to explain that most of the money to pay for the new park would come from visitors to the city by way of a 2 percent increase in the hotel-motel tax. He saw me walk in and shouted: "Hey, Phil Rock. I'll buy you a beer!"[9] We stayed a while longer, and then we all went over to the old Comiskey for a ceremony before the game. Thompson and Mayor Sawyer sat at a table behind home plate to sign the historic legislation. Reinsdorf and Einhorn were there, and I was standing with a small group of legislators. The crowd cheered Thompson when he predicted a Cubs–White Sox World Series in that new park and when he said, "Chicago is the most American of all the cities. . . . We don't give up anything. We don't let anyone take anything away from us."[10]

20. Another Tax Increase and Another Mayor

*Thompson came out not only for another income
tax increase but also for a sales tax on services.
That was almost revolutionary at the time.*

O NE ISSUE THAT DID GET AWAY FROM GOVERNOR THOMPSON in
that summer of 1988 was his attempt to get another increase in the
state income tax. In fact, he had tried for a tax increase the year before,
too, in 1987, just four years after we had passed the temporary increase in
1983—the one that expired after eighteen months. I suppose most voters
think that a temporary tax increase will *always* become permanent, but
the 1983 one did not. It expired, and the state was feeling the consequences
of diminished revenue.

So in 1987, Thompson came out not only for another income tax increase but also for a sales tax on services. That was almost revolutionary
at the time. His proposal was, to say the least, bold—and unpopular. His
tax reform commission, headed by James Furman, had proposed it five
years earlier, but it had gone nowhere. He tried again. There was talk about
paying a sales tax on a round of golf and to your barber, plumber, and car
mechanic but not to your lawyer and doctor. The lawyers and doctors had
been included in Thompson's proposal five years earlier, but both groups
have very powerful lobbies in Springfield. Thompson took the preemptive
strike of exempting them from the possible sales tax because one of the
groups or both working together would have put all their influence into
killing it. Thompson also wanted to raise the personal income tax from
2.5 to 3 percent. I thought that was reasonable, given the state's needs, so
I went on Chicago radio and spoke to Chicago groups about the state's
finances and the benefits of an income tax increase. I said I wanted to
make sure that education and social service and mental health programs
got their fair share of the new revenue. But I couldn't support the sales
tax on services, primarily because I didn't think it would go anywhere.

Once again, I was the first legislative leader out of the box to get behind the tax increase. It turned out to be a lonely position, though, because the other three leaders never backed it. We ended the 1987 session without coming close to getting an income tax increase. The proposed new sales tax on services fared even worse; it had died two months before the session ended. Thompson couldn't get anyone to back that one.

The next year, 1988, Thompson tried again. There was an early distraction for me that year when Illinois Supreme Court justice Seymour Simon announced his resignation. My mentor and friend William Clark, former attorney general, was on the supreme court then, too, and there was widespread speculation that I would be appointed to replace Justice Simon. Even Chief Justice Thomas Moran, a Republican, advised me to go after it. I considered it but then decided against it because I didn't want to walk away from my responsibilities in the Senate, especially as Senate president. Clark was a little disappointed that I didn't join him on the bench.

I stayed in the Senate, and Thompson again proposed an income tax increase. He directly challenged the Democratic majorities in the House and Senate to get the tax increase passed. I didn't think that was fair. I advised him that I would support the increase and that he should spend his time convincing members of his own Republican Party to support it, too. I guess everyone knew I would be behind the increase, but Mike Madigan, as late as June 1988, was less forthcoming. The *Chicago Sun-Times* called Madigan the "wild card" in the deliberations, saying he "continued to keep everyone guessing about his intentions."[1] Pate Philip and Lee Daniels didn't want a tax increase and said they would rather cut spending than raise taxes. But Philip was probably open to it because the governor wanted it.

In the meantime—and I have to digress a bit to tell this story—on February 18, 1988, my district office manager, Pat Arman, told me we had to go to the deaf-blind center in Glen Ellyn for some kind of function. Because that center was so important to me, I always said yes to such invitations. When I got there, Governor Thompson greeted me, surprisingly enough, and some friends and family members and other members of the General Assembly were present, too. They told me that the state was renaming and dedicating this special place as the Philip J. Rock Center and School. They totally surprised me, and I felt honored. "Thanks largely due to the tireless efforts of Phil Rock," Thompson said during the ceremony, "all Illinoisans can be very proud of the services offered at this school and service center for the deaf/blind. Dedicating this facility in Phil's honor is a fitting tribute to a man who saw a need to help a unique group of students and worked tirelessly to meet that need."[2]

Back in Springfield, as we pushed toward the end of the spring session, we continued to talk to our members about an income tax increase. This year, conservative groups such as the Taxpayers Federation of Illinois, the Illinois Manufacturers Association, and some business leaders actually said they could support Thompson's proposed increase.[3] Thompson then made an unusual appeal to a joint session of the General Assembly late in the session, on June 9. He had the support of education and business groups and was pushing us hard. Then, with less than a week before the end of the session, somewhat to the Democrats' surprise, both Philip and Daniels said they could back the increase, at least conditionally.[4]

Madigan was the only holdout among the legislative leaders. Some of his members grumbled that he would not call the bill to the House floor for a vote, and the truth is the Speaker did not want it, and so it did not happen. Madigan, when asked whether opposing the tax increase should be perceived as a message that he also opposed funding for education, explained that his tax opposition was "predicated mainly on my personal view that government, like everybody else, ought to work within their means. . . . We are not asking education to do something that others have not been asked to do."[5] So the big push for the tax increase died in 1988, as it had in 1987. The only progress in 1988 was to get Philip and Daniels and some of the business groups to budge in our direction.

The political landscape changed dramatically as we moved into the eighty-sixth session of the General Assembly in 1989. The main point of interest was that Richard M. Daley, still the Cook County state's attorney, was making another serious run for mayor of Chicago, challenging the incumbent, Eugene Sawyer. Those elections are held in the spring of the odd-numbered years every four years. Although voted in by a 29–19 city council vote after Harold Washington had died a little more than a year earlier, Sawyer never did have the overwhelming support of Chicago blacks, the Cook County Democratic organization, or the council itself. Timothy Evans, a black alderman, also wanted to be mayor, and he had some support. But instead of running in the Democratic primary in 1989, Evans chose to be a third-party candidate in the new Harold Washington Party. So Evans was on the sidelines when Daley challenged Sawyer in the Democratic primary. Daley beat Sawyer but still had to face Evans and "Republican" Ed Vrdolyak in the general election a few weeks later. That's right; Vrdolyak had switched parties.

By most accounts, Daley was a different kind of politician in 1989 than he had been a dozen years earlier in the Senate. Significantly, he recognized the dilemma that many Cook County Democrats were in, and that many of the blacks were in, because of his candidacy for mayor. Asking people for an endorsement would have escalated racial tensions. So Daley made a smart move: before the Cook County Democratic organization met, he called his own meeting and told everyone, "I do not want your endorsement. Don't make an endorsement if you can get away with it." That helped everybody. For one thing, endorsements would have been an absolute distraction, because the party faithful would have worried that their jobs would be in jeopardy if they endorsed the wrong candidate. Party workers were also off the hook because they didn't have to make an announcement: they didn't have to go public with support of a white candidate over a black one or vice versa.

A lot of the deep animosity that some of us had experienced toward Daley had settled down quite a bit, except for Jane Byrne. There was still no love lost between Daley and Byrne, but she didn't push it. With most of the rest of us, there had been what I would describe as a cooling-off period. There was even a change of heart along the way for Dawn Clark Netsch. It's fair to say that Netsch was anti-Daley in the 1970s—and I mean all the Daleys—but she actually endorsed Richard M. Daley for mayor in 1989. Recalling all of the things she had said over the years, I kidded her about whether she was getting something in exchange for that support.

David Axelrod, whose consulting business was flourishing, was one of Daley's advisors in the 1989 campaign. So was Senator Tim Degnan, who was well schooled in Chicago politics.[6] Degnan's dad had been favored with a job in city hall by the first Mayor Daley; Tim himself, when he was younger, was one of those neighborhood guys who had gotten a city job. He was accustomed to city politics, so it wasn't surprising that he became one of Daley's biggest advocates.

In any event, 1989 turned out to be Daley's year, because he won the first of many terms as mayor of the city of Chicago by getting 55.4 percent of the vote and beating Evans of the Harold Washington Party. Table 4 shows the final tally. Vrdolyak had become a Republican by then, after all the turmoil during the 1980s, but obviously, he didn't fare well as a Republican candidate.

I'm pleased that my own relationship with Daley changed over the years, too. I supported him during his entire twenty-two-year career as mayor, openly and privately. In my opinion, he did a very good job before deciding not to run in 2011 and turning the office over to Rahm Emanuel. Certainly, Daley was a better mayor than he was a senator. I think he would tell you that were it not for my support as Senate president, he would not have received the funding for the third expansion of

McCormick Place when he really wanted it to happen. His ascendancy to city hall, while not welcomed by everyone, helped to settle down what had been tumultuous times in city politics for more than a decade.

Table 4
General election results for Chicago mayor, 1989

Richard M. Daley	577,141	55%
Democratic Party		
Timothy Evans	428,105	41%
Harold Washington Party		
Edward Vrdolyak	35,998	3%
Republican Party		

At the beginning of the 1989 session, I finally dumped Frank Savickas from my leadership team, but I had to pay a big price for a few months. The truth be known, in getting rid of Savickas, I was acceding to the request of George Dunne, the Cook County Democratic chairman, and Congressman Dan Rostenkowski of Chicago. The latter had gone to Dunne and conveyed to him that he wanted a leadership position in the Illinois Senate for Senator Ted Lechowicz. That left Savickas as the odd man out as the representative of the white ethnics. Savickas was livid. I told him, "If you have a problem with it, don't complain to me; go see Dunne, because I'm doing what he wants me to do." Savickas withheld his vote from me as Senate president when I was elected to my record sixth term. But no one else held out, and again I got the minimum thirty votes. Unfortunately, Jeremiah Joyce of Chicago, another regular troublemaker, then decided to show his support for Savickas by preventing us from establishing standing committees and adopting the rules for the session. Adopting the rules is usually so routine and all worked out ahead; it's "inside baseball" stuff. But the defections of Savickas and Joyce on adopting the rules left us with only twenty-nine votes, one short of the majority needed. I took the position as the presiding officer that the rules of the previous session would continue until they were replaced. I then wrote a letter to all the Republican members suggesting that this was not the way to operate a chamber, that just because two of my members were recalcitrant didn't mean that they had to engage in a wholesale destruction of the process. I wrote that letter because Pate Philip was plotting with his twenty-eight members, plus Savickas and Jeremiah Joyce, to get thirty votes to adopt rules detrimental to the Democrats. But as the presiding officer, I wouldn't call their ideas for a vote, so they couldn't make any progress. Some

Republicans bought my thinking that what was happening was bad for the Illinois Senate. Enough of them agreed with me, saying, "You know, this could happen to us, too, if we got in the majority, and we wouldn't want that." This was not fun.

Once they figured out what was going on, the press had a field day. I don't disagree with a columnist who wrote that Savickas "is not—to put it delicately—known as a terribly deep thinker."[7] I was so mad at Savickas and Joyce that I didn't want to give them the time of day, and for a long time I didn't. Finally, though, we sat down, and I said, "We aren't getting anything done, and you guys aren't looking so hot on this one. What can we do to settle this thing?" The answer was, "You've got to put Frank Savickas back on the leadership team." I said, "Fine, done." So I did. I created a new position and put Savickas back on the team, but it came at great cost to him. I never talked to him again, except to say, "Frank, as far as I'm concerned, you can stay in your office and play gin rummy all day long. I don't need you and don't want you. Don't come to me for any help with your bills; I'm not calling them." Though I was serious about that, the straw that really broke the camel's back occurred when I did try to call him one time and was told that he couldn't come to the phone. Given all that happened, I didn't think it made any sense that he would say he couldn't come to the phone to talk to the leader of his caucus. For the rest of the session, he got no work, and I never asked him to do anything.

We moved into the final month of that 1989 session having dealt with a lot of tension and having a new mayor in place. The fact that Daley occupied the mayor's office on the fifth floor of city hall might have influenced what happened next with the tax discussions. Mayor Washington had never weighed in when Thompson proposed the income tax increase two years earlier. But this year, after being unsuccessful for two years, Thompson did not propose an income tax increase.

In 1989, it turned out to be the Speaker who surprised the world. After adamantly blocking a tax increase for two years, Madigan himself proposed a state income tax increase on the morning of May 17. Maybe Daley had talked to Madigan about the revenue needs for the city of Chicago. Under Madigan's plan, the personal rate would increase from 2.5 percent to 2.96 percent and the corporate rate from 4 percent to 4.736 percent. I don't know how he came up with those kinds of percentages, but he did. Press reports indicated that Madigan did not want the money to go to state government but to local governments and schools. "I don't trust the Thompson administration," Madigan said. "I've had too much experience with them in terms of misrepresentations, inadequacies and inefficiencies."[8] Thompson and other Republicans did not immediately support Madigan's plan because it did not include property tax relief and additional funding for state-supported human services. Thompson also didn't like the fact that Madigan proposed a two-year "surcharge," not a permanent tax increase.

Even though this was a different plan from the one Thompson had proposed over the past two years, I got behind it. I decided to try to push it through the Senate, where I sponsored Madigan's bill. I got it through the Senate Revenue Committee on May 30, but I was never sure I had thirty votes in the Senate itself. When the bill got to the Senate floor at the amendment stage, the Republicans attempted six different amendments—all intended, in my view, to kill the bill entirely. Instead, I managed to kill off all amendments, and then I let the bill sit until June 23, which was the last day the Senate could have considered this bill at this stage in the process. I was confident. I was telling my members privately and saying publicly that I thought this was the best tax increase bill we could get. Unfortunately, we had only twenty-one aye votes when the bill was called; I needed nine more. I used a procedural move called a "postponed consideration" and talked to my members while Madigan dealt with my black caucus. We voted again and this time got six more votes, but with twenty-seven, we still fell short of passing it. I took this defeat a little harder than most because this was my third year pushing for an income tax increase, and I couldn't get it done in my chamber.

Thompson and Philip started cooking up a new scheme with only a few days left in the session, but Madigan and I came up with a new plan ourselves just one day before the scheduled adjournment day, which was, again, June 30. We did not have legislative leader summits this year with the governor. Instead, Thompson and I played the role of shuttle diplomats going back and forth among the leaders. In our new plan, Madigan and I included some property tax relief so that homeowners could deduct more on their state income tax returns. The absence of such relief seemed to be a big reason the tax bill had failed earlier. We also reduced the amount that local governments would get as a result of the new tax break and changed the percentages so that the temporary income tax surcharge would go to 3 percent for individuals and 4.8 percent for businesses.[9] The Republicans offered no alternative, which was quite different from the 1983 tax increase scenario when Lee Daniels had come up with a last-minute plan for a temporary tax hike. This year, with Madigan's strong support, the House passed our new plan first, with six Republicans voting affirmatively along with most of the Democrats, who were following their leader. It came to the Senate, where we knew it would be tested. I did not want to lose again. The critics complained that a temporary two-year increase was only a Band-Aid, that we weren't offering "real" property tax relief, and that a lot of the revenue was going to municipalities, not state programs. I urged my colleagues to vote for it because we didn't get this close very often. I did indeed get two more Democratic votes than I got when the earlier bill failed, because Democrats Thomas Dunn of Joliet and Richard Kelly of Hazel Crest were with me this time. We also got one Republican vote, from Ralph Dunn of DuQuoin. That meant thirty votes, just enough to win. But Thompson didn't sign off until we also gave him additional revenue with a six-cent increase in the gasoline tax and a ten-cent increase in the cigarette tax. Often, a major tax increase becomes a "package" of tax increases, which is what happened. I still preferred a permanent increase for all state services, but at least we got some money for elementary and secondary schools and higher education.

Thompson signed the bill, which immediately set the stage for a very big issue in the governor's race the next year: whether to extend the surcharge beyond two years. We were indeed already looking ahead to the 1990 statewide elections. We didn't know if Thompson would seek a fifth term and, if he didn't, how that would shake up the lineup of statewide candidates. Netsch was thinking about running for attorney general because everybody knew the incumbent Democrat, Neil Hartigan, would be taking a shot at governor. I thought Netsch belonged on the statewide ticket. We had had our differences, but she was very bright and a hard worker, and we Democrats had not elevated any women to statewide office. However, comptroller Roland Burris was also making a push to run for attorney general, so I encouraged Netsch not to run against Burris but instead to run for comptroller. I told her I would support her. State party chairman Vince Demuzio joined me in approaching Netsch to run for comptroller, not attorney general. We didn't want fights within the party, and we were able to avoid them.

What I didn't know that October, as we prepared for the candidates' filing period in December, is what would happen to me the following month. At the urging of my daughter Meghan, I went to my doctor for a checkup not long before Thanksgiving. He decided to do a stress test. The results concerned him, and he put me in an ambulance that took me to Loyola University Medical Center in Maywood. My doctor looked at my angiogram and said that I had blockage in two arteries; I needed double-bypass heart surgery to correct the problem, which was the normal procedure in those days. I had the heart surgery the day before Thanksgiving, on November 22, and the doctor was very pleased with the outcome. Then I spent a week or so in the hospital before heading home to recuperate. The wedding of my daughter Kathleen was only a month away, set for December 30. I realize now I might have died at the age of fifty-two if my doctor had not discovered the problem during the checkup, but thankfully, he did.

I had been a smoker, so every time I saw my doctor after the surgery, he would ask me, "Are you smoking?" I quit, but I also went through the same trials that many other people encounter when they try to quit. It wasn't easy. The gum didn't work for me. I was hypnotized at least twice, but I went back to smoking a little, and so I got to be on a first-name basis with my hypnotist. I think hypnosis was the tool that finally worked for me. Eventually, I did quit. I honestly can't remember exactly when that happened, but I do recall that by the time my first grandchild arrived home about eighteen months later, I had quit for good.

I recuperated during December. The really good news was that I was healthy enough not only to attend but to enjoy and celebrate Kathleen's wedding. She had gone to Boston College, and so had her husband, Steve Snow, who was from Connecticut. So aside from all the Oak Park and River Forest High School friends whom Kathleen had invited, we had many guests from Boston and other places out east. I had a great time at the wedding, and then the next day, we wound up having a big New Year's Eve party at our house. Friends and wedding guests just kept coming in. I was standing in the door watching all these people, and one of the guests told me there was some Irish story about the blessing of getting married on December 30. I had never heard that one, but having such a festive celebration was indeed a great way to end the year.

21. Riverboats and Governor Edgar

*I wasn't particularly enthused about riverboat
gambling, but one of my members really wanted
it, and so I believed that I had to support it.*

I FELT GOOD AS WE ROLLED INTO 1990, when the biggest news would
be about all the statewide elections.

An issue that became urgent for a few of my members resulted from
action in Iowa just across the Mississippi River from Rock Island and
Moline, Illinois. The news came out in 1989 that Davenport, Iowa, was
going to launch a casino riverboat in 1991. Senator Denny Jacobs of East
Moline told us how terrible that would be for the Illinois side of the Quad
Cities. He said the Iowa boat was going to eat up all the money up and
down the river, and Illinoisans would go across the river and spend their
money in Iowa. Jacobs wanted to make his Illinois communities competitive. In the House, Representative E. J. "Zeke" Giorgi, a Democrat from
Rockford and known as the "father of the state lottery," was also pushing
for riverboat casinos in Illinois. Jacobs's first attempt at passing riverboat
gambling had not been successful in 1989, so that summer, he conducted
some hearings about the issue. That's another strategy commonly used:
if at first you don't succeed, raise awareness of your cause with public
hearings sanctioned by the legislature.

I did not have strong feelings about riverboat gambling, but I was not
particularly enthused about it. However, it was in fact a Democratic initiative that was urgently wanted by one of my members, for good reason,
and as the Democratic leader of the Senate, I didn't believe I could be
against it, even if I was so disposed. It was just too important to some
of my members and to some of the House Democrats, too. Giorgi really
wanted it. Jacobs was passionate, saying things like, "Our bill could make
the Quad Cities one of the tourism capitals of the world."[1]

Giorgi and Jacobs understood what not too many people in the general public understand: that there are three critical times to try to pass a major initiative. The first is in the spring of every year, usually near adjournment of the session. The second is during the "veto session" in October or November. The General Assembly returns for two or three weeks with the assumption that it will consider vetoes sent to members by the governor over the summer. But frankly, the veto session is a time to slip something in or deal with something postponed in the spring. The third and final time is in early January, when legislators always come back for a few days to wrap up the work of the previous year.

Riverboat gambling proponents couldn't get a bill passed in the spring or fall of 1989, so they were ready with the Riverboat Gambling Act when we returned to Springfield after the new year in 1990. Republicans, with the exception of Governor Thompson, were lining up against it, many of them on moral grounds. Speaker Madigan wasn't too thrilled about it, either, but said he would support it as an economic development plan.[2] Madigan also reminded Republican legislators that their Republican governor believed the boats were good for the northwestern region of Illinois (namely, Galena), the East St. Louis area, and maybe Peoria or even Beardstown, which is a really small Illinois River town. The initial riverboat gambling bill said four licenses could be issued on the Mississippi River and one on the Illinois River by January 1, 1991, which would beat Iowa by three or four months. The bill also said the new Illinois Gaming Board could issue another five licenses on any navigable stream outside of Cook County after March 1992.

I was disappointed that both Mayor Daley and Cook County chairman George Dunne told us to take Chicago and Cook County out of the sweepstakes for a license. I said to them, "We ought to leave it in, even if we don't use it, because someday, some years from now, future leaders will want gambling in Cook County. It will cost them an arm and a leg to get it twenty years from now, if they get it at all. Right now you can have it for nothing. Just tag on to what the people in the Quad Cities and Joliet want." But I never really got an answer from them. I asked them individually, and they simply said no. There wasn't much discussion at all. So the bill excluded counties with more than 3 million in population—Cook being the only one—from getting one of these licenses. Meanwhile, a number of senators were concocting all kinds of plans for riverboats. At one point, they were talking about giving licensees two riverboats each. Then somebody would say, "If you get two boats, I want four," and I would have to say no and keep everybody in line. On January 11, 1990, the House passed the bill with no Republican votes at all. In the Senate, Jacobs and I rounded up a few Republican votes because a couple of our members, as usual, were missing in action. (This time it was John D'Arco and Ethel Alexander, not the usual suspects.) We passed it by a 31–22 margin in the Senate, getting one more vote than we needed.

We had very little debate that day. Only Jacobs spoke up. He pointed out that 75 percent of the new state revenue from riverboat gambling would go to education and the other 25 percent would be for local governments. To say the money would go for education sounded good to everybody, but frankly, everyone knew what would really happen. Legislators had made the same argument when we created the state lottery during the Walker years in the 1970s, that the money generated by the lottery would go to education. In addition to the zealous types always opposed to any sort of gambling or drinking, we had a division at that time according to region. Some regions wanted the lottery and others didn't, but Walker won with the argument that it would provide a terrific influx of money for the state's school system. That argument is still going on. But here's what happened: say the lottery generated $600 million in new revenue. Instead of that money being added on top of the pie for schools, the budget makers took $600 million away from the general revenue education pile and gave it to something else, so funding came out virtually a net draw for education. It didn't matter that the law said the money was going to be used for the common school fund. It was, I suppose, but other money was taken away. The big pitch in the 1970s was that the lottery was going to solve the problem of funding the school system, but it didn't. Had it been a real addition, it would have been some serious new revenue for the schools. Everybody played around with that fiction. Now, in 1990, it was the same with the projected riverboat revenue. But the story helped us get riverboat gambling in Illinois, Thompson played it up, and some of our members were satisfied that we could compete with Iowa and generate some tourism and revenue for cities around the state.

Besides that issue, almost all the big news in 1990 was election-related, starting with those who were lining up to compete in the March primary. Thompson began a statewide shakeup by announcing that he would not run for a fifth term as governor. He had served in that position since 1977 and was active nationally in the Republican Party. I talked to him once in a while about his national ambitions. He thought he had a lock on, or at least was close to, the vice presidential nomination in 1988 when Vice President George H. W. Bush became the Republican nominee for president, running against Michael Dukakis. For whatever reason, the Republicans decided Thompson wasn't their guy. Bush picked Dan Quayle, the young U.S. senator from Indiana. There was no comparison between Quayle and Thompson. In my view, Quayle was a little short in a lot of departments. So since it didn't work out for Thompson to become the national candidate, I think he started to consider going out and making some serious money, which he has done at the Chicago law firm of Winston & Strawn.

Thompson revved up his delivery when we went to the House chamber for his final State of the State address early in the 1990 session. He still had a year to go, but it was a farewell address of sorts. I had literally stood behind him eleven times and listened to him give this speech every year since 1979—except for 1981, when he had tried to take over the Senate and we boycotted his big speech. He spoke for seventy-four minutes, giving a great performance and talking about his accomplishments in his four terms as governor.[3] He had modest goals for the session, and he gave a nod more than once to the two people in the front row who might succeed him: Secretary of State Jim Edgar and Attorney General Neil Hartigan, who would indeed become the 1990 Republican and Democratic nominees, respectively. Seventy-four minutes is long for a State of the State speech, but I was among those who thought he deserved to take that kind of bow after serving so long and, in my opinion, so effectively. He was not afraid to govern. He took some chances—three times calling for an income tax increase, for instance. He also floated the idea of expanding the sales tax to include services, but that one never passed. Also, in my judgment, he had the best interests of the city of Chicago and its people uppermost in his thinking, understanding the state's impact on the city's culture and economy. He was behind us when we went after funding for the second and third expansions of McCormick Place, even though he knew that citizens didn't care about that in Peoria and that downstate would complain about money going to Chicago. He stood up to that criticism and pushed for what he thought was right. Thompson knew that Chicago was being pushed out of the convention business by cities that were building bigger convention halls and therefore understood that Chicago needed one; indeed, McCormick Place has done wonders for the city over the years.

Thompson's last year wasn't particularly memorable in the legislature—not because of anything bad but just because we didn't do a whole lot—and everyone was focused on the elections. Although Thompson said in his speech there would be no "Build Illinois" type of initiative, we did spend some time grappling with the possibility of a $1.4 billion expansion for McCormick Place and a new domed stadium for the Chicago Bears, combining both projects. Then someone got the idea to spend $70 million on new marinas all over Illinois, and the downstaters started pushing their own projects with or without "McDome" for Chicago. In fact, the Senate passed a bill for the downstate projects, but without any Chicago projects, Speaker Madigan never called it in the House. It was a lot of show without many results. Thompson was a lame duck and Mayor Daley stayed neutral on McDome; without their clout, the McCormick Place expansion and new dome for the Bears weren't going to get approved, and they didn't.

The big news, anyway, was about the elections. We all figured, correctly, that Hartigan would be the Democratic candidate for governor. As I explained earlier, we lined up Roland Burris to run for attorney general and Dawn Clark Netsch to run for comptroller.

I supported Hartigan for governor, but it proved to be another Republican year at the top, with Jim Edgar winning his first term as governor after being a highly visible and popular secretary of state. That election was especially interesting because many pundits and reporters were saying that Democrat Hartigan was talking like a Republican while Republican Edgar was talking like a Democrat. That was true to a certain extent. Edgar came out early and said he wanted to make the income tax surcharge permanent—in other words, keep the income tax at 3 percent for individuals instead of going back to 2.5 percent. Meanwhile, Hartigan blasted Edgar for wanting higher taxes, saying it would be better to cut state spending by 2 percent. That is usually what the Republicans say.

In any event, the Democrats won three of the statewide positions— Burris as attorney general, Netsch as comptroller, and Pat Quinn as treasurer. Jerry Cosentino, state treasurer, was bounced out of statewide office when he ran for secretary of state but lost to George Ryan. What's unusual is that no incumbent constitutional officer won reelection—

Table 5

New Illinois constitutional officers elected in 1990 (and party designation)

Office	Winning candidate	Losing candidate	Departing incumbent (won in 1986)
Governor	Jim Edgar (R)	Neil Hartigan (D)	James R. Thompson (R)
Lt. governor	Bob Kustra (R)	Jim Burns (D)	George Ryan (R)
Attorney general	Roland Burris (D)	Jim Ryan (R)	Neil Hartigan (D)
Secretary of state	George Ryan (R)	Jerry Cosentino (D)	Jim Edgar (R)
Comptroller	Dawn Clark Netsch (D)	Sue Suter (R)	Roland Burris (D)
Treasurer	Patrick Quinn (D)	Greg Baise (R)	Jerry Cosentino (D)

Notes: Winning candidates were sworn in on Monday, January 14, 1991. D = Democrat, R = Republican.

because none was running for reelection. There was a complete turnover in the six offices, with three Democrats and three Republicans taking over.

When the Senate met to organize on the second Wednesday of January in 1991, Thompson still had five days left in office, and he presided at our ceremony because by law the governor always does. My election to a record seventh term as Senate president by the Democratic members of the Senate went without a hitch. We Democrats still held our 31–28 margin in the Senate after the 1990 elections, and I won all thirty-one Democratic votes on the first ballot. My friends and family were there; Father John Smyth from Maryville Academy delivered the opening prayer. I publicly noted that twenty years earlier, when I first was sworn in as a senator, my four children ranged in ages from one to five, and there they were, all young adults, between the ages of twenty-one and twenty-five. Supreme Court justice William Clark, my first boss in the late 1960s when he was attorney general, was there to swear me in. Netsch, who would become state comptroller the following Monday, ceremoniously nominated me for the Senate presidency. She acknowledged from the floor that we had had our differences, but I certainly appreciated it when she said I had a "reverence for the process of self-government, which means in this case the legislative process."[4] I felt some nostalgia when Thompson called me a leader with "guts, smarts, savvy, knowing when to hold them and when to fold them, compassion and caring, and more ears than two, because that's what the job takes."[5] Then, after my friend Justice Clark administered the oath of office to me, I did some reminiscing myself. I guess I had an inkling that this would be my final time, although I had not decided firmly and certainly had made no announcement. I talked with a sense of history about our economic development programs, tax incentives, and job training, but mostly I talked about children:

> We have made the children of Illinois our important constituency, trying, as best we can, to protect them from harm, with child abuse and neglect laws, the I-SEARCH program, foster care and adoption, day care, youth services, infant mortality, and the list goes on and on and on, and clearly, in my judgment, the Senate has been the initiator and the leader in this effort. And it is the state Senate which has made the intellectual development of our children and young adults of this state our present and future commitment.
>
> Education reform, a competitive higher university system, alternative education—all have been, if you reflect upon it—all have been products of this chamber. . . .

For the last fourteen years Jim Thompson and I, I think, have accomplished a great deal for the people of this state, and I am truly,
really proud to call him my friend. Thank you, Jim. . . .

I am truly humbled by all that we have accomplished together on
behalf of those we serve. Our experience literally is an arch, upon which
to build a better future. We have erected the arch, and with God's help
and guidance, we will continue to build an Illinois that is free of hunger
and disease and discrimination and helplessness.[6]

The same day, over in the House, Madigan was being elected to his
fifth term. Of course, he has gone on to have many, many more. Once
the ceremonies were over, we faced a heavy agenda in the spring: more
education reform, legislative and congressional redistricting, and health
care accessibility, among other issues. But the nation and Illinois were
in another recession, a bit milder this time, and Edgar indicated that he
would deal firmly with a $300 million budget shortfall. Our new comp-
troller, Dawn Clark Netsch, said it was worse than that. She reported
that "at least thirty states are in fiscal crisis, Illinois among them. . . .
[A]s the state's chief fiscal officer, I have been forced to assume the role
of a traveling Grinch as I travel across the state, warning that the state
is nearly one billion dollars in debt."[7] While Edgar was calling for layoffs
of 1,400 state workers, Netsch said massive layoffs by states generally
provide only short-term answers, and she also bemoaned states making
unacceptable cuts in human services.[8] So there we were again, right after
another gubernatorial election, and we were hearing how bad the state's
budget was. Edgar set the tone for his administration in his first budget
address to the General Assembly in March by saying it was time "to tear
up our credit cards and put a screeching halt to the spending spree in
state government."[9]

Many other Democrats and I thought Edgar was going too far and
threatening services truly needed by the poor and others unable to fend
for themselves. I went on WBBM radio's *At Issue* program in Chicago and
said we would not support Edgar's budget. It wasn't unusual for reporters
with microphones from WBBM or WMAQ to catch me in the hall in the
Capitol or to ask me to sit down for a few minutes and record something
that would be played over the weekend. I tried to accommodate those
reporters, but it wasn't as organized or as formalized as you might think.
It wasn't like getting ready for a national Sunday morning television news
program. People in Chicago on Saturday or Sunday might have thought I
was at the station, but it was all recorded rather quickly before I headed
out of Springfield.

It wasn't long before all sides were comparing that year's rhetoric with what had happened under fourteen years of Thompson. Netsch talked about fourteen years of "smoke and mirrors budgets" under Thompson—which I didn't agree with, but you get the point. While Edgar did not directly blame his fellow Republican predecessor, the new governor did refer to a "spending binge" that had allowed old bills to pile up. I countered that Edgar's budget was the first time I had seen a "truly Republican budget" in years.[10] I was concerned that under Edgar, citizens who could not take care of themselves would no longer be taken care of by the state. The administration was talking about cutting human services and education—two issues that I supported for my entire career. I proposed borrowing $300 million for one year to tide us over, but Edgar said borrowing was not an option. He meant what he said about tearing up credit cards.

That public standoff stayed tense even behind the scenes as we neared the scheduled adjournment date, June 30. There was not a lot of interaction between the governor, the Speaker, and me. In style, Edgar was like a hands-on micromanager. That was his background—serving on the Senate Republican staff before he entered the legislature and became secretary of state—and he didn't let go of details easily. As a downstater from Charleston, he also didn't like to come to grips with political problems in Chicago and didn't want to address the city's problems head on. He wasn't quite sure of himself when he started talking about the needs of the city of Chicago, so he was almost nonchalant about Chicago's problems and how we were going to deal with them. He recognized from his staff background, though, that there had to be communication with us leaders. So there was some communication with us, but not as much as we had had with Thompson.

One special personal moment occurred the night we were supposed to adjourn. I was presiding at the podium, taking care of business, when Nancy Fritzsche, my secretary, interrupted and said, "Your wife is on the phone, and it's very important."

"Nancy," I said, "you know my rule. I don't get off this podium."

It was just before midnight. In those days, we still went through the fiction of legally stopping the clock just before midnight so that bills could be passed on June 30. If we waited until July 1, we had different rules and it wasn't so easy. So we declared that it wasn't midnight yet; it was a routine way of finishing up business. I had to be there when we stopped the clock, to deal with the usual objections from the floor, especially from Republicans, about the actual time being past midnight. I would simply rule them out of order, and my ruling would stand. Then we would proceed with business on "June 30."

It was that close to midnight, and Nancy said the magic words: "Well, you have a new grandchild. I wasn't going to tell you; I was going to let Sheila tell you." So I ran off the podium and went to the phone, and I said, "Sheila, if you can hold on for about two minutes, I'll get right back to you, but I have to get back to the podium now." Then I returned to the Senate chamber and stopped the clock. Things were rolling right along, and I was able to leave again to call home. I found out all of the vital information about my first grandchild, Emily Snow, who was born June 30. What a thrill that was!

I came to believe that all of Edgar's public laments about the budget had been totally premeditated. He was planning all along to work the General Assembly against itself by going into overtime, into July. Nobody wanted to stay overtime. Starting at the end of June, he tried to frame the big question in terms of the budget. He said the budget wasn't to his liking, and we the General Assembly had done a lousy job, and we would stay until it was done right. The facts were otherwise. The budget was in pretty good shape, and we had taken full responsibility for it.

He wanted to keep us overtime so that he could coerce the assembly into enacting property tax caps for counties and municipalities and other local units of government. In doing so, he wanted to go against the towns and villages and park districts—everybody who levied property taxes—and limit them to a 5 percent increase. His theory was that homeowners were tired of seeing their real estate taxes go up and up, and he was going to lower them, or at least limit the rate of increases, irrespective of what school districts, park districts, or library districts wanted. Edgar was going to try to put caps on those autonomous units of local government. He had called for capping property taxes during his State of the State speech in February and had called a special session to deal with it, asking that we approve the tax caps by the end of March. But we didn't do it. It's something he really wanted, and we were at the end of the regular session, and he still didn't have it.

As an aside, I will say that I made my final attempt during this session to move Illinois's primary date from March to the second Tuesday in September. I still felt that the state's political season was too long, and I said so. I thought voters might get more interested in the electoral process if we shortened the campaign season considerably. I got it through the Senate easily by a 52–4 vote, but it got stuck in the House, where Madigan, Republican minority leader Lee Daniels, and our party's state chairman, Gary LaPaille, all had various reasons for not wanting to subject their members to a September primary election. So the idea died once again— one of those good ideas I could never get enacted.

Something else at stake was the continuation of the half-percent surcharge on the state income tax. Edgar supported it, I supported it, and so did
many others. We wanted to make permanent the 1989 temporary income
tax increase because the state and municipalities needed the revenue. It was
that simple. Edgar wanted to make it permanent, but Madigan was talking
about just a two-year extension. Edgar rejected that idea because he wanted
to deal with the surcharge only once, not every two years. He especially did
not want it to be an issue when he would be up for reelection.[11]

We went into overtime without an agreement, and I was really upset
with Edgar. I took to the Senate floor and reminded members that the
surcharge had expired the previous night as of midnight. I was concerned
about holding up $2 million in checks for people around the state most
in need of assistance. I blamed Edgar because he did not present us with
any real alternative plan for the state's budget. "We convened [today]," I
said, "but [Edgar's] plan is not here. . . . Now that he has gotten his way,
it's time for him to produce a plan. I just left his office, where there is
no plan." We offered an alternative plan that included some borrowing,
but the governor said no. He also said no to a one-month budget to keep
the state operating. "We offered many alternatives, but they have not
moved off the dime because their plan was to have us here this summer,"
I continued. "The government has ground to a halt at his request." What
happened was that the Republicans were insisting on property tax caps
in exchange for continuing the surcharge. As a compromise, I joined
Madigan in suggesting a two-year extension of the surcharge instead of
making it permanent, but Edgar and the Republicans said no to that, too.
There was a lot of back-and-forth, but the main thing was the Republicans
wanted those tax caps, especially for the suburbs. Homeowners probably
wanted the caps, but the units of government would be severely limited
by a 5 percent increase, such as the school districts, wanted nothing to
do with state-imposed caps.

In mid-July, everyone knew that Edgar's plan for overtime was not
the budget but property tax caps. We finally struck an agreement and
passed it just after midnight on July 19—a record nineteen days into
overtime. I was not a happy camper in those three weeks, and neither
were my members. In addition, I was not pleased by the outcome. The
new budget included $1 billion in program cuts, including a big whack at
the Department of Public Aid. Welfare cuts meant that we were hurting
thousands of poor people in Illinois. Ultimately, I voted for it but told
the press that the agreement "is not that happy an event. It inflicts some
severe cuts. . . . But I think it's fair to say it is a realistic attempt to deal

with a bad situation."[12] We made permanent the portion of the income tax increase designated for public schools but phased out the portion of the surcharge intended for local governments. It was all a compromise, and it became the first permanent increase in the income tax since we had enacted it in 1969.

Meanwhile, the Republicans won tax caps, sort of. They didn't get state-wide caps, and they didn't get them for Cook County, either. We wouldn't allow that. What they did get were annual increases in real estate taxes limited to 5 percent or the rate of inflation, whichever is less, in the five collar counties of DuPage, Kane, Lake, McHenry, and Will. A major reason we excluded Cook County was to help the Chicago school system; we didn't want to put a noose around it. In later years, of course, the concept of tax caps expanded to other counties. But not long after we passed those first property tax caps, local districts across the state—schools, libraries, parks, mosquito abatement, you name it—were all starting to say, "Take off these caps. We can't live with these caps, and you in Springfield ought not be telling us what to do." I agreed with that. I did not think it was the Republicans' finest hour when they insisted on those caps.

We had an agreement and we had a budget, but we weren't quite finished. I got a call from the governor as the final bills were being printed and prepared for a vote; he told me we still had a problem. I asked him what it was. His staff had discovered that we had appropriated $400,000 more than we had budgeted to spend. That concerned Edgar a great deal, and he told me we couldn't have a budget that is out of balance. I listened to him, and I reminded him that we were dealing with a $28.9 billion budget. To be off by $400,000 wasn't too bad; nor was it unusual. I listened for a while and had a brief response: "Governor, chill out," I told him, adding that we weren't going to make any more changes. Edgar doesn't mind telling this story on himself, and he called it some of the best advice he ever received.[13]

A social change occurred after the exhausted General Assembly adjourned for the summer. Not everyone wanted to attend the traditional after-session party at the Governor's Mansion, just three or four short blocks from the Capitol. Thompson always had thrown such a party, and it was a great deal of fun. But Edgar changed things and decided not to serve alcohol at any functions at the mansion, and that was his prerogative. If you wanted soda or apple cider, it was fine to go there or drop by. But this year, LaPaille, who was Madigan's chief of staff as well as our party chairman, had a beer truck in his driveway and a very large bipartisan crowd in his backyard.[14] That's where lawmakers wound down well into the night.

22. The Final Year

Although I was not seeking reelection in
1992, I remained committed to the belief that
public service is the highest of callings.

A LONG WITH DEALING WITH A NEW GOVERNOR IN 1991, we faced a worsening economy. As a result, the state was falling short of projected revenues. We had to be creative to make up the budget deficit since our normal reliance on natural revenue growth from income taxes and sales taxes, our largest sources of revenue, was in jeopardy. Illinois was losing jobs in addition to losing revenue. The Illinois Economic and Fiscal Commission reported a loss of 238,000 Illinois jobs, seasonally adjusted, from early 1990 to late 1991.[1] The commission also said that Illinois would lag behind the nation in recovering from the recession. In short, all the economic news seemed bad, and the state's reduction of services and funding for poor people bothered me a lot.

Then came another blow on September 5, 1991: Secretary of State George Ryan pulled the name of Al Jourdan out of a crystal bowl. Jourdan was the Republican Party's state chairman. The name of a Democrat was also in the bowl, but it no longer mattered. It was a redistricting year, and we went through the whole routine that had been so favorable to the Democrats in 1981. When Jourdan's name was drawn, the map victory went to the Republicans in 1991. They would create new districts that would be effective for the elections of 1992. Everybody would have to run for election or reelection in all 118 House districts and all fifty-nine Senate districts, including my new one.

That presented two problems for me. In the new district maps, the Republicans gave parts of Oak Park to three Senate districts and four House districts. Obviously, that could be confusing to voters. I had represented the Eighth District, but the new Fourth Senate District in which I lived included precincts that had been part of Senator Earlean Collins's district. My second problem was that the new maps gave Republicans a good chance of taking majority control of the Illinois Senate after the 1992 elections. We had been in the majority since 1975. I knew I would not like being in the minority after serving as the Senate president for fourteen years, and that was assuming I would get reelected in whatever district I found myself.

I wasn't sure what I was going to do, but the map became a major factor in helping me decide. After twenty years, I had this feeling that we were no longer making the kind of progress that I wanted to make in the General Assembly. The economy and the budget were in trouble again, and funding for the poor and disadvantaged was in danger under Governor Edgar. I determined I had had enough and rather quietly decided that I would not run for reelection. It was time to let somebody else try.

That did not mean I was finished with politics, though. It was interesting how my career was on some path that paralleled the career of William Clark, my first boss when he had been the attorney general. Clark had become an Illinois Supreme Court justice in 1976 and announced in December 1991 that he was stepping down. I knew ahead of time that his announcement was coming. In Illinois, we elect the seven supreme court justices. Three are in the First District, which is just Cook County. The other four are in districts covering the rest of the state. With Clark and me being from Cook County, I thought it was my turn to try for one of those seats. My name had come up previously for the supreme court. So after Clark's announcement, my name was floating around before I even put it out there. I received a great deal of support from the legal community and labor leaders and started putting together a strategy to get the campaign documents filed. Then, sitting at my kitchen table one December evening with all the paperwork in front of me, Sheila and I talked it over, and I finally just said: "What am I doing? I'm not doing this." That is how and where I decided not to run for the supreme court or any other office in 1992. I never filed the paperwork. Instead, on December 12, 1991, I issued a statement that, frankly, surprised a lot of friends:

> Yesterday, as I was in the midst of planning all that would need to be done to make this announcement, I stopped to reflect on what I again would be asking of my wife Sheila and my family and friends.
>
> I began to reflect on the fact that my family, my business partners and my friends have been giving of their time, energy and their love in my election campaigns for nearly 22 years. . . .
>
> I came to the decision yesterday that I would not seek the Democratic Party's nomination for the Supreme Court, nor will I seek reelection

to the Illinois State Senate. The time has come for me to give back to my family and friends some of the time and attention they have so selflessly given to me for over 20 years. . . .

I look forward to spending more time with my family, our new granddaughter, and my law partners and friends. And while I am not seeking reelection in 1992, I remain committed to the belief that public service is the highest of callings.[2]

Quite a few Democrats, including Mary Ann McMorrow, entered the supreme court primary in my absence, because in all likelihood, the winner of the Democratic primary would win the Cook County seat in November. McMorrow did indeed win the primary and went on to become the first woman elected to the Illinois Supreme Court.

I had one more year to go in the Senate, one more year as Senate president. I had no intention of sitting back and doing nothing, and I let the rest of the world surmise about who would take my place and what would happen after my departure.

The two issues that drove everything in our 1992 legislative session were the bad economy and the upcoming November elections. Edgar was still in budget-cutting mode, but we had to put money back into the Department of Children and Family Services because of a lawsuit in the federal courts.[3] Edgar wanted to increase the liquor tax and impose a new tax on tobacco products to raise $182 million to close the budget gap, but Speaker Madigan and the rest of the General Assembly would have nothing to do with those tax increases.

For reasons of his own, Madigan led the way in 1992 to try to cut state services and lay off state workers. He released a figure of $372 million in budget cuts, and he and Edgar really went after one another in the press all during the month of June. I wasn't supporting Madigan's spending cuts, so we were in a deadlock. Edgar, the other leaders, and I finally persuaded Madigan to go along with reducing his proposed level of cuts. We restored $210 million and spread that money around to various state agencies, such as the Department of Corrections, DCFS, and the Department of Mental Health and Disabilities. There was the usual haggling over the details, but we got the budget done and got out of town.

It was a big election year, and everyone was in a hurry to get home. With the new maps shifting power to the suburbs, I wasn't optimistic about our chances of maintaining control of the Illinois Senate. We tried to sound upbeat, but when Election Day rolled around in November, the Senate Democrats did indeed lose our majority: we went from thirty-one Democratic members to twenty-seven, giving the Republicans a 32–27 majority starting in 1993. Two of my incumbents, Ted Leverenz of Maywood and Joyce Holmberg of Rockford, lost their bids for reelection, primarily due to newly drawn districts. That set up James "Pate" Philip, the Republican chairman in DuPage County, to replace me as Senate president in January 1993. Madigan, meanwhile, lost a total of five seats and dropped to sixty-seven members, still enough, though, to keep his position as Speaker. Earlean Collins won the Senate's new Fourth District Seat, and James DeLeo, who had been in the Illinois House, became the new state senator from the new Tenth District, which included a portion of Oak Park. After a lot of speculation about who would replace me as the leader of the Senate Democrats, the new group of twenty-seven selected Emil Jones of Chicago as the Senate minority leader. He held that position for ten years before becoming the Senate president himself in 2003. The Illinois Senate would have a total of twenty-two new members in January 1993—more than one-third of the members.

I spent 1992 wrapping up my Springfield career. One thing that happens when a top official leaves is that his or her senior staff members have to find other things to do. I had many wonderful and loyal staff members. Judy Erwin, for instance, my longtime press secretary, won a seat as a Chicago Democrat in the Illinois House of Representatives in 1992 and had a stellar career as a legislator for ten years. Later, she became the executive director of the Illinois Board of Higher Education. Bill Holland, my chief of staff, was named the Illinois auditor general in 1992 and then was reappointed to a second ten-year term in 2002. The auditor general has a vital independent role in auditing state agencies in a comprehensive way, analyzing whether agencies are in compliance with state laws and tracking how agencies are spending taxpayers' money. It's an important role, and Bill has done a great job. Another brilliant staff member was Paul Vallas, a really bright and remarkable leader. He became an innovative CEO of the Chicago public schools, later went to Philadelphia to run that city's public school system, and then took an even more challenging job: he went to New Orleans after Hurricane Katrina to literally rebuild a school system called the New Orleans Recovery School District. Vallas also ran in the Democratic primary for governor in 2002. I supported his candidacy and certainly was sorry that he lost to Rod Blagojevich. My last chief of staff, Linda Kingman, left government shortly after I did in 1993 and went on to an outstanding career in communications and public relations. Since leaving the Senate, she has worked for two large public relations firms, counseling clients in public affairs, crisis management, and employee communications. She also spent seven years as vice president of corporate communications for Kemper Insurance Companies, where she led the company's external and internal communications efforts. I think I worked with more than three hundred staff members during my Senate career. I stay in touch with quite a few of them. I'm proud of their careers, many of them in public service.

A few of them were regulars over the years at barbecues and other informal gatherings at my white frame house, located at 222 West Cook Street, just a little southwest of the Capitol, on the corner of Cook and College Streets. We had a lot of fun there. For one thing, it was only two blocks from the Stratton Building, the Capitol, and the parking lots. It was also just a block south of the former Boone's Saloon, a very popular spot. On many spring days, when our day's work was over, we would have a barbecue and beer in the backyard with legislators, lobbyists, and journalists, all of whom were welcome in what the *Chicago Tribune* called "a decompression zone for Springfield's itinerant band of lawmakers."[4]

For a while, Governor Thompson would have an annual dinner for the press corps and the union leaders at the Governor's Mansion, so I decided to host a big dinner, too, at our house. I brought in Charlie Robinson, who became famous because of Chicago journalist Mike Royko. The witty columnist, also known for his love of sixteen-inch softball games, once boasted that he himself made the best barbecued ribs. He invited others to compete at the Mike Royko Ribfest in 1982. Charlie Robinson entered and won the contest, earning a lot of attention for it.[5] Charlie also happened to be a precinct captain, and his main restaurant, Robinson's No. 1 Ribs, is in Oak Park, just a few blocks from where I had my district office. I called Charlie and had him bring his whole apparatus down—the big grill, the truck, everything—for the dinner at my Springfield house. I invited a lot of people, including Thompson. "I didn't get invited to your party; well, you're invited to mine," I told him. A lot of the press corps used this opportunity to have their picture taken with the governor, which is something they don't do while on duty in the Capitol. It would violate protocol there.

Charlie came down two or three times for these big dinners. I also had smaller barbecues in the backyard many other times. Sometimes a committee hearing in the Capitol would be running a little long, and I would just tell the members to wrap things up and go down to the house and have a burger and beer. It would not be a legal continuation of the committee meeting, but I would talk to committee members and ask them questions. At the end of the cookout, I knew how they were going to vote. It was a good way for me to talk with my members and to influence their positions on issues—kind of clever as well as relaxing, I thought.

I had bought the house as an investment. I owned it jointly with Jerry Mayberry, an old-timer from the attorney general's office, who was from southern Illinois. Jerry and his wife lived there, and I had a room upstairs. We also rented to other people. George Sangmeister was in there for a while before he went to Congress. After Mayberry passed away and I was getting ready to leave the Senate, the timing seemed right to sell the place. The Illinois Federation of Teachers offered to purchase the building, since they knew I was leaving. I told them to get a legitimate appraisal from somebody in Springfield. "You're not going to spend a million dollars for this building or any other figure that's too high," I told them. "This is not a political deal, nor should it be perceived as one. Get the appraisal, and then I won't quibble about the price." I ended up selling it for $115,000, and we completed the transaction in May 1992. The IFT built a nice headquarters at that corner. The address now is 700 South College, but it's the same location on the corner, though. I guess the teachers wanted the address and front door to be on College, not Cook Street.

When we returned to Springfield for my final veto session after the elections, our agenda, frankly, wasn't all that busy. Mayor Daley was pushing for a privately owned $2 billion casino and entertainment complex in downtown Chicago. We had adjourned without taking action on the casino in the spring, and we had to deal with it again in the fall. There was considerable opposition from the usual naysayers, with other strong opposition coming from Governor Edgar, from Lake County, and from the new riverboat owners, who didn't want competition from Chicago. I was on my way out, and we couldn't muster enough support to get the bill voted out of committee. I didn't make a big deal out of it, but I had strongly advised the Chicago people to get their deal when we had passed the original riverboat bill a couple of years earlier. Now they couldn't get a casino deal done.

It was time to bid farewell.

I returned to Springfield after the new year for one final day of the Eighty-Seventh General Assembly, January 12, 1993. There are always a few technical issues to deal with before a General Assembly adjourns for the last time and a new one takes over; 1993 was no different. The House had sent us a few bills on which we had to vote up or down or just ignore. If we didn't pass them on that last day, the bills would die. It was all routine. It's also customary on the final day to hear from people who won't be returning and to consider some resolutions honoring them for their service. I was at the podium for the final time. When it came time for the resolutions, I turned the gavel over to Senator Vince Demuzio, my good friend from

Carlinville, who had become a trusted leader and a skilled presider. We did a little more business, including the adoption of a resolution honoring former Speaker Bill Redmond, who had died the previous month.

It was almost time to adjourn, and Senators Demuzio and Philip and "all Members" introduced a resolution to recognize my twenty-two years of service in the Illinois Senate.[6] Sheila was in the chamber, as were all four of my children, along with the husbands of Kathleen and Meghan. They came up and stood behind me during the Senate's final farewell to me. By then, my children were young adults. I pointed out "that when we first came down [in 1971], we came down with three or four [children] in diapers and a dog, and it was an awful trip."[7] Demuzio and Philip, along with a few other members, spoke up and expressed heartfelt sentiments of friendship and thanks. Both Demuzio and Philip found one word to describe my leadership style—"fairness"—and I appreciated that very much. I knew I had to say something, but I had little to say. "I want to thank you for all that you have done for me, with me, to me," I said in my final, brief Senate speech. "I truly, as I'm sure you know, love this institution, this process and you people. I am proud to be numbered among you, and I thank you very, very much. God bless you."[8] It was time to go. Demuzio asked for the Committee of Escort, a tradition in our chamber, to come to the podium and lead me out of the chamber. Demuzio asked for all the senators to line up behind my family as an honor guard, and they did. Somebody arranged for a group of bagpipe players to be there as well.

The bagpipes led me out of the Senate chamber, down the stairs from the third floor, and past the entrance to the press room on the mezzanine level, where I stopped, looked up, and waved to those who were watching from the big open area on the third floor around the rail. Then the bagpipes led us out of the building, heading south. We marched to Baur's restaurant on First Street, one block south of the Capitol. The name of that placed has changed at least a couple of times since then; it seems to keep closing and reopening with a different name. Many people were there for this party: Dan Fusco and some others from the law office, friends from Oak Park, and my staff. We had dinner, and then Sheila and I went to the Caucus Room, a saloon on the other side of the Capitol.

Soon I would return to Oak Park and my law practice, but never would I give up on public service or set aside the belief that government should step in to help people, especially those who cannot adequately care for themselves.

Epilogue: After the Senate

I am a part of all that I have met.

—Alfred Lord Tennyson

WHEN I LEFT THE SENATE, I WAS FIFTY-FIVE YEARS OLD. My children were almost grown up, and I had one grandchild—the first of twelve. I was ready for the next phase of life after twenty-two years in the Illinois Senate, the last fourteen as Senate president.

I can say without hesitation that if there had not been a Danny Fusco, I would not have been Senate president. Danny Fusco was the first person I met as a first-year law student at Loyola. From the earliest days, we talked about going into practice together. A few years after we graduated from law school in 1964, Danny decided to start his own practice, and I agreed to join him in a little office in Chicago. We didn't have a lot of work at first, but we knew it would be that way. Our general civil practice grew over the years. He and I never needed a written agreement. It's really an amazing relationship I had, and still have, with Danny. He is my friend and is as trustworthy as can be. Danny and I and our wives, Sheila and Dorothy, are all very close.

When I first decided to run for public office, Danny supported me totally and handled all of the firm's business while I was in Springfield. At the law office, I never had to worry about a thing, not the phone bill, not the staff, nothing. He handled the whole practice. Not only that, but he also prepared and filed all of my campaign reports and all of the official paperwork you have to file to run for office and maintain a political campaign committee with the Illinois Board of Elections. In a typical week most of those years I was in the Senate, I would be in Springfield from Tuesday to Thursday. Then I would go into the law office on Thursday afternoon and Friday, spend Saturday in the ward office, and often have political events on Sunday. Then I'd be back in the office on Monday and return to Springfield on Tuesday. That's not a lot of time to give to the law practice. Danny made it work. In the earlier years, I would usually take the train back and forth between Chicago and Springfield. As time went on, several state planes flew every day from Meigs Field in downtown Chicago to Springfield. That was more convenient for me, with my law office being downtown.

I became busy practicing law after retiring from the Senate, but I never did have what could be called a routine. Things were too helter-skelter. I still felt an obligation to go to some political events, and that's true even today, although they are fewer and fewer for me. There always were a great number of invitations; it began to feel strange to start saying no after going for years without saying no to any kind of event, it seemed.

I became a registered lobbyist for two years after leaving the Senate. My biggest clients were the owners of various entities in the horse-racing industry. I was close friends with the owners of a couple of the racetracks. They wanted more gambling opportunities at the tracks—slot machines, for one thing. I also represented a horseman from Louisiana, a man named Louie Roussel III, who owned the Fair Grounds in New Orleans and also owned some thoroughbreds. He wanted to lend his name to help the industry in Illinois in any way. I finally told him, "I don't think that what you want is ever going to come to pass. You don't have a governor [Edgar] who wants this stuff. You don't have a House leader [Madigan] who wants it. I'll stay with it if you want, but I don't think it's going anywhere."

Also, I came to realize rather quickly that being a lobbyist is different from being in the inner offices. I used to enjoy being in Springfield; I loved the camaraderie and the process. But as a lobbyist in the capital city, people would slap me on the back and say, "How are you? I wish you were still here." More than once—too often, frankly—friends would say, "We need another person like Phil Rock down here in Springfield." I was uncomfortable hearing that—a lot uncomfortable—as nice as it was for people to say. I think some had the idea that I was walking around and shaking hands because I wanted to hear that kind of stuff. I really didn't. I felt so awkward about it. When people said, "I wish you were still here," I would say, "Well, I'm not still here. So carry on." I didn't know what to do about it except to stay away, so that's what I did. It's a big reason I stopped the lobbying, and I haven't been a registered lobbyist since 1995. Standing in the outer office or hanging around the rail on the third floor of the Capitol wasn't fun, and I didn't want to do it.

But my feeling about service never went away. I stayed active in the church and occasionally was called upon by local clergymen for advice. Anyone who has ever been in the seminary, as I was for ten years, knows

you never entirely lose your connection to it. Some people are better off
for the seminary experience, and some are worse off. I've known them
both. I have never worn my religion on my sleeve, but I have some serious principles, and I can't walk away from them. I won't, and I never will.

So in my post-Senate years, I responded affirmatively to invitations to
serve on some boards of organizations I supported, such as Loyola University and its medical school, Loretto Hospital, West Suburban Hospital,
the Brookfield Zoo, Maryville City of Youth, *Illinois Issues* magazine at
the University of Illinois Springfield, and quite a few others. When my
friend George Ryan was elected governor in 1998, he asked me to serve as
chair of the Illinois Board of Higher Education, and so I said yes to that,
too. George knew how important higher education was to me, and I took
that role as IBHE board chair very seriously. I served on a lot of those
boards at the same time, and I did what I could to help. I spent a lot of
time working on the board that develops continuing legal education for
Illinois attorneys, under the auspices of the Illinois Supreme Court. There
also was the Oak Park Development Corporation, which contributes to
the economic progress of my home community. Just as I was proud to be
from Chicago and proud to be a regular Democrat in the Cook County
organization, I was equally proud of my life and service of more than
three decades in Oak Park. Sheila and I sold our Oak Park house late in
2010 and downsized elsewhere in the Chicago area.

I have backed off considerably from many of my previous responsibilities. Danny and I have passed along our longtime law practice to a very
capable group of lawyers in a new firm named Rock Fusco, LLC, where
we still have offices in downtown Chicago and have been "of counsel" to
that firm since 2005. That means I can arrive at 10:00 A.M. and leave at
3:00 P.M. and say, "See you tomorrow" or not show up at all. It's a different lifestyle, and Danny can play golf or do whatever else he wants to do.

I still go to Cubs games, too. I love the afternoon games and rarely if
ever attend at night or on weekends. Someone asked me if I had a favorite player of the past seven decades. I suspect my response will surprise
you: Phil Cavarretta. He was a great ballplayer who played first base and
sometimes the outfield for the Cubs for twenty years, from 1934 to 1953
(I was born in 1937).[1] He played in three World Series for the Cubs: 1935,
1938, and 1945—all series losses, of course. Then Cavarretta became the
Cubs manager but was fired; he next played for the White Sox for two
years before retiring. The reason I liked him so much was that he was a
Chicago boy who went to Lane Tech High School and lived in the Wrigley
neighborhood. In those days, he would walk home from Wrigley Field

after every home game; he lived within walking distance. Kids who were around my age would hang around and wait for him and walk him home. It was like the Pied Piper with all of us kids around. Cavarretta, along with Andy Pafko, another favorite of mine, would just hang around the kids and put their arms around them and talk. It's fair to say we idolized them. So when I wrote that people always say I was born a Catholic, a Democrat, and Cubs fan, but not necessarily in that order, I guess that will never change.

I need to mention that even while I covered a lot of ground in this book, I didn't give as much attention to some topics that I might have. On some of the issues, my memory failed me completely, and some of the people who might remember aren't around any more or weren't available to consult. Other issues are just so complicated, and the way they developed was spread out over such a period of time, that it seems impossible to adequately reconstruct all the critical, relevant details in some comprehensible way. I'm thinking about such issues as branch banking and interstate banking, the many annual deliberations about education funding and reforms, Chicago school reform, collective bargaining for teachers, the various McCormick Place expansions, the establishment of the partnership of colleges and universities that is called the University Center of Lake County, and the disposal and transportation of radioactive nuclear waste, a topic of considerable concern to my good friend in the Senate Jerome Joyce of Reddick in Kankakee County.

I could have written a much longer book to cover all those topics and more, such as the Illinois Domestic Violence Act, but I recognize something inside of me that feels that publishing a book constitutes a level of self-aggrandizement that is out of character for me. Another part of me recognizes the value of helping people understand what we did all those years in Springfield, how the legislative process can indeed work in a bipartisan manner, and that I had a hand in it.

Two people in particular who did not make these pages in adequate detail are Gregory Coler and Father John Smyth. I mention them together because the three of us shared a heartfelt compassion for children, especially children who are disadvantaged. Coler directed the Department of Children and Family Services in the 1980s. He was not a hard-nosed ideologue but a child-care expert and not at all interested in our politics. We set up a study group—House members at our joint invitation, Senate members at my invitation, and a couple of agency administrators at Coler's request. Out of that, quite a bit of legislation emerged, such as the bill to make adoptions easier. We also organized a statewide conference on child support enforcement. That led to a new law in 1983 that made it possible to go after deadbeat dads and allow for court orders to withhold child support payments from their paychecks. I think we sent a strong message that the state of Illinois was going to support divorced or single women who were trying to raise children by themselves.

Father Smyth ran Maryville Academy in Des Plaines, not far from O'Hare Airport. I met him in the seminary. John is a big man, about 6 feet 5 inches tall, and had been a star basketball player at Notre Dame University in the 1950s. He was drafted in the first round by the old St. Louis Hawks, but he chose the seminary over professional basketball. He was ordained a priest in 1962 and then went to Maryville as his first assignment. Maryville was well established in the Archdiocese of Chicago, having been founded in 1883. By 1972 or so, most of Maryville's clients were wards of the state, and it was natural for DCFS and Maryville to work together closely to take care of troubled kids not only on the campus but elsewhere in the Chicago area.[2] One of those shared programs was a twenty-four-hour shelter program for teenagers. Maryville took over a children's hospital that had closed on Montrose at Lake Shore Drive. When police would pick up teenagers for various reasons—for getting into mischief and other less serious offenses—and those teens had no place to go, police could drop them off at the shelter. DCFS moved in to help with the intake. The agency had staff for triage and then could determine the best place for these children—maybe a foster home or some other place. Having everything on one floor in one building was a good thing for everybody and the system. DCFS could conduct evaluations and determine the teens' long-term needs. The shelter became a "front-door model" for taking care of children in the state of Illinois, and it was very successful.[3] Governor Thompson helped us, too, because he was a supporter of Father Smyth's and understood the value of the state and Maryville working together. Coler eventually was lured away to the state of Florida to help set up similar programs there.

It is laudable how the state of Illinois has enacted policies and services to provide assistance to people who have been victimized, harmed, and traumatized in unimaginable ways. Those are the kinds of services I have in mind—helping those most in need—when I say that government is not self-executing. It is vital for professionals in public service to perform such work. It's a shame that dedicated state employees or people working under contract for the state don't get enough credit—or, even worse, sometimes get a bad rap.

As I wrap this up, I want to acknowledge with great appreciation the hundreds of people who served with me in state government, in Cook

County, and in Oak Park. Too few of them are mentioned in this book. I never did stop being an unofficial advisor, and certainly a friend, to some of those people. I was happy, and am happy, to share my insights with those who are interested. That happens privately, and that's as it should be. Meanwhile, some of what happened during all of our meetings, trips, and conversations will just live in our memories. That's as it should be, too.

I have quoted Alfred Lord Tennyson many times to help me describe what I'm thinking. "I am a part of all that I have met," he wrote in his masterpiece on Ulysses.[4] That's how I felt when I left the Senate and how I still feel today.

I could never emphasize enough how important it is to respect the institution of the Illinois Senate and, frankly, all the other institutions of government, too. The Senate has important work to do, and it exists for the people's benefit, despite the glories, the errors, and the sins that any of its members bring to it. Also, it was designed to keep functioning (and does) as members come and go. As I told the gathering in my honor at the Maryville City of Youth just before leaving the Senate: "I am part of all that I have met, and truly, each of you is an important part of me, and I am a better person for it. My success is a shared success. Any failures or mistakes, I will, as I have always done, wear the jacket by myself for those. . . . I have long believed that to whom much is given, much is expected. I am a very lucky man, and tonight, a very grateful one."

Appendix

Notes

References

Index

Appendix

Illinois Governors, Senate Leaders, and House Speakers, 1965–2011

General Assembly	Year	Governor	Senate president	Senate minority leader	House Speaker
74th	1965	Otto Kerner (D)	W. Russell Arrington (R)	Thomas A. McGloon (D)	John Touhy (D)
	1966	Otto Kerner (D)	W. Russell Arrington (R)	Thomas A. McGloon (D)	John Touhy (D)
75th	1967	Otto Kerner (D)	W. Russell Arrington (R)	Thomas A. McGloon (D)	Ralph Smith (R)
	1968	Otto Kerner (D)[a]	W. Russell Arrington (R)	Thomas A. McGloon (D)	Ralph Smith (R)
	1968	Samuel Shapiro (D)	W. Russell Arrington (R)	Thomas A. McGloon (D)	Ralph Smith (R)
76th	1969	Richard Ogilvie (R)	W. Russell Arrington (R)	Thomas A. McGloon (D)	Jack. E Walker (R)
	1970	Richard Ogilvie (R)	W. Russell Arrington (R)	Thomas A. McGloon (D)	Jack. E Walker (R)
77th	1971	Richard Ogilvie (R)	Cecil Partee (D)	W. Russell Arrington (R)	W. Robert Blair (R)
	1972	Richard Ogilvie (R)	Cecil Partee (D)	W. Russell Arrington (R)	W. Robert Blair (R)
78th	1973	Dan Walker (D)	William Harris (R)	Cecil Partee (D)	W. Robert Blair (R)
	1974	Dan Walker (D)	William Harris (R)	Cecil Partee (D)	W. Robert Blair (R)
79th	1975	Dan Walker (D)	Cecil Partee (D)	William Harris (R)	William Redmond (D)
	1976	Dan Walker (D)	Cecil Partee (D)	William Harris (R)	William Redmond (D)
80th	1977	James Thompson (R)	Thomas Hynes (D)	David Shapiro (R)	William Redmond (D)
	1978	James Thompson (R)	Thomas Hynes (D)	David Shapiro (R)	William Redmond (D)
81st	1979	James Thompson (R)	Philip Rock (D)	David Shapiro (R)	William Redmond (D)
	1980	James Thompson (R)	Philip Rock (D)	David Shapiro (R)	William Redmond (D)
82nd	1981	James Thompson (R)	Philip Rock (D)	David Shapiro (R)	George Ryan (R)
	1982	James Thompson (R)	Philip Rock (D)	James "Pate" Philip (R) [b]	George Ryan (R)
83rd	1983	James Thompson (R)	Philip Rock (D)	James "Pate" Philip (R)	Michael Madigan (D)
	1984	James Thompson (R)	Philip Rock (D)	James "Pate" Philip (R)	Michael Madigan (D)
84th	1985	James Thompson (R)	Philip Rock (D)	James "Pate" Philip (R)	Michael Madigan (D)
	1986	James Thompson (R)	Philip Rock (D)	James "Pate" Philip (R)	Michael Madigan (D)
85th	1987	James Thompson (R)	Philip Rock (D)	James "Pate" Philip (R)	Michael Madigan (D)
	1988	James Thompson (R)	Philip Rock (D)	James "Pate" Philip (R)	Michael Madigan (D)

86th	1989	James Thompson (R)	Philip Rock (D)	James "Pate" Philip (R)	Michael Madigan (D)
	1990	James Thompson (R)	Philip Rock (D)	James "Pate" Philip (R)	Michael Madigan (D)
87th	1991	Jim Edgar (R)	Philip Rock (D)	James "Pate" Philip (R)	Michael Madigan (D)
	1992	Jim Edgar (R)	Philip Rock (D)	James "Pate" Philip (R)	Michael Madigan (D)
88th	1993	Jim Edgar (R)	Pate Philip (R)	Emil Jones (D)	Michael Madigan (D)
	1994	Jim Edgar (R)	Pate Philip (R)	Emil Jones (D)	Michael Madigan (D)
89th	1995	Jim Edgar (R)	Pate Philip (R)	Emil Jones (D)	Lee Daniels (R)
	1996	Jim Edgar (R)	Pate Philip (R)	Emil Jones (D)	Lee Daniels (R)
90th	1997	Jim Edgar (R)	Pate Philip (R)	Emil Jones (D)	Michael Madigan (D)
	1998	Jim Edgar (R)	Pate Philip (R)	Emil Jones (D)	Michael Madigan (D)
91st	1999	George Ryan (R)	Pate Philip (R)	Emil Jones (D)	Michael Madigan (D)
	2000	George Ryan (R)	Pate Philip (R)	Emil Jones (D)	Michael Madigan (D)
92nd	2001	George Ryan (R)	Pate Philip (R)	Emil Jones (D)	Michael Madigan (D)
	2002	George Ryan (R)	Pate Philip (R)	Emil Jones (D)	Michael Madigan (D)
93rd	2003	Rod Blagojevich (D)	Emil Jones (D)	Frank Watson (R)	Michael Madigan (D)
	2004	Rod Blagojevich (D)	Emil Jones (D)	Frank Watson (R)	Michael Madigan (D)
94th	2005	Rod Blagojevich (D)	Emil Jones (D)	Frank Watson (R)	Michael Madigan (D)
	2006	Rod Blagojevich (D)	Emil Jones (D)	Frank Watson (R)	Michael Madigan (D)
95th	2007	Rod Blagojevich (D)	Emil Jones (D)	Frank Watson (R)	Michael Madigan (D)
	2008	Rod Blagojevich (D)	Emil Jones (D)	Frank Watson (R)	Michael Madigan (D)
96th	2009	Rod Blagojevich (D)c	John Cullerton (D)	Christine Radogno (R)	Michael Madigan (D)
	2009	Patrick Quinn (D)	John Cullerton (D)	Christine Radogno (R)	Michael Madigan (D)
	2010	Patrick Quinn (D)	John Cullerton (D)	Christine Radogno (R)	Michael Madigan (D)
97th	2011	Patrick Quinn (D)	John Cullerton (D)	Christine Radogno (R)	Michael Madigan (D)

Source: Illinois Blue Books, published biennially by the Illinois secretary of state, and Illinois Issues magazine.

Note: D = Democrat, R = Republican.

[a] Kerner resigned to become a federal judge.

[b] Philip was chosen minority leader in the fall of 1981 after David Shapiro died on August 1, 1981.

[c] Blagojevich was impeached and removed from office in January 2009.

Notes

Preface, by Ed Wojcicki

1. Thomas Hardy, "A Man for All Sessions: Phil Rock's Mission Is to Make the System Work, and Even Opponents Admit He's Good at It," *Chicago Tribune Sunday Magazine*, July 30, 1989.

2. Linda Kingman, interview by Ed Wojcicki, Chicago, January 29, 2007.

3. Hardy, "Man for All Sessions."

4. Senator John Cullerton, interview by Ed Wojcicki in the Senate president's office, Springfield, March 12, 2009.

5. Michael Burlingame said something similar about Abraham Lincoln in his important work *Abraham Lincoln: A Life* (Baltimore: Johns Hopkins University Press, 2008), 1:xii.

Introduction: Try to Be Fair and Evenhanded

1. Thomas Hardy, "Rock Will Be Missed on Both Sides of the Aisle," *Chicago Tribune*, January 10, 1993.

2. Thomas Hardy, "A Man for All Sessions: Phil Rock's Mission Is to Make the System Work, and Even Opponents Admit He's Good at It," *Chicago Tribune Sunday Magazine*, July 30, 1989.

1. They Told Me It Wasn't My Turn

1. 35th Quadrennial Convention of the Democratic National Committee, 1968. Transcript of proceedings published by Alderson Reporting Company, Washington, D.C., 354.

2. Rakove, *Don't Make No Waves.*

2. Getting My Opportunity in Springfield

1. *Austinite*, October 14, 1970.

2. Jerry Owens, a columnist for the *Illinois State Register*, as quoted in "Sen. Phil Rock Singled Out as Promising Senator," *Austin News*, June 16, 1971.

3. Official vote from the Illinois State Board of Elections.

3. Battling Walker and Fighting for Children

1. Jim Donnewald, telephone interview by Ed Wojcicki, April 24, 2008. Donnewald died on September 18, 2009, at the age of eighty-four.

2. "The Law: Children's Rights: The Latest Crusade," *Time*, December 25, 1972.

3. Dianne Witkowski, "Nurses' Long Vigil of Love," *Chicago Today*, July 9, 1972.

4. Editorial, *Chicago Tribune*, September 2, 1972.

5. Dianne Banis and Dorothy Collin, "Meet Adrianne, a Battered Child," *Chicago Today*, June 8, 1973.

6. William Syers, "Child Abuse," *Illinois Issues*, August 1977.

7. Illinois Department of Children and Family Services, "Child Abuse Neglect Statistics, Fiscal Year 2005" (Springfield: State of Illinois DCFS, October 2005), 3, table 1. See http://www.state.il.us/DCFS/docs/cants97_scr.shtml.

8. Senate transcript, May 29, 1973, p. 27. Illinois Senate and Illinois House transcripts from floor debates since 1971 can be found on the Illinois General Assembly website; see http://www.ilga.gov/PreviousGA.asp.

9. Ibid., 37.

10. The "conscience bill" was HB 650, which we passed in the Senate on June 22, 1973.

11. Senate transcript, June 22, 1973, p. 21.

4. My Finest Accomplishment

1. John Elmer, "Richie Shoots for the Stars," *Chicago Tribune*, July 2, 1975. Also see Ed McManus, "Young Richie Faces a Fight," *Chicago Tribune*, December 9, 1975.

2. Gerald Shea, interview by Ed Wojcicki, Springfield, July 18, 2007.

3. Elmer, "Richie Shoots for the Stars."

4. Senate transcript, February 4, 1975, pp. 24–25.

5. Ibid., May 21, 1975, 47.

5. A Scandal I Didn't Deserve

1. Whitney Tower, "The Racing Lady of Chicago," *Sports Illustrated*, August 20, 1962.

2. According to a study done for Ed Wojcicki by the Illinois Legislative Research Unit, Springfield, Illinois.

3. Sue Dinges, "Equal Rights Amendment: Will the 80th General Assembly Ratify It?" *Illinois Issues*, March 1977.

4. Ibid.

5. Senate transcript, December 16, 1976, pp. 30–32.

6. Mike Lawrence, "Corruption in the Legislature: Cement Bribery Trial," *Illinois Issues*, December 1976. This article is a good source for the background of this scandal and the convictions resulting from it.

6. The Crazy Eight Emerge

1. George Gunset, "Donovan out as CBOT President," *Chicago Tribune*, April 15, 2000.

2. Senate transcript, January 12, 1977, p. 10.

3. Ibid., 15.

4. Ibid., 21.

5. Ibid., January 27, 1977, 2–3.

6. Ibid., 9–11.

7. Ibid., February 2, 1977, 3.

8. Ibid., February 15, 1977, 23.

9. Ibid., 27.

10. Edward S. Gilbreth and Robert G. Schultz, "Phil Rock: Shuttle Diplomat," *Chicago Daily News*, February 17, 1977.

11. Bill O'Connell, "Rock May Hold Key to Democrat Truce in Senate," *Peoria Journal-Star*, February 17, 1977.

12. Ibid.; Gilbreth and Schultz, "Phil Rock."

7. A Move to Oak Park

1. See a letter to the editor by Ann Armstrong and Galen Gockel, "Opponent Says Rock Using Chicago Base," *Oak Park Oak Leaves*, March 15, 1978. Also see Edward S. Gilbreth and Robert G. Schultz, "Rock Move Shakes Oak Park," *Chicago Daily News*, June 28, 1977.

2. Gilbreth and Schultz, "Shea, Rock Eye Power Plays," *Chicago Daily News*, March 10, 1977.

3. Armstrong and Gockel, "Opponent Says Rock Using Chicago Base."

4. The authors thank Pat Arman for sharing her recollection of district office activities.

5. Senate transcript, December 12, 1984, p. 62.

6. "Widow of Slain Lawyer Calls for Handgun Ban," *Wednesday Journal of Oak Park and River Forest, Illinois*, February 1, 1984.

8. Finally, the Senate Presidency

1. Hartley, *Big Jim Thompson of Illinois*, 164.

2. Senate transcript, January 10, 1979, pp. 12–13.

3. Michael A. Bilandic Papers, biographical sketch, n.d., University of Illinois at Chicago Library. Also see Milton Rakove, "Bilandic Filling Daley's Shoes," *Illinois Issues*, May 1978.

9. Choosing Leaders and Saving Chrysler

1. Diane Ross, "STOP Stopped; Thompson-Byrne Penny Goes Through," *Illinois Issues*, December 1979. Also see Jeff Brody, "Approval of 1 Cent Tax Cut Expected Today in Senate," *Chicago Tribune*, November 8, 1979.

2. Hartley, *Big Jim Thompson of Illinois*, 178.

3. Ross, "STOP Stopped."

4. Kathy Gill, "What Was the Chrysler Bailout?," About.com, http://uspolitics. about.com/od/economy/a/chryslerBailout.htm (accessed July 2009).

5. Senate transcript, June 25, 1980, p. 344.

6. Ibid., 346.

7. Ibid., 350.

8. David Axelrod, "Senate Dems Want Piece of the Rock," *Chicago Tribune*, January 6, 1981.

9. "State High Court Studies Senate Issue," Associated Press, January 28, 1981.

10. Ibid.

11. Tom Schaefer, "Battle over Senate Presidency Becomes Violent," Gannett News Services, February 4, 1981.

12. Daniel Egler and Larry Sandler, "Elections of Shapiro, Rock Void," *Chicago Tribune*, February 10, 1981.

10. A Redistricting Fight

1. "Charges Fly as Senate Adjourns Without Vote on Boundaries," Associated Press, June 28, 1981.

2. Ibid.

3. Senators and reporters who were there tell slightly different versions of what happened. Senator James "Pate" Philip, the Republican minority leader from Wood Dale, for example, said Vadalabene smacked Rhoads in the Adam's apple, and for a week Rhoads was unable to speak (interview with Philip by Ed Wojcicki, February 22, 2007, in Philip's home in Wood Dale). Mary Bohlen wrote for United Press International on June 29, 1981, that Vadalabene claimed to hit Rhoads "right on the jaw." Dennis McMurray of the *Alton Telegraph* reported on the same date that Vadalabene started with a quick left jab and followed with a "haymaker right to Rhoads' jaw." Then came the headlock that Rock talked about.

4. Ken Buzbee, interview by Kyle Dooley, Springfield, April 12, 2007.

5. Mike Royko, "We Elected Sluggards: A Knockout Bunch," *Chicago Sun-Times*, July 1, 1981.

6. "Recession, Revenue and the Budget Reserve," *Illinois Issues*, January 1981.

11. Going National and Beefing Up Our Party

1. *Intergovernmental Issues*, September 1980.

2. William Holland, interview by Ed Wojcicki, Springfield, December 3, 2008.

3. Ibid.

4. "Two Groups Named to Advise Governor on Federal Block Grants," *Illinois Issues*, February 1982.

5. Mike Lawrence, "Illinois Democrats Seek a Party Cure," *Decatur Herald and Review*, August 14, 1981. The *Herald and Review* was among more than forty newspapers in Illinois to carry a weekly column and other articles on Illinois politics written by Lawrence, then the Springfield bureau chief for Lee Enterprises.

6. Shelley Davis, "Phil Rock: A Little Less Than Even-Handed and a Desire to Be Governor," *Illinois Issues*, July 1981.

7. Jon Margolis, "U.S. Dem Leaders Hope Rock Gets State Helm," *Chicago Tribune*, January 19, 1982.

8. "Legislative Life: The Rules of the Game," *State Legislatures*, October 1981.

9. Robert Davis and David Axelrod, "Vrdolyak Announces Race for Dunne's Job," *Chicago Tribune*, March 26, 1982.

10. John Lattimer, telephone interview by Kyle Dooley, December 12, 2008.

12. Speaker Madigan

1. Daniel Egler and Philip Lentz, "83d State Legislature Opens—Smaller and More Democratic," *Chicago Tribune*, January 13, 1983.

2. Charles N. Wheeler III, "Thompson's Tax Hike: The Reasons and the Politics," *Illinois Issues*, April 1983.

3. Illinois House Speaker Michael Madigan, interview by Ed Wojcicki, Springfield, November 3, 2007.

13. Getting Behind the Tax Increase of 1983

1. State of Illinois, *Report of the Tax Reform Commission* (Springfield: State of Illinois, 1982).

2. Daniel Egler, "Tell It Like It Is on Tax, Rock Urging Thompson," *Chicago Tribune*, January 16, 1983.

3. That's what I said on the Senate floor on June 30, 1983, as we were trying to wrap up months of debate about the tax increase issue.

4. Charles N. Wheeler III, "Thompson's Tax Hike: The Reasons and the Politics," *Illinois Issues*, April 1983.

5. Diane Ross, "Thompson's Gamble," *Illinois Issues*, March 1983.

6. Wheeler, "Thompson's Tax Hike."

7. Governor James R. Thompson, from the Illinois House transcript, February 8, 1983, p. 18.

8. Wheeler, "Thompson's Tax Hike."

9. Parker, *Illinois Tax Increase of 1983*, 28.

10. Ibid., 34.

11. Ibid., 37–39.

12. Wheeler, "Thompson's Tax Hike."

13. Parker, *Illinois Tax Increase of 1983*, 43–44.

14. Ed McManus, "The Key to Byrne's Undoing," *Illinois Issues*, April 1983.

15. Paul Green, "Washington's Victory: Divide and Conquer," *Illinois Issues*, April 1983.

16. Levinsohn, *Harold Washington*, 202.

17. Ibid., 203.

18. Paul Green, "Chicago Election: The Numbers and the Implications," *Illinois Issues*, August 1983.

19. Ibid.

20. Michael Briggs and Ted Scott Matthews, "Scant Senate Support for State Tax Increase," *Chicago Sun-Times*, April 3, 1983.

21. Thompson, testimony before the Senate Committee of the Whole, Senate transcript, May 5, 1983.

22. James R. Thompson, interview by Ed Wojcicki and Kyle Dooley, Thompson's Chicago law office, August 1, 2006.

23. Parker, *Illinois Tax Increase of 1983*, 64.

24. Ibid., 113.

25. Ibid., 112.

26. Associated Press, "Thompson Signs Tax Hike Bills," *Springfield State Journal-Register*, July 2, 1983.

27. Again, I want to thank Joan Parker for noting many of these details and recording them in her *Illinois Tax Increase of 1983*.

28. Senate transcript, June 30, 1983, pp. 138–39.

29. Ibid., 154.

30. Ibid., 151–54.

31. Jeff Brody, "Illinois 14th State to Increase Taxes this Year," *Springfield State Journal-Register*, July 3, 1983.

14. Boosting Regional Transportation

1. Joseph A. Tecson, "The Regional Transportation Authority in Northeastern Illinois," *Chicago Bar Record*, May–June 1975 and July–August 1975, 13. Tecson was a lawyer, a delegate to the Illinois constitutional convention of 1970, an early member of the RTA board, and its temporary chairman from 1974 to 1975.

2. Paul Gapp, "Civic Leaders Press for OK of Transit Proposal," *Chicago Tribune*, November 14, 1973.

3. David Gilbert, "Vote Means RTA Is Dead, Leaders Say," *Chicago Tribune*, November 17, 1973.

4. Senate transcript, November 29, 1973, pp. 134–35.

5. Tecson, "Regional Transportation Authority," 18.

6. James A. Lesser, "Reading the Future of the New RTA," *Illinois Issues*, December 1984.

7. Philip Lentz and Daniel Egler, "RTA Vote Too Close to Call: Bill Facing Final Test in State Senate," *Chicago Tribune*, November 2, 1983.

8. Several of Rock's former staff members related in interviews that Rock's floor speech on July 2, 1984, was among his best, if not his very best, of many great floor speeches in his twenty-two-year career. Republican senator Aldo DeAngelis stood up after the vote and said, "[In] my years in the senate, I stand real proud to hear the eloquence of a speech that I think is the most eloquent I've ever heard on Senator Rock's part."

9. Diane Ross, "Tying the Strings to the RTA," *Illinois Issues*, January 1984. See also Basil Talbott Jr., "Mayor, Thompson Try for RTA Deal," *Chicago Sun-Times*, August 19, 1984.

10. Stanley Holmes, "The Tortuous Tale of a Serial Killer—Gacy," *Newsweek*, April 25, 1994.

11. "John Wayne Gacy," Biography.com (accessed July 2009).

12. "How Pogo the Clown Killed More Than a Score of Youths," *Time*, January 8, 1979.

13. J. D. Podolsky, Bonnie Bell, and Joni H. Blackman, "Day of Reckoning: As John Wayne Gacy's Execution Nears, He Makes No Concessions to Death," *People*, May 16, 1994.

14. National Center for Missing and Exploited Children website, www.missingkids.com (accessed July 3, 2009).

15. Senate transcript, May 25, 1984, p. 49.

16. This information comes from Pat Arman, March 3, 2009.

17. Ibid.

18. Diane Ross, "Economic Development: Four Handles for the Future," *Illinois Issues*, July 1983.

19. Some of the information in this section comes from an interview that Ed Wojcicki conducted with Peter Creticos, Chicago, December 9, 2006.

20. I mentioned this on the Senate floor the day we passed the bill, May 26, 1983, p. 234.

21. Ibid.

15. A U.S. Senate Race against Paul Simon

1. Simon, *P.S.: The Autobiography of Paul Simon*, 155.

2. David Axelrod, "Boosted by Poll, Simon Weighs Bid for Senate," *Chicago Tribune*, June 23, 1983.

3. Ibid.

4. Simon, *P.S.*, 154–57.

5. Dana Priest, "Rock Tells Senate Bid; Mayor Says He Fits It," *Chicago Sun-Times*, July 31, 1983.

6. From text of prepared remarks in Phil Rock's personal papers, August 29 and 30, 1983.

7. Charles N. Wheeler III, "The Democratic Primary for U.S. Senator: Harmonious Rivalry," *Illinois Issues*, March 1984.

8. James R. Thompson, interview by Ed Wojcicki and Kyle Dooley, Thompson's Chicago law office, August 1, 2006.

9. David Axelrod, "Rock: Intelligence and Party Loyalty Give His Career the Look of a Survivor," *Chicago Tribune*, March 2, 1984.

10. Editorial, *Chicago Tribune*, February 26, 1984.

11. "Rock's Car Gets Vote of Thieves," *Chicago Sun-Times*, March 17, 1984.

12. Results from the Illinois State Board of Elections. A fifth candidate, Gerald M. Rose, received 17,985 votes (1 percent), and there were also forty-nine write-in votes recorded around the state.

13. R. Bruce Dold, "Reality Sinks in on Day After: Unsuccessful Candidates Assess Political Futures," *Chicago Tribune*, March 22, 1984.

14. Mike Lawrence, "Sen. Rock, Legislator of Principle, Remains Misunderstood by Many," *Oak Forest Star Herald*, April 1, 1984. At the time, Lawrence was syndicating his popular weekly column to individual newspapers and newspaper groups. The column would have run in Lee Newspapers, which included the *Quad-City Times*, the *Decatur Herald & Review*, the *Southern Illinoisan* of Carbondale, and the *Kewanee Star-Courier*.

16. Year of Major Education Reform

1. National Commission on Excellence in Education, *A Nation at Risk: The Imperative for Educational Reform* (Washington, D.C.: U.S. Government Printing Office, 1983). Archived at http://www2.ed.gov/pubs/NatAtRisk/risk.html (accessed June 1, 2011).

2. Illinois Commission on the Improvement of Elementary and Secondary Education, *Excellence in the Making* (Springfield: Illinois Commission on the Improvement of Elementary and Secondary Education, 1985), 1.

3. Cynthia Peters, "Madigan's Conference on Education Reform," *Illinois Issues*, May 1984.

4. Illinois Commission on the Improvement of Elementary and Secondary Education, *Excellence in the Making*, 5–8.

5. Ted Sanders, "Illinois Educational Reform: A Thoughtful Response to Crisis," *Illinois Issues*, May 1986.

6. Donald Sevener, "Education Reform: The Outcome," *Illinois Issues*, August–September 1985.

7. Tim Franklin and Daniel Egler, "Rock Asks Summit on School Reform," *Chicago Tribune*, May 11, 1985.

8. John Maitland testimony, Senate transcript, July 2, 1985, pp. 103–4.

9. Sevener, "Education Reform."

10. Ibid.

11. From my remarks during the debate, Senate transcript, July 2, 1985.

12. Sevener, "Education Reform."

13. James R. Thompson, *Illinois State of the State: 1977–1991, The Thompson Administration* (Springfield: State of Illinois, 1991), published at the conclusion of Thompson's fourteen years as governor.

14. Diane Ross, "Build Illinois: The Governor's Grand Plan Approved," *Illinois Issues*, August–September 1985.

15. Ibid.

16. We included language in a series of bills about what the General Assembly has learned about Alzheimer's. See especially Illinois Public Act 84–378, which came from HB 301, and Illinois Public Act 84–513, which came from SB 388.

17. Now called Rush University Medical Center in Chicago.

18. Illinois Public Act 84–513, from SB 388.

19. Illinois Department of Public Health, "Alzheimer's Disease and Other Related Dementia State Plan," a report to the governor and the General Assembly in response to Senate Joint Resolution 43, from the Alzheimer's Disease Advisory Committee, January 2009.

17. The Debacle of the 1986 Elections

1. Debbie Willard, "The 1992 Chicago World's Fair: Fortune or Folly?" *Illinois Issues*, June 1985.

2. Debbie Willard, "Fair Flops and Other Chicago Woes," *Illinois Issues*, August–September 1985.

3. Peter Creticos, interview by Ed Wojcicki, Chicago, December 9, 2006.

4. John Camper, "Madigan Rules State House with Firm Hand," *Chicago Tribune*, November 17, 1985.

5. Senator John Cullerton, interview by Ed Wojcicki in the Senate president's office, Springfield, March 12, 2009.

6. Illinois Public Act 84–1468, effective July 1, 1987. It was passed as HB 2486 in the 84th General Assembly.

7. Cullerton interview.

8. Ibid.

9. "Rock in the 8th Senate," *Oak Park Oak Leaves*, March 5, 1986.

10. Charles N. Wheeler III, "Adlai's Candidacy," *Illinois Issues*, May 1986.

11. Michael D. Klemens, "Don't Vote for Nobody Nobody Knows," *Illinois Issues*, December 1986.

12. William B. Crawford Jr., "Ex-Sen. Nedza Gets 8 Years for Fraud," *Chicago Tribune*, October 22, 1987.

13. Chicago Office of the City Clerk website (http://www.chicityclerk.com), official biography of Miguel del Valle (accessed July 2010).

18. Illinois Women in Government

1. Thanks to Linda Kingman, Linda Hawker, Bonnie Ettinger, and Judy Erwin for sharing their recollections of these conferences.

2. For more information about these two groups in Illinois, see www.iwilinfo.org (Democrats) and www.lincolnseries.com (Republicans).

3. Center for American Women and Politics, www.cawp.rutgers.edu (accessed

November 2009).

4. Ibid. Statistics are from the "Fast Facts" link on this website, which has numbers for every state.

5. Ibid.

6. Daniel Egler, "Rock Re-elected after Bargaining," *Chicago Tribune*, January 16, 1987.

19. The Cubs and the Sox

1. Carrie Muskat, "Wrigley Lights up the Night for 20 Years: A Timeline of Struggles and Successes to Host Night Games," written for www.mlb.com and posted on www.cubs.com, August 7, 2008 (accessed 2009).

2. Michael D. Klemens, "Horse Racing, Sox Stadium, Insurance for the Uninsurable," *Illinois Issues*, January 1987.

3. Matt Krasnowski, "Sox Plan Offered to Legislators," *Springfield State Journal-Register*, June 2, 1988.

4. Brett D. Johnson, "Saving the Sox," *Illinois Issues*, August–September 1988.

5. House transcript, June 30, 1988, p. 205.

6. Ibid.

7. Ibid.

8. Mark Brown and Fran Spielman, "OK for Sox: Stadium Saved by Late Rally," *Chicago Sun-Times*, July 1, 1988; Johnson, "Saving the Sox."

9. Ray Sons, "Gov Big Hit with Sox—Bar None," *Chicago Sun-Times*, July 7, 1988.

10. Ibid.

20. Another Tax Increase and Another Mayor

1. Charles N. Wheeler III and Mark Brown, "Thompson Tax Plea: 40%," *Chicago Sun-Times*, June 10, 1988. In a separate column for *Illinois Issues*, June 1988, Wheeler wrote: "As usual, the most candid of the legislative leadership has been Senate President Philip J. Rock, who early on acknowledged that higher taxes were needed; the most enigmatic, as always suits his purpose, was House Speaker Michael J. Madigan."

2. "Governor at Dedication," *Glen Ellyn News*, February 24, 1988.

3. Michael D. Klemens, "Mike Madigan and the Party of Economic Opportunity," *Illinois Issues*, August–September 1988.

4. Tim Franklin, "Thompson: Tax Hike is Dead," *Chicago Tribune*, June 29, 1988.

5. Klemens, "Mike Madigan and the Party of Economic Opportunity."

6. Robert Kieckhefer, "Daley's Cabinet: Symbol of a New Beginning for Chicago?" *Illinois Issues*, June 1989.

7. Harvey Berkman, "Senate Democrats: Will Savickas Lower the Majority by One?" *Southern Illinoisan*, March 19, 1989.

8. Michael D. Klemens, "Madigan's Tax Increase for Education, Local Government," *Illinois Issues*, June 1989. Many of the details here explaining the 1989 tax increase come from this article and another written by Klemens, "The Tax Increases of 1989: Structurally Similar to 1983 but Politically Opposite," *Illinois Issues*, August–September 1989.

9. Michael D. Klemens, "Phil Rock: Defender of Government," *Illinois Issues*, August–September 1989.

21. Riverboats and Governor Edgar

1. Ray Long and Peggy Boyer, "Gambling on Illinois Riverboats: Morally Wrong or Profitably Right?" *Illinois Issues*, October 1989.

2. Sean Noble, "Lawmakers Pass Riverboat Gambling," *Springfield State Journal-Register*, January 12, 1990.

3. Charles N. Wheeler III, "Memorable Farewell by the Iron Horse of Illinois Politics," *Illinois Issues*, February 1990.

4. Senate transcript, January 9, 1991, pp. 4–5.

5. Ibid., 18–19.

6. Ibid., 19–22.

7. Dawn Clark Netsch, "State Fiscal Crises: From Connecticut to California," *Illinois Municipal Review*, June 1991.

8. Charles N. Wheeler III, "1,400 Jobs Slashed in Edgar's Budget," *Chicago Sun-Times*, March 7, 1991.

9. Charles N. Wheeler III, "Edgar Calls for Layoffs, Welfare Cuts," *Chicago Sun-Times*, March 7, 1991.

10. Lynn Sweet and Charles N. Wheeler III, "Tough Odds for State Budget," *Chicago Sun-Times*, March 11, 1991.

11. Jim Edgar, interview by Ed Wojcicki, Urbana, Ill., November 20, 2008.

12. Charles N. Wheeler III, "Governor Gets Budget; Session Finally Adjourns," *Chicago Sun-Times*, July 19, 1991.

13. Edgar interview.

14. Lynn Sweet, "Legislators Wrap It Up and Head for Home, Parties," *Chicago Sun-Times*, July 20, 1991.

22. The Final Year

1. Michael D. Klemens, "The Morass in State Government's Fiscal Affairs," *Illinois Issues*, March 1992.

2. Rock's personal papers, December 12, 1991.

3. Michal D. Klemens, "Budget and Posturing Dominate Session," *Illinois Issues*, August–September 1992.

4. Thomas Hardy, "Rock Will Be Missed on Both Sides of Senate Aisle," *Chicago Tribune*, January 10, 1993.

5. See "The Charlie Robinson Story" on Robinson's No. 1 Ribs website, http://www.rib1.com/about-us.php (accessed October 2009).

6. Senate Joint Resolution 196, adopted by the Illinois Senate on January 12, 1993, my last day in the Senate.

7. Senate transcript, January 12, 1993, p. 109.

8. Ibid.

Epilogue: After the Senate

1. Information on Philip Joseph Cavarretta from Baseball-Reference.com (accessed April 12, 2011).

2. Ames Boykin, "Maryville at 125," *Daily Herald*, July 27, 2008.

3. Rev. John Smyth, interview by Ed Wojcicki, Des Plaines, Ill., February 22, 2007.

4. Alfred Lord Tennyson, "Ulysses," written in 1833 and published in 1842. Explanation from The Victorian Web (www.victorianweb.org); the first publication of the poem occurred in *Poems by Alfred Tennyson*, 2 vols. (London: Edward Moxon, Dover Street, 1842).

References

Byrne, Jane. *My Chicago.* New York: W. W. Norton, 1992.

Cornelius, Janet. *Constitution Making in Illinois, 1818–1970.* Urbana: University of Illinois Press, 1972.

Fremon, David K. *Chicago Politics, Ward by Ward.* Bloomington: Indiana University Press, 1988.

Gove, Samuel K., and Louis H. Masotti. *After Daley: Chicago Politics in Transition.* Urbana: University of Illinois Press, 1982.

Green, Paul M., and Melvin G. Holli. *The Mayors: The Chicago Political Tradition.* 3rd ed. Carbondale: Southern Illinois University Press, 2005.

Hartley, Robert E. *Big Jim Thompson of Illinois.* Chicago: Rand McNally, 1979.

Kilian, Michael, Connie Fletcher, and F. Richard Ciccone. *Who Runs Chicago?* New York: St. Martin's Press, 1979.

Levinsohn, Florence Hamlish. *Harold Washington: A Political Biography.* Chicago: Chicago Review Press, 1983.

Merriner, James L. *Mr. Chairman: Power in Dan Rostenkowski's America.* Carbondale: Southern Illinois University Press, 1999.

Parker, Joan A. *The Illinois Tax Increase of 1983: Summit and Resolution.* Springfield: Illinois Issues and Sangamon State University (now University of Illinois Springfield), 1984.

Pensoneau, Taylor. *Powerhouse: Arrington from Illinois.* Baltimore: American Literary Press, 1996.

Pensoneau, Taylor, and Bob Ellis. *Dan Walker: The Glory and the Tragedy.* Evansville, Ind.: Smith Collins, 1993.

Rakove, Milton L. *Don't Make No Waves—Don't Back No Losers: An Insider's Analysis of the Daley Machine.* Bloomington: Indiana University Press, 1975.

———. *We Don't Want Nobody Nobody Sent: An Oral History of the Daley Years.* Bloomington: Indiana University Press, 1979.

Simon, Paul. *P.S.: The Autobiography of Paul Simon.* Santa Monica, Calif.: Bonus Books, 2003.

Watson, Joanna M. *Electing a Constitution: The Illinois Citizen and the 1970 Constitution.* Urbana: University of Illinois Press, 1970.

Index

Leverenz, Ted, 208
license plate fees, 121, 131, 133
Lincoln Series for Excellence in Public Service, 175
Lindley, Maralee, 174, 175, photo section
Lindquist, Johnny, 36–37
Lindquist, William, 36
liquor taxes, 120, 121, 130, 207
lobbying work, PJR's, 213
Local Government Advisory Committee, 108
Lockhart, Richard, 29
lottery, state, 196
Love, Ruth, 158
Luft, Richard, 154–55
Luxembourg, 21
Lynn, Naomi, 175
Lyons, Bill, 24

Macoupin County, 133, 170
Madigan, Michael J.: baseball legislation, 182, 183; budget legislation, 207; during Chicago's council wars, 126; economic development legislation, 162; education legislation, 44–45, 160; family medical leave legislation, 116–17; first House election, 21; gambling legislation, 195; on leadership team, 83; legislative skills, 115–16, 118; PJR relationship generally, 114–18, photo section; PJR's U.S. Senate campaign, 153; primary date legislation, 202; redistricting conflict, 100; in Senate presidency contest, 96–97, 118; speakership contests, 200, 208; tax legislation, 89, 122, 127, 129, 130–31, 132, 186, 187, 190–92, 203, 231n1 (ch 20); transportation policy, 140; World's Fair, 164–65
Madison County, 156–57, 167
Mahar, William, 133
Maitland, John, 106, 159, 161
Manatt, Charles T., 112
Mandeville, Robert, 124

Manufacturers Association, Illinois, 122, 187
Marovitz, William, 101
Maryville Academy, 216, photo section
Mathematics and Science Academy, Illinois, 162
Mayberry, Jerry, 26, 210
mayoral elections, 80, 83–84, 124–26, 187–89
McCormick Place, expansion, 197–98, photo section
McDonnell, Kathy, 9
McGloon, Art: Byrne-Bilandic contest, 83–84; Clark's introduction of, 12; judicial legislation, 20–21; PJR swearing-in ceremony, 82; State Fair outings, 110, 111; tutelage of young PJR, 14, 18, 21–22, 32, 73
McHenry County, 137–38, 204
McMaster, Tom, 27
McMorrow, Mary Ann, 207
McMurray, Dennis, 226n3
McPartlin, Robert, 22, 25, 26
McPike, Jim, 140, 183
Michigan, 90, 105
minimum wage legislation, 28
minority leaders, terms listed, 220–21
missing children legislation, 142–43
Mondale, Walter, 112
Moran, Thomas, 186
Morris, William, 63–64, 111
Mulcahey, Richard, 158–59
Municipal League, Illinois, 123
Murphy, Marty, 100–101
Murphy, Morgan, 16–17
Murphy, William T., 16

National Conference of State Legislatures (NCSL), 104, 105–7
National Organization for Women, 151
Nation at Risk, A: The Imperative for Educational Reform, 157
NCSL (National Conference of State Legislatures), 104, 105–7

Philip J. Rock served fourteen years, 1979–93, as the Illinois Senate president, longer than anyone in state history. He was a leading advocate for women and children and sponsored landmark legislation to assist abused and neglected children. A former seminarian and a product of the Democratic organization of Cook County, he demonstrated that a public official could be both a partisan politician and a public official with great integrity. He interacted regularly with several giants in Illinois history, including Governor James R. Thompson, Illinois House Speaker Michael J. Madigan, and Chicago mayors Richard J. Daley, Harold Washington, and Richard M. Daley, which gives him a unique insider's perspective on Illinois and Chicago politics. Many say he was the greatest statesman in Illinois politics in the last quarter of the twentieth century. Rock has had a private law practice in Chicago since 1970 and lives in the Chicago area.

Ed Wojcicki was a longtime journalist with extensive experience in reporting on local and state government in Illinois. For ten years he was the publisher of *Illinois Issues* magazine, which has received national acclaim for its coverage of state politics and government. Wojcicki also was the project director of two research and citizen engagement projects at the University of Illinois Springfield: the Illinois Campaign Finance Project and the Illinois Civic Engagement Project. A native of St. Louis, he is the author of *A Crisis of Hope in the Modern World* and a contributing author to four other books. He lives in Springfield, Illinois.